DRIVING SOMA

DRIVING SOMA

DRIVING SOMA

A Transformational Process in the Analytic Encounter

Patrick Miller

Routledge
Taylor & Francis Group

LONDON AND NEW YORK

First published in French in 2001 as
Le psychanalyste pendant la séance: expérience de la psychanalyse
by Presses Universitaires de France (PUF)

First published 2014 by Karnac Books Ltd.

Published 2018 by Routledge
2 Park Square, Milton Park, Abingdon, Oxon OX14 4RN
711 Third Avenue, New York, NY 10017, USA

Routledge is an imprint of the Taylor & Francis Group, an informa business

British Library Cataloguing in Publication Data

A C.I.P. for this book is available from the British Library

ISBN 9781782200017 (pbk)

Translated by David Alcorn

Edited, designed and produced by The Studio Publishing Services Ltd
www.publishingservicesuk.co.uk
e-mail: studio@publishingservicesuk.co.uk

CONTENTS

ACKNOWLEDGEMENTS

Jose-Luis Goyena encouraged me to publish this book, and he welcomed the news that I had signed a contract with Karnac Books in his own warm and cheerful manner. His sudden and premature demise is a terrible loss.

I shall be forever grateful for his friendship and generosity, remember his clinical intelligence, his wide psychoanaytic knowledge, and deep commitment to his patients, and miss his joyful humour and permanent criticism of all kinds of conformists. He was such a lively *Mensch*.

I wish to express my gratitude to my friends and colleagues who have helped me to pursue my work and overcome moments of discouragement by giving me good advice when needed and/or some of their precious time to read and discuss the work in progress: Marilia Aisenstein, Jacqueline Amati-Mehler, Betsy Brett, Eric Glassgold, Deanna Holzmann, Monica Horovitz, Edward Nersessian, Rosine Perelberg, Alan Pollack, Ana-Maria Rizzuto, Sherry Turkle.

My thanks to L'Esprit du Temps for the authorisation to publish in English "Metabolisations psychiques du corps dans la théorie de Piera Aulagnier", first published in 2001 in *Topique*, 74: pp. 29–42, and to *Revue Française de Psychosomatique* for the authorisation to publish in

English "Auto-engendrement ou auto-excitation. Quelques réflexions concernant le rôle qualifiant de l'objet", first published in *Revue Française de Psychosomatique*, *18*, in 2001.

I would like to express my special gratitude to Presses Universitaires de France for their great generosity in graciously permitting me the English copyright for several chapters of my book, *Le Psychanalyste Pendant la Séance*, PUF, 2001.

None of this would have been possible without Maria Vlachou's perseverance and faith in editorial ethics.

The experience of discussing matters of translation or revision with David Alcorn was always lively and enriching, though sometimes exhausting! Thank you, David.

Patrick Miller discovered Freud's *Three Essays on the Theory of Sexuality* on a bookshelf when he was thirteen years old. After reading it with the vivid intensity of his age, he asked for Freud's address because he wanted to meet him. He had missed him by just twenty years. Psychoanalysis has become, ever since, an important part of his life.

He had just begun his literary studies when he started his first analysis, and then moved on to medical school after completing his MA, having decided he wanted to become an analyst some day.

He was lucky enough to be in Paris during the cultural and intellectual turmoil of the 1970s, where he could follow the bumpy road of the French psychoanalytical controversies, from Lacan's seminar and Françoise Dolto's case presentations to the meetings of Confrontation (René Major), to Wladimir Granoff's and Conrad Stein's seminars.

After completing his psychiatry residency, he decided to begin his training at IVè Groupe, because what Piera Aulagnier, Micheline Enriquez, Nathalie Zaltzman, François Perrier, and J. P. Valabrega had elaborated about the complexity of analytic training seemed to him to be the deepest and most subtle approach at the time. He later participated for many years in Piera Aulagnier's private seminar, and in André Green's seminar at the Paris Society, two major encounters in his psychoanalytical training.

He became an active member of IVè Groupe, serving as scientific secretary and Vice-president. After ten years of controversies within the IVè Groupe (1994–2004) he co-founded with a number of his colleagues the Société Psychanalytique de Recherche et de Formation (Paris) in 2005, of which he was President (2007–2011).

He is currently a training and supervising analyst of the IPA, and is a member of CAPS (Princeton).

He has written numerous articles in psychoanalytic journals and collaborated on several collective books: among others, "How Emmy silenced Freud into analytic listening", in *On Freud's "On beginning the treatment"* (Karnac, 2012), and "Le Moi-Corps de l'analyste", in *Le travail psychanalytique*, edited by André Green (PUF, 2003).

An earlier version of the present volume was published in French in 2001: *Le psychanalyste pendant la séance* (PUF).

Introduction

Freud had a monistic approach to the relationship between body and psyche (*Seele*), the psyche being solidly rooted in the soma and progressively emerging from it through the formation of more and more elaborate representational capacities. His very sophisticated theoretical model, an attempt at describing this reversible passage from soma to psyche, is contained in his definition of the drive:

> If now we apply ourselves to considering mental life from a *biological* point of view, an 'instinct'[1] appears to us as a concept on the frontier between the mental and the somatic, as the psychical representative of the stimuli originating from within the organism and reaching the mind, as a measure of the demand made upon the mind for work in consequence of its connection with the body. (Freud, 1915c, p. 122)

A work of transformation enables the passage from the endo-somatic stimulus to its equivalent, perceived from the standpoint of mental life, the psychical representative (of the endosomatic stimulus). The controversy surrounding the translation of *Trieb* (see note 1) is only the reflection of a much deeper difficulty in describing in a monistic way phenomena which we usually look upon from a dualistic point of view: that of body and soul. The vague area concerns the capacity to describe how the work of transformation is being carried out. Freud's opening remarks in "Instincts and their vicissitudes" stresses this epistemological difficulty:

> We have often heard it maintained that sciences should be built up on clear and sharply defined basic concepts. In actual fact no science, not even the most exact, begins with such definitions. The true beginning of scientific activity consists rather in describing phenomena and then in proceeding to group, classify and correlate them. (1915c, p. 117)

In this book, I shall try to explore some aspects of this difficult topic of the relationship between soma, body, and mind, as it can be experienced within the process of analysis by both analysand and analyst, and from both intra- and intersubjective points of view. I shall also attempt to delineate some of the different ways of theorising this.

Alongside the definition of the drive as a model of a way of thinking about the soma–body–mind transformational continuity of substance despite differences of aspect, I have in mind two other tools related to thinking: Freud's assertion, in *The Ego and the Id*, that the ego is "first and foremost a bodily ego; it is not merely a surface entity, but is itself the projection of a surface" (1923b, p. 26) and the concept of the hallucinatory satisfaction of need as one model of the origin of mental life. In the absence of the real source of satisfaction, the urge to satisfy a need is met by a capacity to elicit a pseudo-experience of satisfaction, which is a representative equivalent of what is usually experienced in the body when an actual satisfaction of need occurs. This hallucinatory satisfaction of need is a first level of mental life that creates an illusion of the bodily sensations experienced during actual satisfaction. Mental life begins as the negative realisation of a somatic activity: it causes bodily sensations to be evoked in the absence of actual somatic need fulfilment. Or, to put it differently, it allows the individual to deny the endosomatic excitation of need by a presentation of bodily sensations that do not have an actual somatic source. The *as if* bodily sensation is used as a representative of an actual somatic sensation. A recreated somatic sensation functions as a first degree of psychical representation. As Freud remarked in "Formulations on the two principles of mental functioning" (1911b), at some point a difference must be established between the hallucinatory satisfaction of need and the actual satisfaction of need in reality. If some kind of reality testing is not introduced, mental life as hallucination of need would eventually lead to the death of the soma.

The clinical perspective

Some patients represent a greater challenge to the boundaries of our mind, our bodily ego, and our theories than others. Because of the intensity of the demand made on the capacity for figurability and representability of the analyst's mind, they compel us to be more aware of the importance of the subjective involvement required from the analyst.

This is often the case with patients presenting somatic diseases when we are confronted with the possibility of a figurative use of the soma in order to find some "meaning" beyond the psyche and its capacities for representational transformations. How can we respond to such an enigma when it seems that something that should be in the mind is not even in the body, but in the soma. How can we conceive of a possibility, within the process of psychical metabolisation taking place in the work of an analysis, of bringing it from the soma to the mind through the body?

When this does occur, it is usually channelled through the analyst's bodily ego's response manifested by a feeling, which is a first step in the integration of a process of working through concerning the patient, but which cannot take place in the patient's mind. There are many clinical examples in this book which aim to illustrate how the attempt by both analyst and analysand to work together seems to reach a limit, and how the analyst's mind has to modify its functioning in order to try to encounter the patient at a different level of communication (this might or might not occur; it has nothing to do with the analyst's free will or resorting to a "technique"). We usually call this adaptive phenomenon "regression", or, more precisely, "formal regression" of the analyst's mind at work. Naming it makes it more familiar, but might also prevent us from exploring when, how, and why it happens, and how it can deeply affect how we think about intersubjectivity.

To illustrate this, let me take a clinical example taken from a session with a psychotic patient, a young man in his twenties, who had been diagnosed as schizophrenic. The patient is sitting in front of me; the couch is to my right. The patient recalls a nightmare he used to have repetitively when he was a child. This nightmare would wake him up, screaming and in a state of terror, as if he found it impossible to come out of the nightmare.

> He is lying in the grass, he hears a loud and horrifying sound and sees coming towards him at full speed a train that blows his brains out.

As I am listening to the patient while looking at him, I am suddenly plunged into an experience which, subsequently, is very difficult to describe: I am looking at the empty couch and I see on the couch a plate full of spaghetti covered with tomato sauce. Then something happens in my mind which I can only describe afterwards as a thought indicating something like "this is weird", which dissipates the hallucination.

This phenomenon—an analyst having a hallucination in response to listening to a patient's narrative of a nightmare—seems to be a far cry from what we usually think of as being an interpretation.

An extremely traumatic original event cannot be processed by dream-work into a dream. What is being experienced in the nightmare, and what is horrifying beyond thinking, is the blowing up of the brain's capacity to metabolise the internal trauma of endosomatic excitation into some psychical representation. Something that has to do with the capacity for bringing about the satisfaction of a need through primary hallucination does not function the way it should, and prevents the dream from accomplishing its function as the guardian of sleep.

The hallucinatory experience taking place in the analyst's mind operates the kind of transformation which repetitively fails in the patient's psyche. In a state of wakeful sleep, the analyst's mind transforms the blowing of the brain, the bloody scattering and fragmentation of the mind, into the integrative representation of an object, an appetising enough object which can be eaten and digested, and which can contribute to the growth of the body-mind. This could be viewed as an elemental aspect of the capacity for reverie, or, following Bion's hypothetical model, a transformation of beta elements by the alpha function.

This, therefore, is one possible way of trying to think theoretically about this psychical event suddenly happening in the analyst's psyche. Some of its important features are:

- its total spontaneity;
- the fact that it occurs in response to an incapacity in the patient's mind to maintain a hallucinatory function necessary for dreaming;
- the analyst's mind seems to "lend" a primal aspect of its functioning to the patient's mind, seemingly coming to its "rescue", somehow enacting the "interpreting function" of the primary object or primary environment.

At this point, some very difficult questions arise: where does it take place? What is the topography of such an event? Are we in the logics of two separate minds? Of one mind for two people? Of two minds creating a "third topography", a co-constructed common body-mind ground?

These questions follow on logically from that of the nature of the event and of its potential mutative effect on the patient's psychical functioning.

Is this event (the hallucinatory experience) solely for the use and benefit of the analyst's mind? Does it have a defensive and protective function only for the analyst? Or is it an experience which can somehow benefit the patient's psychical functioning, one that can be shared by him/her, even though it is not verbally communicated? Or is it only the changes brought about in the analyst's capacity for listening that will benefit the patient in the long run?

This example is of an extreme nature, and not of the kind that happens often in our clinical work. However its extraordinary dimension emphasises and lays bare some potential aspects of the involvement of the analyst's mind in the intersubjective dimension of the analytical process.

Let us now turn to the more usual and temperate, or well-tempered, interplay of two minds as they can be experienced by analyst and patient during the analytic hour.

A young woman in her late thirties had felt a need for a consultation some months after an extremely traumatic event in her family involving the brutal death of a close relative. What she initially expected to be a kind of "debriefing" within the context of a post-trauma syndrome developed, after a few encounters, into a long-deferred need to have psychoanalysis. She is intelligent, very articulate, and quite sensitive, but somewhat on her guard emotionally and, defensively, prefers to be in charge of taking care of the distress of others. My overall impression was that she seemed to have developed what could be schematically described as "a mildly neurotic way of being".

For the purpose of my description, I simply want to isolate two elements from the initial interviews in my experience of listening to her. I noticed, two or three times during the first interview, an emotional response on my part, going beyond the usual emotional response that I can usually experience while listening to a patient—a response sufficiently intense to bring tears to my eyes. During the second interview, as I had been listening to her for some time, I began to feel the rapidly growing pain of a headache. Headaches or migraines are not at all part of my usual set of somatisations, so that I was immediately alerted to the fact that this could have something to do with what she was telling me, or, rather, with what she was not able to tell me. Some time later in the session, she mentioned the fact that she was prone to migraines, especially when confronted with emotionally disturbing events, as had been the case, for instance, since the tragic death of her relative.

My way of thinking about these two aspects of my listening to her during the initial consultations is manifold. A movement of identification with the patient that indicates a kind of proximity to her that needs to be called into question. Is this identification a defensive way of being too close to the patient, in order to put aside any capacity for listening to her and to hear what she had to say from a greater distance: in other words, a "third-party" position? Or is it a capacity for coming closer in spite of her guarded and defensive stance: "I can deal with this on my own"? This would imply that she had not managed to induce, as a repetition in the transference, some kind of phobic avoidance from the transference object. Is it countertransference as resistance on the analyst's part, or countertransference as receptivity?

What struck me about the second event, the headache, was the anticipation of an element of her symptoms enacted within my bodily mind. This seemed to indicate not only a specific kind of permeability, but also a capacity to lend my mind to being the "theatre" of a figurative bodily enactment of her psychical pain. This, to me, is not part of a defensive countertransference, but a kind of intersubjective enactment which bears witness to a capacity to communicate at a formally regressed level. In that respect, it reinforces a positive indication for psychoanalysis between this patient and this analyst. This kind of enactment is, to me, an initial profound level of understanding.

What follows is a description of the way things can unfold in the dynamics of transference and countertransference during a session, once the analysis has been going on for several months.

She begins the session with a silence, and then remarks on becoming aware that her disposition at this moment is that she would like to make me feel comfortable. She wonders why. The analyst says that this wish might indicate a fear she might have of making him uncomfortable. The patient remains thoughtful, and wonders what kind of thoughts she might have that would make the analyst feel uncomfortable. And why would she even fear that?

"Well, would it be a fear that I may decide to close the door of my office?" This was a precise reference to how her mother, a successful businesswoman, would shut herself in her office and deny her daughter access while she was working.

She says she knows very well that I am listening to her. Then she adds, laughing, "And you just can't walk away anyway!"

I say that, well, she might also fear that I could walk away intellectually and emotionally, and leave her in loneliness even if I am physically present.

The session continues and, at one point, I become aware of the fact that I am making conscious efforts to memorise the session. I am departing from my usual way of being with her in the session, outlining theoretical links in my mind, thinking of a forthcoming conference where I could use some of this material. After a while, I have to acknowledge to myself that I am actualising, enacting in the session, precisely the mother's closing of the door of the mind and the kind of narcissistic abuse that the patient felt subjected to during her childhood, one that she is beginning to become aware of: I am giving precedence to my intellectual work, and to the narcissistic use I can make of it, over being with her during the session and caring for her.

As I progressively disengage myself from this countertransference enactment, I am again more in contact with her, and, to my surprise, I realise that she is now talking about wars in Africa, about young children enrolled as soldiers, how they are forced into becoming killers, the atrocities, the abuses, the rapes, the unthinkable violence of traumatised children who become abusers themselves. When the war is over, how could they ever get back to any kind of normal childhood?

Beyond the articulate description she is making of these situations, I can sense a whole assortment of chaotic atrocities, of painful violence, which I immediately associate to her migraines. The door of my mind had indeed closed, the receptivity and permeability had shut down, and she had been left alone, developing in her mind all the painful atrocities of an unspoken war with her mother, whom I can now see as having a severe borderline personality, which could now develop in a narrative within the transference and counter-transference intersubjective interplay, instead of being regressively manifested through the painful atrocities of the migraines.

After exploring her narrative with her, I was able to tell her that although she had felt so lonely while her mother had shut her out, she had forced herself to be a good little soldier to her mother, keeping all the war atrocities painfully pent up in her mind, instead of making her mother feel uncomfortable with them.

From feeling a headache while listening to her to being able to describe metaphorically to her an evocative narrative of her intra-psychical pain, there is a long path of processing. This work of process-ing is made possible by a specific treatment of the analyst's subjectivity, how it is invested in the process, and how it comes into play with the analysand and for the analysand's sake. Creating the conditions for this specific use of subjectivity is what we call the analytical frame and method. However, it never works magically simply through its own good merit. The analyst is subjected to the setting just as the analysand is, but, contrary to the analysand, he/she must also be guardian of the setting, while at the same time being part and parcel of the process. Exploring the metapsychology of the analyst at work is also an attempt at dealing with this difficult paradox.

Questions of and about metapsychology

Anticipation and anxiety characterise the situation into which both protagonists of the psychoanalytical experience are plunged. We prob-ably tend to minimise the traumatic aspects of the first encounter between patient and analyst, where so many psychical and bodily events are precipitated, mobilising powerful drive forces. Initially, we have very little representation of what is being actualised. Our capacity to survive this potentially traumatic experience, without becoming a "wise baby" (Ferenczi), will determine the transformation of the encounter into a process with an ending.

Bion underlined the traumatic aspect of psychoanalysis during a seminar at the Tavistock in 1976: "It took me a very long time to realize that the actual experience of being psychoanalysed was a traumatic one and it takes a long while before one recovers from it" (Bion 2005).

This idea links together the epistemology, the history, and the clinical practice of psychoanalysis. Every beginning of an analysis again summons up some traumatic aspects of the beginnings of the psychoanalytical movement, and, perhaps even more fundamentally, the traumatic impact of Freud's discoveries from which we might not yet have recovered. Alluding to "The dream of the wise baby" brings Ferenczi to our minds for obvious reasons: his formidable anticipation of analytical theorisation when he wrote his paper on Introjection, at a time when he had had no personal experience of analysis and had been familiar with Freud and his work for barely two years. A wise baby indeed, dealing with the trauma of psychoanalytical thinking with the prematurity and the hypertrophy of theoretical thinking. His prematurity of mind, intuition, and feeling (*Einfühlung*) was not offered the psychoanalytical treatment it deserved in order to grow into a creative integration of body and mind. Creative he remained, constantly trying to tackle the paradoxes and contradictions that he encountered in his experience of psychoanalysis, but the price to pay for this dissociation was very high. Not long before his death, he wrote in his "Clinical Diary" that he was confronted at the age of fifty-nine with this radical dilemma: to change or to die. He died.

Many Cassandras claim that the doomsday of psychoanalysis is coming; others talk of a Golden Age of psychoanalysis that is forever gone. This is not simply nowadays, as each generation tends to believe; it has always been the case, ever since the beginning. Nothing really new.

The fear of doomsday sounds a bit like the fear of breakdown described by Winnicott: it does not refer to a catastrophe about to happen in the future, but to a disaster which has already occurred in the past. Is this disaster what nostalgic people call the Golden Age of psychoanalysis?

After more than a century of existence, and so many Cassandras prophesying the death of psychoanalysis, could we perhaps think that it has not yet actually begun to exist? And what if, after more than a century of existence, psychoanalysis was only in its earliest stages?

Freud's new theories of the mind, no matter how revolutionary they might have been, are not, in themselves, traumatic. They might have caused the same kind of narcissistic injury that Copernican and Darwinian theories had done in their time. What seems potentially more traumatic is that theory does not stand alone: it is fundamentally linked to, and dependent upon, an experimental field of realisation, one that was never explicitly theorised by Freud.

This experimental field is one of the dynamic forces powerfully brought into action within the setting of the encounter. This is not only the meeting of two minds; it also engages the somatic and the libidinal body, and the changes that might occur will affect mind, body, and soma. Come to think of it, this sounds far more frightening than the coming into consciousness of a repressed representation or a rearrangement of signifiers.

I remember many years ago a discussion panel in a television talk show involving a few psychoanalysts (one of whom was André Green) and a neurobiologist, Alain Prochiantz. After listening to the analysts for a while, Prochiantz said that he had never been in analysis, and now he knew why he would never begin an analysis. He said something along the lines of: "If I have understood you correctly, what you say about the therapeutic action of psychoanalysis implies that it must go as far as touching and changing something in living matter, and I shall never let anybody mess with mine."

A powerful argument, in its radicality based on an intuition of the potentialities of intersubjectivity within the analytic encounter. Freud's answer, quoting Ambroise Paré, a surgeon of ancient times, was: "Je le pansai, Dieu le guérit" ("I bandaged him, God healed him"). Analysis would be about the undoing of false connections. Once these are undone by the action of analysis, new connections, what he called the synthesis, take place spontaneously. There is a lifting of barriers (repression, defences, resistances) set up in the course of development and reappearing during the analysis, allowing for a free-flowing of libido, reorganising the connections between affects and representations and enriching the network of connections between representations. This can be implemented following the rule of free association, while the analyst by following the rule of free-floating attention allows for some suspension of his/her secondary-mode thought processes. This enables links to be made in the patient's discourse by being closer to the logics of primary processes.

The implication of the analyst's subjectivity here remains one of understanding and of enabling a new way of understanding in the analysand's mind.

By recommending free-floating attention for analytical listening, Freud opened up a path for the involvement of the analyst's subjectivity, one which went much further than his explicit theoretical intentions. This is one of the main threads followed and explored in this book: why and how the psychoanalytical encounter creates the conditions for an intersubjective construct which has no equivalent in "ordinary", "real" life, one which implies the analyst's bodily ego, hence giving the possibility of sometimes having access to the analysand's bodily ego.

Free-floating attention amounts to a return of hypnosis in psychoanalysis, in the form of self-hypnosis applied to the analyst. It opens up a path of formal regression for the analyst's mind, bringing him/her closer to the primary processes, hence closer to the bodily forms of his/her own ego

The setting that turned the psychoanalytical method into a psychoanalytical experience was defined in an apparently pragmatic way. It seemed reasonable enough, once memory, repression, and resistance were at stake, to see a patient frequently and for a good length of time. This pragmatic disposition corresponded to explicit aspects of theory of which they were, somehow, an application. However, once they were actually experienced, they engaged patient and analyst in psychical and bodily events that far exceeded what had been anticipated.

The potential for exploring the unknown, the unanticipated, for realising a theory of the body-mind in action resides first and foremost in the actual encounter of two body-minds subjected to a method within a particular setting. Method and setting are constantly being overtaken by the experiences in progress, just as the theory cannot be but inadequate to what is being experienced. But theory, method, and setting are the necessary conditions for the emergence of whatever is excessive and its working through into a new body of knowledge. Just as transference was conceived by Freud as an enactment (*agieren*), the method and the setting could be seen as an enactment of potential implicit theories that have not yet been thought through.

When I write "first and foremost", I think of Freud's assertion that the ego is "first and foremost a bodily ego". In my view, Freud's work is essentially an attempt to go beyond a dualistic approach to the body and the mind, towards a continuity of thinking about trans-formative progressions from soma to body to mind and back via a regressive path. The capacity for regression is a condition for thinking about the possibility of change. This description of progression and regression remains too linear and caught up in Euclidean geometry, whereas what is required, given the complexity of phenomena involved—especially time, space, simultaneity and reversibility—would have more to do with the instruments offered by quantum theory. In my view, Freud's thinking is essentially somato-psychical and psycho-somatic and offers the possibility of a general theory of figurability and representability, including not only the libidinal body, but also the physiological soma, the potentiality for representability arising from both thanks to the action of a third element: the care provider's mind or the primary environment. The importance of this third factor in the capacity for constructing a psyche was to be empha-sised by Freud's followers, and, in particular, by Ferenczi, Melanie Klein, Winnicott, Bion, and Piera Aulagnier.

Lacan was too cautious about (and, I think, frightened by) the issue of regression (including that of the analyst) in the psychoanalytical process and by that of primary dependence (he loathed them with a good deal of grandiosity), so that he did not include the soma and the body in his general theory of representability or develop further the model of the drive proposed by Freud. He went more and more into a formalised approach to the mind while, in a sort of parallel process, his technique tended to reduce more and more the length of the actual encounter between patient and analyst. His quest was for a "mathème de la psychanalyse", and the return of the body, in his thinking, happened through his fascination with the great Catholic mystics: Theresa of Avila and Saint John of the Cross.[2]

However, the question of mathematical thinking should not be looked upon as alien to the issues of psychoanalysis. Is mathematics a language? If this is the case, is it a pre-verbal language? If so, why is it intuited by some, sometimes to the point of prevailing on language, and not by others? Since Henri Poincaré's assumption, we are familiar with the fact that there exists a very strong connection between mathematics and intuition:

> I have said how much *the intuition of pure number*, whence comes rigorous mathematical induction, *differs from sensible intuition* to which the imagination, properly so called, is the principal contributor.
>
> . . . It is the intuition of pure number, that of pure logical forms, which enlightens and directs those we have called analysts. This it is which enables them not only to demonstrate, but also to invent. . . . The majority of us, *if we wished to see afar by pure intuition alone, would soon feel ourselves seized with vertigo*. Our weakness has need of a rod more solid, and, despite the exceptions of which we have just spoken, it is none the less true that sensible intuition is in mathematics the most usual instrument of invention. (Poincaré, 1907, pp. 24–25, my italics)

However, there is also a strong connection between mathematical logic and its discoveries and the reality of the external world. Mathematics may result from a capacity to formalise a self-perception of the functioning of the brain and of its relationship to the body. This would imply that a self-perception of the workings of the organism has a deep connection with the logics of the rules governing the universe.[3]

Mathematical thinking and discoveries can be used in physics to establish general rules. When it comes to the sciences of living matter, biology, the level of complexity would appear to make it more difficult to use mathematics in order to modelise principles of functioning into general rules. When it comes to the phenomena of consciousness (including unconscious phenomena), this seems even less feasible. Is this because mathematics is too far removed from the scientific object called consciousness, or is it because it is too close?

What is the use of metapsychology?

Metapsychology (literally: beyond psychology) is a kind of modelisation, an imaginative one. It is an attempt to give a descriptive representation of the workings of the psyche.

This modelisation draws on previous knowledge, a knowledge which is not quite adequate to its object. In that respect, we could say that Freud's metapsychology is also a metabiology or a metaneurophysiology.

The confrontation in Freud's mind of new events needing some kind of conceptualising description led him to borrow images, meta-phors, shapes, patterns, and systems that belonged to the area of knowledge with which he was most familiar: neurology.

Yet, intuition plays a major role in the shaping of a theory, in this case a theory of the mind—or, as I would say, of the body-mind.

This intuition has to do with the phenomena of self-perception, similar to what Freud says about consciousness being a sense organ, or when he describes the capacity in a dream of accomplishing the self-diagnosis of an incipient somatic illness.

This self-perception of an organic process, this intuitive perception of the functioning of the bodily ego, would have to be projected out in order to take on a form that can be thought about. The trajectory of projection finds on its way some more or less adequate representa-tions that can be used as a provisional form, or perhaps they might end up on a surface in the form of a drawing or a diagram that is no more than a kind of squiggle game giving shape to what has been intuited and projected.

This way of thinking about the origin of theory in the intuition of a self-perception being projected out seems to me to be in continuity with Freud's final writings on 22 August 1939: "Space maybe the projection of the extension of the psychical apparatus . . . Mysticism is the obscure self-perception of the realm outside the ego, of the id" (1941f, p. 300).

This book is an attempt to deal with the issues of what Ferenczi called a metapsychology of the analyst: more precisely, a meta-psychology of the analyst at work. I shall examine in particular what the analytical setting, implementing the method within a precise structure, *demands* from the analyst's psyche, how it transforms it during the session and enables it to have access to modalities of intrapsychic and intersubjective functioning that are not reachable in "real" life. How, and to what extent, does this enable the analyst to modify the workings of his/her body-mind in order to engage in a specific intersubjective *rapport* with the analysand that might create the conditions required for bringing about mutative changes in the analysand's self-organisation?

Freud's assertion in "Observations on transference love" (1915a, p. 166)—"The course the analyst must pursue is neither of these; it is one for which there is no model in real life"—will be repeated on several occasions in the course of this book.

Metapsychology seems to me to be necessary because it gives us the instruments of understanding, but these instruments of understanding are still rudimentary and provisional. They are always lagging behind the growing complexity of what they have helped to open up in the field of thinking about what we call "clinical data". Let us not forget that "data" means not only "facts" but also—etymologically—"givens". Nothing is "given" in any kind of observation, even less so when the observer is implicated in what is observed.

In *An Outline of Psycho-Analysis*, Freud brings this epistemological question to our attention:

> In our science as in the others the problem is the same: behind the attributes (qualities) of the object under examination which are presented directly to our perception, we have to discover something else which is more independent of the particular receptive capacity of our sense organs and which approximates more closely to what may be supposed to be the real state of affairs. We have no hope of being able to reach the latter itself, *since it is evident that everything new that we have inferred must nevertheless be translated back into the language of our perceptions, from which it is simply impossible for us to free ourselves.* (1940a, p. 196, my italics)

In his neo-Kantian way, Freud postulates the unknowable character of reality itself, or, as he puts it, "the real state of affairs". The observer can only infer and interpolate the unknown processes and translate them into the descriptive language of conscious ones. The analyst is part of the experiment, but tries to describe it when no longer in the experiment. The "knowledge" which is being developed during the session cannot be described if we maintain the distinction between an observer and "an object under examination". During the session, should we say that the analyst is there to observe and to understand, or, rather, that he/she is part of the experiment and of the understanding as it develops in a form which remains unknown to us, as Freud put it? What is being experienced by the analyst during the session is known to him/her while it is happening *hic et nunc*, precisely in this form which, later, after the session, will again become "unknowable" and indescribable. If it remains unreachable by us again, after we come out of the experience that we have been through during the session, this does not mean that the modifications experienced in this different state of being do not have a retroactive impact on our conscious way of thinking about the phenomena that we call "clinical". This "form" was explored by Freud in terms of primary processes, where the notions of timelessness, of suspension of oppositions, of reversibility, of the coexistence of logical opposites, of the capacity to apprehend the same "object" from different points of view at the same time render it difficult to describe in terms of secondary thought processes.

Some authors (in particular, Botella and Botella (2007)) have indicated that, just as modern physics could not account for realities at the subatomic level with descriptive instruments that belonged to nineteenth-century physics, so that they needed to forge the concepts of quantum theory, so analysts need to construct instruments of thinking that might be more adequate to describing what is being experienced at the "subatomic level" which patient and analyst can sometimes reach and "share" in the course of an analytical session.

This, to me, does not mean that quantum theory should be "applied" to psychoanalysis, but that analysts ought to open themselves up to such questions as, for example, if Freud had embarked on theorising psychoanalysis, having in mind the most recent developments of our contemporary biology, neurobiology, and immunology, as well as the revolutionary approach to physical reality introduced by Einstein, Planck, and Niels Bohr, how would he have conceptualised the psyche, what would have been his metapsychological modelisations?

Recalling a challenging analytic case

I would like now to recall one of my oldest of psychoanalytical adventures. Mr K was, in fact, just the second patient who was referred to me at a time when I was beginning my analytical training.

The psychiatrist who referred him was a primal scream therapist. She had seen Mr K in consultation and had decided that it was too risky to embark him on the road to primal scream. She thought that he was too brittle and that primal scream therapy might precipitate a psychotic breakdown.

Mr K, almost thirty, was at the end of his tether, feeling that he was about to let go of a rope he was still desperately clinging to. He was extremely depressed, sometimes suicidal, his life was a wasteland,

and he was invaded by extremely demanding obsessional rituals that took up most of his free time. He was vegetating in a menial job, quite inferior to his real potentialities and capacities.

He conveyed to me an atmosphere of lead and ozone, the texture of having to wade through some kind of thick paste, yet there was something very gentle in him and an eagerness to try to do something for himself that moved me deeply. As I was enthusiastically beginning my analytic training, I thought that I could not offer him anything better than to begin an analysis. Without much hesitation, while acknowledging the severity of his psychopathology, after two interviews I explained to him the setting—three sessions per week, lying on the couch—and the method. He agreed, we set his hours and began our work the following week.

Nowadays most analysts, faced with the same kind of patient, would be more inclined to be "careful": they would see the patient face to face for a longer period, one session per week, testing the patient's and their own capacity to engage in more frequent sessions, and perhaps not even considering the possibility of analysis (with the possible exception of some British colleagues, perhaps?). I think that there is a possibility that I might be less daring today and think twice before offering analysis to Mr K. Would that be better? I am not sure. It would certainly be more comfortable for the analyst, but might deprive the patient of a mutative experience.

Mr K was, thus, my second patient in analysis. Quite different from the first, and quite different from anything I had anticipated as being a "classical analysis".

Mr K kept talking profusely, breathlessly, endlessly, without any pause that might offer some kind of breathing space. When I would tell him that the session was over, he would continue, I would stand up, make some throaty noises to attract his attention, but he would still go on. I would have to insist, explaining that the time of the session was up. He would then give a start and come out of a state I later identified as a kind of trance. I soon realised that this abundance of words had not much to do with free association. Instead of triggering my mind and making it roam freely, it suffocated me, it lulled me into a kind of nightmarish magma, where words were not words any more but part of a kind of undifferentiated paste. Needless to say, I felt drained and exhausted after the sessions, with a terrible sense of having no memory of what he had said. The profusion of words, instead of filling me, had emptied me of all thoughts and even images; what was left was a terrible sense of helplessness.

However, Mr K had developed a very efficient way of forcing me to remember him and his bodily presence. As the session progressed, he would release a strong body odour, which developed into a powerful stench that saturated the whole space of my consulting-room. After he had left I had to open the windows wide and ventilate the room by creating draughts. But even that was not sufficient to dissipate his presence. His smell clung to every fibre of the fabrics in the room, tenaciously incrusted so as to remain present until the next session, and remind my other patients that he had been there and would not be dislodged. That much I realised because it was so figuratively depicted. But what was I to make of it?

It was all about being overwhelmed and saturated. Mr K did not seem to be aware of any of that, not even the stench, and I was immersed in it, so much so that I had a growing sense of being forced to experience it without having much capacity left, during the sessions, to think about it and to become aware of anything other than a threat of annihilation.

The more I tried to pay attention to the content of what he said, the more I had the feeling that it was evading my grasp. This painful and enigmatic experience occupied a lot of my thinking between sessions. I was very aware of the fact that, in this way, he managed to be very much present in my mind. I was trying to understand, I was trying to make sense of it all. In what I remembered of the sessions, there were no dreams, no day-dreaming, no fantasying. Everything seemed to revolve, in a very repetitious manner, around recollections of very painful separation anxieties. His parents had left him in the care of an aunt when he was just a few months old, and would come to visit him from time to time, while they had kept with them his older brother. That situation lasted until he was five years old. The excruciating wait for their visits, the knowledge that it would end all too quickly, that they would leave again, that there was nothing he could do about it, and then the torturing questioning: why don't they want me, what can I do to force them to take me back, what does my brother have that I don't have? On the other hand, his aunt was married but childless: she had engulfed him in a very possessive kind of love, very controlling, very suffocating, and very incestuous. He was often in her bed and she would allow him to caress her breasts, and, so it seems, even encouraged him to do so and maybe more.

So there I was, having to experience, all at once, the excruciating pain of separation and the suffocating, engulfing incestuous atmosphere of his aunt's bed with all of its body smells, numbing and wrapping in a mist the sharp contours of the pain of separation—the exertion of a powerful and archaic anal retention, constantly enacted in the room, in a somatic as much as in a libidinal way, in the place of a capacity for dreaming and thinking which implies a necessary distance from the object. But as I say this, I am jumping ahead in time, because at the time, in the first three years of the analysis, I was not able to go that far in thinking theoretically about what was going on, a situation in which I was caught and trapped.

I did not remain silent. I would sometimes make a comment, at other times offer an interpretation, including transference interpretations, but I had the impression that the meaning of what I said, with its potential for evoking meaning in him, went unheeded, like a *lettre morte*, a dead letter. It was like water sliding off a duck's feathers. What was meaningful, however, seemed to be more the fact that he would hear my voice, that I was paying attention to him, that I was signalling my presence.

This was so much not what I thought a psychoanalytical process should or could be. My overall sense was that I did not understand him, could not help him, was not able to grasp what he was saying or remember it, and I felt guilty about it. At odds with myself, I eventually decided to do something that was the opposite of what I thought analytical listening should be: free-floating. I decided, for a limited period of time, to take notes during the sessions. It was a strange experience: I was writing automatically everything he was saying, without listening, in a kind of trance. Then I would read my notes that evening or the next day. They were strangely non-evocative, like a foreign body, like a dead body, dissociated from his voice, which I could not hear any more as I was reading the content of what he was saying. I think that that was painful for me because I missed his voice and its powerful, maddening effect on me, which put me in a slumber and destroyed my understanding. An eerie kind of mermaid.

So, eventually, I decided to surrender, to give up my wish to understand and to accept the reality of what was going on, without trying to change it. "Take in whatever comes and as it comes, endure what it makes you endure and observe what is happening." I was quite aware that this decision was taking me beyond free-floating attention, that it was something I had to experience because free-floating attention was impossible. It was an experience of passivity in which I agreed to be controlled by the patient, invaded by what he needed to induce in me, at the limit of losing my mind and my control over my mind. No matter how disturbing this borderline experience was, I knew that I was able to maintain a cathexis towards meaning: I was allowing this to happen because I believed that this was what he needed in order to eventually, some day, maybe, come out of this repetitive traumatic fixation. So, it remained meaningful, not an exercise of traumatophilia or masochism, even if some degree of both might be necessary to accept undergoing such an experience; indeed, this might also be true in a more general sense of the wish to become an analyst. We may wonder how the sublimation (or transformation, to put it more in Bion's terms) of traumatophilia and of masochism is accomplished in an analyst's everyday working task. It requires a powerful metabolism of destructivity and, when successfully accomplished, it may offer some protection from the tendency to resort to somatic illness. That is one aspect of how the analyst's body may be involved and required in quite a demanding way for the sake of the analytical process. The constant need to metabolise psychical conflict and to remain cathected towards the demands of figurability and representabilty might protect the analyst from the seduction of entropy. This is the optimistic hypothesis.

I eventually decided to increase the frequency of weekly sessions to four and then to five. I thought it might prove meaningful to contain his acute separation anxiety, but, on the other hand, it also possibly meant increasing incestuous proximity. The very fact that I could envisage this increase in our meetings certainly meant that he had not succeeded in deterring me from being in his presence and that his repellent bodily strategies had not managed to disgust or discourage the analyst—they were aimed at a transference object. But was there also a possibility that he might sense that I wanted more of it, that is, that he had, in fact, managed to seduce me in some kind of paradoxical way? There was undoubtedly a great deal of complexity in what could be induced, and there must have been some degree of enactment on my part in increasing the number of sessions, but there was perhaps no other way of conveying to him something about my endurance as analyst and a sense of some difference between analyst and transference object, than through some kind of enactment. At any rate, from whatever angle I might view it, I think it basically meant that I was ready to confront his psychical destructivity and his incestuous seductiveness and that we needed a solid framework in which to do this.

Another aspect in my decision is that in increasing the sessions to five I was deliberately breaking away from the so-called "French model" of three-sessions-per-week analysis—I was not going by the book, in order to adapt to what I thought was needed by this man to continue and develop his analytical process.

For the first three years of the analysis each summer break was accompanied by a repetition of the same events. He expressed a lot of separation anxiety as the break was approaching, and this led to an increase in all the manifestations that I have so far described. When the sessions resumed, he would invariably say that he had been in a sort of limbo, unable to recollect anything having to do with the sessions, and, in particular, trying to remember my face but not succeeding, as if he, too, found it impossible to keep me in his mind. He also reported, on each occasion, that some time after the interruption of sessions, he had begun feeling pain in his anus and rectum. This developed into an anal abscess with a fistula, with bleeding and a great deal of pain, necessitating surgery.

This repeated event impressed me deeply. It was obviously related to the excess of psychical pain produced by the separation and absence, and to his incapacity to process it psychically; also, it was very probably linked to the incapacity, of both analyst and analytical setting, to contain it and facilitate its metabolisation. This was the patient's own somatic way of dealing with psychical pain. Pain was somehow evacuated into the soma; he could not recollect anything having to do with the analysis and the analyst. Instead, there was a somatic collection of pus near the anal sphincter. He seemed not to have at his disposal a symbolised psychical capacity to use the retentive function of the anal sphincter; in order to keep the object from going away, he quite literally had to use his somatic sphincter in a desperate attempt to do so. This struggle to keep the object inside was harmful to both his body and the object, which it destroyed along with the capacity of the sphincter to retain and evacuate. It had been triggered by a failure of the retentive capacities of the mind and resulted in a failure of the somatic functions that had been used to somehow figuratively create a substitute for the symbolising functions of the mind.

This was not a hysterical conversional symptom, using symbolic language to represent something meaningful in the libidinal body, creating a dysfunction which does not correspond to an anatomical or physiological impairment, a dramatised sexualisation of the body.

In Mr K's somatic equivalent of psychical pain, there was a series of physiological events leading to a destructive attack on the physical and anatomical integrity of the body. However, we cannot say that it was entirely devoid of "meaning". It was repeated identically as a consequence of, and also, so it seems, as a response to, a recurring set of identical events. It also appeared to constitute some kind of non-mentalised solution to the pain created by an unthinkable conflict. Unthinkable because happening at a time when the representational capacities of the mind were not sufficient to generate a psychical scene giving a meaning, even a persecutory one, to what was being endured. We can also imagine that, as an infant, he could not come into contact with any psychical capacity for processing because the primary environment was unable to offer a good-enough metabolisation of his unthinkable bodily agonies.

In such cases, I believe that the infant tries to find figurative resources within his/her own bodily sensations and their somatic physiological equivalents, which function as a kind of *ersatz* of an internal object when the needed introjective capacities are lacking. A sort of primitive somatic "grammar" is created, in an attempt to deal with the alternative: feeling alive/feeling dead. This "grammar" cannot create metaphors, only equivalents. It does not contribute to creating a mind, it helps the organism survive, and it protects a potential mind from being deflagrated at the outset by a tsunami of unmetabolised excitations coming from the soma. For instance, if "cold" is the somatic sensation associated with being left alone with a feeling of dying, then triggering a somatic inflammatory process can be a way of "warming up". Who triggers this? No one, not an individual-as-subject, not a psychical agency, but, in my view, the powerful life instinct—that is, an organic instinct for the preservation of the self, not a drive. Resorting to this somatic "grammar" is quite the opposite of the psychical path enabling the construction of a mind described by Freud as the experience of hallucinatory satisfaction. Neither does it result from the introjection of an internal object, even though it functions as an *ersatz*, as an "as if", of an internal object.

After each summer, Mr K was too absorbed with the experience of reconnecting with me, trying to convey to me how terrible it had been not to be able to get back in touch with my presence by summoning up images of me. I would try, very carefully, to raise the possibility of a link between the state of mind he was describing, separation, and the development of the anal abscess and fistula. The connection between separation and his mental states during the summer was only too obvious to him; it was, after all, a repetition of what he had been through during his childhood. But the possible link with the somatic episode was dropped.

When we were in the third year of his analysis and just a few sessions away from the summer break, I heard him talking about a wish to be naked on the couch. After he had mentioned this a few times, I asked him to try to say what this idea brought into his mind. He said that it had just popped into his mind some time ago, he had thought about it; it would be like being a baby on a changing table, handled by his mother. I was disturbed by the factual way in which he talked about it, although this was his usual way. It began to dawn on me that he had in mind the idea of actually *doing* it. This raised a great deal of anxiety in me; I saw this as a potential major acting-out and thought that I had to try to do what I could to bring him to dream about it instead of doing it. But this was precisely what was so difficult for him.

So, shortly after beginning the session, the penultimate one before the break, he began undressing on the couch. It is hard to describe what went on in my mind. There were too many things at once, and I had to come to a decision very quickly. Something quite overwhelming was happening which exceeded the usual limits of the framework of psychoanalysis. I had to decide what would make "the best of a bad situation" in order not only to save the analytical setting, but, above all, to help this man find his own way in a process of psychical working through. Of course, I could not state this in my mind quite so clearly in that moment of vertigo. My mind was in turmoil: should I tell him to stop, or let this go on? I considered both possibilities, racing quickly from one to the other, in a length of time which stretched out of time, which seemed so terribly long when in fact it must have lasted just a split second. A thought forced its way into my mind: "If you

stop him you'll kill him, psychically. Don't let the fear of being unacceptable take over, try to be with him in this moment and to
stretch your mind a little more in an attempt to keep this within the
boundaries of what could become analysable."

He was almost naked, but had not removed his clothes completely,
so that his movements were restricted and his remaining clothes
looked like bonds fettering him. He eventually decided to free himself
of this hindrance.

Suddenly, there was an unusual kind of silence. He was making
little sounds, which seemed to be of pleasure and relief, he seemed
to be plunged into an intense experience which it was much too
soon to want to qualify. After the anxiety, fear, and turmoil that I had
experienced, to some extent linked to the manifestations of a hostile
analytical superego, I, too, felt at peace—although with a slight
feeling of unease, which, I think, had more to do with the positive
trembling and quivering of my epistemophilia than with guilt.

There was a baby on the couch, for sure, at times babbling in sheer
delight, with all his craving for a good-enough holding, but also with
all of his infantile sexuality. And there was an analyst trying his best
to be a skilful father and/or mother, very much aware that his infantile sexuality was also part and parcel of what was going on.

At that time, I had not read Ferenczi's "Child-analysis in the
analysis of adults", or Winnicott's "Metapsychological and clinical
aspects of regression within the psycho-analytical set-up" (1954), or
Margaret Little's sequel in the form of her narrative of her analysis
with Winnicott (Little, 1990).

I was quite on my own in this one, with my own mind-set, my
personal experience of analysis, my personality, and my analytical
ideals (not to be confused with an analytical superego, which I also
had, in all of its ambivalence) mostly forged through my encounter
with Freud's writings and my strong, mainly positive, transference to
him—and I think that this was fortunate, because it made this experience a more deeply formative one. It reinforced my awareness that it
is a dangerous illusion to think that there is anything like "technique"
per se in the field of analysis. There is a method, a theory with its
successive reinterpretations, and a very particular way of thinking,
which is that of the analyst during a session, involved as he/she is in
an experience with a patient that should always keep a critical eye on
both method and theory. It would be omnipotent to say that method

and theory are constantly reinvented; but they are constantly being reappraised, and this reappraisal sometimes goes so far that it eventually transforms our own relationship to both. Very rarely does it generate new concepts. It is far more important to be able to maintain the potentialities of transformation of the analyst's mind that can turn a couch into a changing table.

But do we really need new concepts in order to become better analysts? Yes, we do, provided we manage not to fetishise them or idolise those who have devised them, on condition that they be authentically new, and do not arise from someone's wish to be known and become famous by a brand name.

The session continued. Mr K would sometimes utter some simple phrases: "It's so marvellous!", "It feels so good!" What came into my mind and remained in the aftermath was this phrase: "A gentle breeze caressing the skin", although I am not sure that he actually did say that. It might have been my own representation of what he was experiencing. Except for encouraging him from time to time to voice what he was experiencing, I remained silent.

As the end of the session was drawing near, I began to worry that I would have to interrupt the session while he was still naked on the couch. I knew how difficult and painful the ending of each session was for him, so I told him that we had ten more minutes left and that it might be better for him to start putting his clothes back on, since it might feel quite awkward for him to find himself naked after the end of the session. He did so, slowly, and then the session ended.

When the analysis resumed in early September, Mr K was very impatient to *share* with me the story of what had happened during the summer that had surprised him a great deal because it was so totally *new*. He had been able to remember, and to recall when needed, the session during which he had undressed and spent time naked on the couch. He had day-dreamed about it, recalling all the pleasurable feelings, emotions, and sensations that he had experienced. It had kept him company all through the summer; he had not felt the usual anxieties, and had been able to summon up images of me and of my face. Moreover, he had not felt any peri-anal pain, no abscess, no fistula. This, to him, seemed quite miraculous, and he sounded almost cheerful.

The tonality of the sessions had changed palpably: the lead, the ozone, the paste, and the magma had lifted. I could listen to him.

Words were differentiated, polysemous, there were distinct sentences, with pauses for breath.

In one of the following sessions, for the very first time he recounted a dream, a dream that he had had during the summer. He was in his car, in the driver's seat; it was night and very dark. He shifted into reverse gear and turned his head to look out the rear window. The rear light was on, and as he was moving backwards he could see a terrifying dog with its jaws wide open, barking, at the back of the car.

This dream seemed to be a graphic transformation of the somatic figuration worked through by the process of the dream work into a psychical scene where even the regressive movement in the transference was represented.

Gradually, his body smell diminished and eventually disappeared over a period of a few months. It was later replaced by a discreet fragrance of cologne.

In one way, we could say that this was the beginning of his analysis, an analysis that turned out to be very fruitful, but also very long. For a while I thought it would be interminable and that it would end only when one of us died. But Mr K eventually entered a phase in which ending became conceivable and he said that he knew, once he felt ready to stop, that he would go for good and never come back. That was exactly how it happened, and I have never heard from him since.

Writing about this analysis, almost thirty-five years after it began, reawakened in me so many vivid memories of the challenging experience that it proved to be for the young analyst in training that I was at the time. I shall forever be grateful to Mr K for his sufficient trust, beyond my analytical skills, in my capacity to navigate with him in such troubled waters. He allowed me, very early on, to face up to the unpredictable nature of some psychical events that happen in the course of an analysis. I believe that no analytical process can be mutative without the analyst being, at some point and to a varying degree of intensity, confronted with such unpredictability, where skills show their limits and he/she has to resort to the more intimate resources of what we call his/her "being", for lack of a better word. This does not mean that the analyst's knowledge should not be as sophisticated as it can be, in as many areas of knowledge as possible. What is potentially mutative might occur precisely at the interface between this knowing and the unknown, where the limits of what is thinkable need to be stretched. By thinkable, I do not mean only cognitive, but something more in line with what Freud described as a finality of psychoanalysis: *Wo Es war, soll Ich werden*, provided that the *Es* and the *Ich* of the analyst are part and parcel of the analysand's *werden*. This means that the more intimate aspects of the analyst's self do not *react to* what is happening, but are allowed to become, for a while, part of the process for the analysand's sake. The capacity to allow this to happen in a non-narcissistic way depends on the analyst's personal experience of analysis, on how this is worked through in his own training, and on the subjective aspects of the personal encounter with each specific patient. This challenge is always being renewed; we can never be certain each time of being equal to the situation. Psychoanalysis is certainly not for the meek or for the faint-hearted.

The story of Mr K's analysis as I have described it in its beginning offers more questions than answers, especially with regard to what seems to have been the pivotal role of the session during which he undressed, leading to fundamental and sustained changes in his capacity to metabolise separation anxiety and to deal with psychical pain in a psychical way instead of evacuating it via somatic discharge.

I do not believe that the fact that this patient found himself naked on the couch had any curative virtue *in itself*. If it can be understood in its potentially mutative aspects, it is only as one moment in a lengthy dynamic process of intersubjective interaction, including the transference–countertransference situation, within the containing function of the analytical setting. Something had to happen, in the form of an act, which would threaten not only the analytical setting, but also the analyst's frame of mind. That was how it happened in the dynamics of the analysis with this particular analyst, but no doubt it might have happened in a different way with another analyst. What I do believe is that an analytical process of working through might not have been possible if something of the sort had not happened.

The analysand had to *do* something which meant obtaining something *real* from the analyst: by "real", I mean that something had to shift in the analyst's mind in his way of perceiving what is "proper" or "improper" in that specific moment; the analyst's mind had to adapt in order to discover the most appropriate way of facilitating self-development—with the risk of failure or of going directly to an acting-out, with a destructive impact on the process and on the setting. This "doing something real" had to do with going beyond the usual boundaries of analysis without destroying the analytical setting or the analyst's mind. When we think of Winnicott's now famous definition: "After being – doing. ... But first, being" (Winnicott, 1971, p. 85), there seems to be, in this kind of analytical situation, a reversal. In trying to reach "being", the analysand is first "doing", and this doing can only bring him to "being" if it is met by the analyst not first doing (resorting to analytical "technique"), but first being (trying to stretch the usual boundaries of his bodily ego in order not to "react").

This can create the conditions for some kind of new beginning. I suppose that, in this instance, Mr K had managed to make use of the analyst and the setting in order to give himself the opportunity of experiencing, even if it were only this once, the long-sought-after illusion of an omnipotence which allowed him to let go of some of his traumatic fixations and rekindled his capacity for dreaming—a "sample" of what had been missing too often in his own development.

The course the analyst must pursue is neither of these; it is one for which there is no model in real life. (Freud 1915a, p. 166)

This book, therefore, is not intended to be the poem of a journey nor the logbook of a wandering dream. On this occasion, the conflict is taken to the very moment of the act, with a refusal to separate, at the foot of the mountain, the poet from the mountaineer, on the river, the writer from the sailor, and, in the open country, the painter from the surveyor or the pilgrim from the topographer; the idea is to catch hold, in the very same moment, of the joy that is in the muscles, in the eyes, in the thoughts and in the dreams. My sole aim here is to try to discover in what mysterious caves in the depths of human beings these various worlds can come together and reinforce one another in all of their plenitude. (Segalen, 1915)

In memory of two remarkable women:
Piera Aulagnier and Laure Kazinetz, my mother.

CHAPTER ONE

Is the analyst a person?

Longe de mim em mim existo [Far from myself in myself I exist]
A parte de quem sou, [Standing apart from who I am,]
A sombra e o movimento em que consisto. [Shadow and movement
   of which I consist]

(Pessoa, 1960)

As soon as one person sits down in an armchair in order to listen, for the duration of an analytical session, to another person lying on a couch, that person is no longer at his or her own personal disposal, and we may well wonder what becomes of him/her. An instrument, said Freud, adding that "it is not so easy to play upon the instrument of the mind" (1905a, p. 262).

I feel tempted to follow that metaphor, with its musical reference: the apparatus of the soul transformed into an Aeolian harp that vibrates to the analysand's words and voice. Rather than a musical instrument, Freud suggested, more prosaically, an analogy with an object that, in his day and age, was at the forefront of technology: a telephone receiver. What is most remarkable in his account is not so much the metaphor of listening, communicating, and transmitting, but his description of an apparatus for transformation, the aim of which is to reconstruct the original object after a whole series of splittings into its component parts, while ensuring the elimination, as far as possible, of any distortions. According to that model, the psychoanalyst's unconscious deals with the various elements of the patient's "emerging unconscious" in such a way as to bring them together into a meaningful whole. In that process, any personal or contingent elements that belong to the psychoanalyst's personality will have been eliminated. In order to achieve a neutralisation of any elements that might give rise to distortions in that reconstruction, psychoanalysts will have carried out some degree of "psychoanalytical purification" of their own minds. Rendering those personal imperfections harmless means that the analyst can make available to the analysand the universal dimension of mental functioning. In that way, Freud attempted to conceive of the scientific character of subjectivity in the analytical process, in the course of which both analyst and patient agree to submit to a certain number of rules: even though Freud saw these as very simple, the effects that they have are surprisingly complex.

A forgetting of oneself

The most viable and scientific manner in which psychical reality can emerge is possible only if conscious intentionality and purpose are put on hold. Wilfred Bion would later say that, at the start of every session, the analyst must be without memory and without desire. The analyst is subjected to a rule—that of free-floating attention, which in itself lends meaning and heuristic effectiveness to the rule of free association to which the patient is subjected. The scientific standpoint of psychoanalysis is the outcome of a gamble, the taking of a risk with respect to the use of memory: "He should simply listen, and not bother about whether he is keeping anything in mind" (Freud 1912e, p. 115). The aim of these rules is to enable the laws of mental functioning to be brought into play in their intrinsic logic so as to undo the false links that, for defensive reasons, are being forcibly maintained. To that end, analyst and patient are invited to free themselves from their respective idiosyncrasies in order to come into contact with something of which they have no advance knowledge—something of which the structure does not depend on their will, but on the laws that govern understanding.

The highly specific action that psychoanalysts bring to bear on their own minds gives rise to unbinding and decomposition with respect to the patient's psychical material. The work of recomposition is done automatically according to the universal rules of organisation: "But on the whole, once begun, [the process] goes its own way and does not allow either the direction it takes or the order in which it picks up its points to be prescribed for it" (Freud 1913c, p. 130).

That somewhat optimistic picture of the curative process brought about by psychoanalysis was called into question by the metapsychological revisions introduced after 1915—these were necessitated by various problems arising in psychoanalytical practice. None the less, two elements remained absolutely fundamental in Freud's conception of psychoanalytical treatment: it implies, on the psychoanalyst's part, a profound change in his or her way of being in ordinary waking life, and the nature of that modification makes a fundamental contribution to the processes of psychical change that the treatment can facilitate— it enables both protagonists to stand back a little and observe, each from his/her own point of view, the mental processes that are unfolding in the course of the treatment.

To put it simply, forgetfulness, which lies at the heart of the analytical method in the way that it involves the analyst in the process, is fundamentally a forgetting of oneself. The quality of the profound modifications—topographical, economic, and dynamic—that the rules of free-floating attention and neutrality bring about involves the relationship which the analyst has with him/herself and with the outside world, and this up to the very frontiers of self-identity and modifications in states of consciousness.

By insisting on that aspect of the psychoanalytical setting, Freud opened up a pathway of thinking to which we psychoanalysts have so often paid little heed, because it is so demanding and anxiety provoking. Ferenczi, Bion, Winnicott, and Lacan have all been very mindful of that aspect, each in his own way. It is at the juncture of the subjective involvement of the analyst in the psychoanalytical process that psychoanalysts have shown the strongest resistance with respect to their own way of working.

When Lacan wrote, in "The function and field of speech and language in psychoanalysis", "Such is the fright that seizes man when he discovers the true face of his power that he turns away from it in the very act—which is his act—of laying it bare" (Lacan 2006, p. 201), and when, later, he said that the analyst is horrified by what he does, I think that he was referring to that highly particular experience of him/herself that an analyst has during the session. I shall try to show, below, how he attempted to respond to that and the impact that this had on his theorisation and, above all, on his conception of the analytical setting.

Let us consider one example, which is paradigmatic of Freud's own use of the method he invented and of his own implication in the treatment, at a time when he was still working on the various parameters of psychoanalytical technique. On 3 October 1907, the "Rat Man" came for his second session. At the beginning of the session, Freud explained the idea of resistance and warned the patient that he would probably have to put in a great deal of effort in order to overcome his difficulty in sharing what he was feeling.

At the point where he seemed ready to talk about the torture described by the cruel captain, which ever since had haunted him, the patient stopped talking, stood up, and asked Freud to spare him the need to go on with the story. Although Freud's reply was put in very simple words, it bore witness to the complexity and the multiplicity of dimensions in which the analyst is implicated, from the sphere of the transference as such all the way to himself as a person. That said, although the patient's remarks were addressed to Freud as the founder of psychoanalysis and inventor of the method of treatment, Freud did not reply in his own name. What fundamental issue was he pointing out to the Rat Man with respect to the particular characteristics of the relationship involving them when he spoke thus: "I assured [the patient] that ... I could not grant him something which was beyond my power" (Freud, 1909d, p. 166)?

It is as if Freud were saying, if the method that I invented is well founded, it is meant to be able to bring into play mechanisms that are governed by rules that are independent of my will. *I, too, therefore, just like you, am subjected to these rules.* It is not I who am subjecting you arbitrarily to the torturing constraint of speaking out (as would do a cruel captain taking sadistic pleasure in someone else's anguish); it is you who, like me, are subjected as a human being to the agonising ordeal of having to make use of a whole series of meaningful constraints that will tear you away from the inner experience, impossible to put into words, of the horror of a kind of pleasure, unknown to you yourself, in your attempt to share with someone else an intelligible representation of it. The nerve-wracking experience of this work of verbalisation is irreplaceable with respect to the kind of unexpected transformations that it may bring about. But nobody can do it for you. What I cannot exempt you from is the necessity of being human and dependent, for your own psychical survival, on the understanding of some other person. Therefore, quite naturally, the method leads the patient to a radical confrontation with primary distress and with his/her ability to make use of the resources of representation and language in order to overcome it and process it on an intrapsychical level through the intersubjective relationship.

It is hardly surprising that this issue came to the fore in the context of thinking about cruelty. Through his response, Freud displaced the transference attribution—"You are the cruel captain"—towards the very roots of cruelty in relationships between human beings. That is why psychoanalytical impassiveness could be perceived as being completely inhuman: because it confronts us with what, in ourselves, is so unbearably human.

In order to illustrate that cruelty, Freud, in his "Recommendations to physicians practising psychoanalysis" (1912e), has recourse to the image of the surgeon: "[He] puts aside all his feelings, even his human sympathy, and concentrates his mental forces on the single aim of per-forming the operation as skilfully as possible" (p. 115). That para-graph ends with an allusion to God via the motto of "a surgeon of earlier times": "Je le pansai, Dieu le guérit".[4] Freud adds: "The analyst should be content with something similar" (1912e, p. 115).

This, of course, is a counterpoint to the megalomaniacal omni-potence that is conveyed by "therapeutic pride". The analyst triggers something, he/she is a vector, a mediator—not a demiurge. What, at the analyst's behest, became disorganised will be able to reorganise itself, find its rightful place, come out right by following pathways over which the analyst has no control. That allusion to the divine tran-scendence that limits the power of the analyst in fact represents, in Freud's thinking, the field of science.

Lacan's ambivalence

In Lacan's writings, the issue is expressed thus in "The direction of the treatment and the principles of its power":

> As an interpreter of what is presented to me in words or deeds, I choose my own oracle and articulate it as I please, sole master of my ship after God; and while, of course, I am far from able to weigh the whole effect of my words, I am well aware of the fact and strive to attend to it. In other words, I am always free in the timing and frequency, as well as in the choice of my interventions, so much so that it seems that the rule has been entirely designed so as not to interfere in any way with my activity as an executor—to which corresponds the aspect of 'material', which is how my action here takes up what it produces. (Lacan, 2006, p. 491)

That statement calls for some comment, because we can see here how Lacan, like Freud, oscillates between two poles, words and acts, those of a desire that is imperative and expressed in one's own name, a process that follows its own path without any control. Lacan joined battle, in what he called a return to Freud, with what seemed to him, in the practice and in the writings of psychoanalysts in the early 1950s, to be a gradual loss of interest in what the analysand says, in language, in speech, and in the part that those elements play in the mutative effect produced by psychoanalysis. That is the underlying meaning of his polemical paper "The function and field of speech and language in psychoanalysis", which he delivered in Rome shortly after the schism that took place in 1953.

When, five years later, he tackled the question of "The direction of the treatment and the principles of its power", his aim was to show that it implies something radically different from a kind of direction of conscience; it consists above all in the application of the fundamental rule of analysis—here we can see something of Freud's paradigmatic stance with respect to the Rat Man, as I pointed out earlier. Lacan, however, emphasises the fact that the meaning of this statement in *words* will be affected by the *tone of voice* in which it is pronounced, given the fact that its modulations convey something of the *body* of the analyst. Lacan does not say so in so many words, but it is very much present in his paper. The point at which the fundamental rule is formulated, he writes, "consists in getting the patient to forget that it is merely a matter of words" (p. 490). That idea would seem to be in agreement with the argument according to which the analyst interprets not only what the analysand *says*, but also what he/she *does*. Lacan, however, draws back somewhat in the remainder of the sentence, thereby immediately reducing the complexity of what he has just envisaged: "This stage consists in getting the patient to forget that it is merely a matter of words, but . . . this does not excuse the analyst for forgetting it himself" (2006, p. 490).

There are other major contradictions in Lacan's paper. Did Pythia ever determine the content of the oracle? The oracular words were conveyed through the priestess, carried by her voice—but moulded by the gods. Why, then, refer to this, or to the power of divine transcendence, when at the same time he claims to be in control of everything that presides over the formulation of an interpretation at the point when it is communicated to the patient, following the rhythm of his interventions? While asserting that, as analyst, he has complete control over how he interprets, he claims that it is in the handling of the transference that his freedom is alienated. "In handling transference, on the other hand, my freedom is alienated by the splitting my person undergoes in it, and everyone knows that it is here that the secret of analysis must be sought" (2006, p. 491).

In fact, this splitting of the analyst's person as a result of the transference, far from being an element of alienation, as he claims in this paper, is more of an opportunity for freedom—not of *his* speech, but of speech *as such*, that is, speech that is no longer that of one particular person in the here-and-now situation. It was, after all, Lacan himself who asked the fundamental question concerning *who* was speaking in any given analytical session.

> But who will say what the analyst is there, and what remains of him when he is up against the wall of the task of interpreting? . . . Thus he prefers to fall back on his ego, and on the reality about which he knows a thing or two. . . . Who is the analyst? He who interprets by taking advantage of the transference? He who analyses transference as resistance? Or he who imposes his idea of reality? It is a question that may pinch a bit harder those to whom it is addressed, and be less easy to sidestep than the question, 'Who is speaking?' (pp. 494–495)

I shall come back later to the issue of *the being of the analyst*.

Is the idea of splitting really correct as a description of what goes on within the analyst's being, subjected as it is to the effects of the transference in the analytical situation?

Most of the time, analysts have the impression that they are working in the relatively temperate sphere of thoughts, conscious or pre-conscious, which Freud defined as trial actions. That sphere is compatible with the relatively silent functioning of free-floating attention and neutrality. Any disturbance in that area of functioning comes from the affects: the analyst suddenly feels touched, moved "in person". When, in a session, analysts feel, in and apparently for themselves, something of the nature of hate, love, desire, anger, boredom, joy, etc., it is better for them not to act as though they had felt nothing.

Neutrality does not consist in *not feeling* affects, but in not allowing them to follow their "natural" path towards internal discharge in the dynamics of intersubjective communication. That said, the *force* that they bring into the analytical process should not be stifled, because it lies at the very heart of psychical transformation. The analyst will, therefore, attempt to apply to his/her own mind what Freud emphasised with respect to the patient: "It is, therefore, just as disastrous for the analysis if the patient's craving for love is gratified as if it is suppressed" (1915a, p. 166). What involves the most intimate level of the analyst's psychical corporeality will be subjected to a specific kind of processing that turns it away from any *personal* use. Instead of acting or reacting with respect to a discharge of affect, the analyst will endeavour to go on feeling, without ceasing to think, and postponing as much as possible any recourse to discharge. This psychical work begins with the acknowledgement "I am the one who is feeling (this affect)" and continues with "No, I am not the one (to whom it is addressed)". Thereupon, the question becomes "What am I feeling, and for whom?"

Something is taking place in the theatre of my mind, something that I can feel, yet it does not involve me directly. The obviousness of what is being experienced, kept constantly on hold as far as attribution and ownership are concerned, acquires a fictitious dimension—hence the possibility of disengaging in the direction of the realm of illusion and the dynamics of mental play. More than a splitting, it is a paradox, close to that of the actor, according to Diderot. These are the modalities of the internal transformation to which the analyst subjects his/her affects during the session; that processing will be a decisive factor in making it possible for the analysand to break free of the compulsion to repeat. In the deflection that results, the analyst brings in the directness of the apparently unwavering reality of what is felt and experienced, in a space for representation in the theatrical sense of the term. Putting discharge on hold enables what was about to be mass-produced, as it were, in an enacted response to be fictionalised and virtualised.

The blind walls encaging the person affected or hurt become a shadow theatre in which *dramatis personae* can come to life. That movement takes up again what was constitutive of a fantasy or dream scenario, and actualises it in the psychical time sphere of the session.

The analyst's fright

Freud laid stress on the excessiveness of the transference: "The peculiarities of the transference . . . thanks to which it exceeds, both in amount and nature, anything that could be justified on sensible and rational grounds" (1912b, p. 100). That excessiveness cannot be processed and become meaningful unless it meets up with an equivalent excessiveness in the analyst in the manner in which he or she brings into play, in the psychoanalytical experience, his/her psychical being—including what is most bodily related in it. Compared with that comment on the excessiveness of the transference, there is this other indication of Freud's concerning the specific nature of the analyst's work: "The course the analyst must pursue is neither of these;[5] it is one for which there is no model in real life" (1915a, p. 166).

From that perspective, *neutrality does not protect the analyst*—quite the contrary: it requires the analyst to ensure at all times that he/she does not respond in person, while at the same time communicating something of what is most alive inside him/herself. It is obvious, then, that abstinence lies at the very heart of the dynamics of psychoanalytical treatment; it is not a fixed state, but a movement within the psyche resulting from a continuous effort towards drive regulation and transformation that analysts demand of their own psychical apparatus.

In his paper on "Observations on transference-love" (1915a), Freud, after some incidental arguments and counter-arguments, finally comes to the conclusion that "we have no right to dispute that the state of being in love which makes its appearance in the course of analytic treatment has the character of a 'genuine' love" (p. 168).

Going on to discuss what is taking place in the analyst, Freud in the end acknowledges that, particularly in the case of analysts "who are still youngish and not yet bound by strong ties" (p. 169), "there is an incomparable fascination in a woman of high principles, who confesses her passion" (p. 170).

What thereupon may endanger the psychoanalytical dimension of the treatment is not the desire to have a sexual relationship (Freud described that as "natural"), but desires that are more "subtle". To that, Freud quite simply set up a series of moral commandments and prohibitions, inviting analysts to adopt them: "It is quite out of the question for the analyst to give way" (p. 170). He went on to elaborate on this in several ways. "For the doctor, ethical motives unite with the technical ones to restrain him from giving the patient his love" (p. 169). "In my opinion, therefore, we ought not to give up the neutrality[6] towards the patient, which we have acquired through keeping the counter-transference in check" (p. 164).

Let us look more closely at this *indifference*. Freud made it clear that psychoanalysts are anything but indifferent; in the course of a session, they are affected by what is transpiring, and this at the deepest and most subtle of levels; that sentence of Freud's does, therefore, sound somewhat like a profession of faith. True, he does say that that neutrality has been *conquered*, which does indicate—without his going into any details, and in a way that is slightly too voluntarist—that some psychical work has been accomplished, although we are left somewhat in the dark about its nature. We could perhaps, with a smile on our lips, draw a parallel between that neutrality/indifference and the *belle indifférence* of the hysteric (Freud, 1895d, p. 135), the co-inventor of psychoanalysis. Another possible connection could be established here. In a very striking paragraph of his paper on transference love, Freud writes of the need to surmount the animal side of the self. Depending on how we read that extract, Freud's recommendation could be addressed just as much to the analyst as to the patient:

> Instead, he must consider that the time has come for him to put before the woman who is in love with him the demands of social morality and the necessity for renunciation, and to succeed in making her give up her desires, and, having surmounted the animal side of her self, go on with the work of analysis. (1915a, p. 163)

What follows shows that Freud is indeed referring to the patient and that this image of virtue in which morality triumphs—the feminine principle having been overcome by its masculine counterpart—is not a description of the path that the analyst must follow. "As we know, the passions are little affected by sublime speeches" (1915a,

p. 164). In the analyst, however, that animal side can be found in the metaphor in which the movement of an interpretation is compared to the manner in which an animal jumps on its prey: "a lion only springs once" (1937c, p. 219). The animal side is sublimated, but it continues to bear witness to a predatory form of epistemophilia.

What might be the relationship between that lion and the analyst's ego? Does it represent the ego of an analyst who satisfies his/her instincts by making use of the patient as a person and revels in the fact of being justified in so doing? Or does it represent the liberated power of an intelligence that surges forth to undo and put to flight the forces of destruction that lie in the very depths of the mind?

The terror that might seize the analyst faced with the drive-related violence that might be unleashed as a result of the psychoanalytical experience was first described by Freud, before Lacan took up the subject. Several elements come together at that point: the scientific project of psychoanalysis and its ideals; the analyst's subjective cathexis in all of its drive-related and sublimated aspects, with its roots in his or her own past history and involvement in the psychoanalytical method; and the mental phenomena aroused by the application of the analytical experience, the transference being an important element in this, but not the only one. It is at that point that issues concerning the analyst's ethical responsibility arise and that the paradox with respect to the analyst as a person becomes more intense.

Whatever the nature of the transference projections *on to* the surface of the psychical being of the analyst (the metaphor of the analyst-as-mirror) or *into* him or her (due to the movement of projective identification)—they divest the analyst, during the session, of his or her own being as a person, drawing it into the virtual dimension of a theatrical drama—it is, none the less, the case that the analyst commits him/herself as a person whenever an interpretation is suggested, no matter the "transpersonal" pathways thanks to which that interpretation came to fruition within the analyst.

Although the aim of psychoanalytical treatment is that of therapeutic psychical change, analysts cannot simply content themselves with facilitating, via the analytical situation, the production of psychical phenomena, without deciding to make some kind of intervention. That is what Freud emphasised quite clearly, with the metaphor of spirits rising from the underworld, in his description of the ethical position of the psychoanalyst:

> It would be just as though, after summoning up a spirit from the underworld by cunning spells, one were to send him down again without having asked him a single question. One would have brought the repressed into consciousness, only to repress it once more in a fright. (Freud 1915a, p. 164)

Freud does not speak here simply of fear or of anxiety. The word "fright" evokes a nameless dread that gives rise to traumatic fascination and paralysis. What comes to the surface and becomes visible here is a monstrosity of some kind, the Medusa's head, or a Gorgon, or, perhaps, even more frightening, a terrifying presence that can be given no figurative representation.

Such representations lead us towards myths and legends, and bring into play the heroic aspects of the analyst. It should be pointed out, all the same, that Freud does not invite the analyst–hero to strike down the beast and kill it so as to make it disappear. The one heroic task that can be demanded of the analyst is not that of doing away with the representation that is the source of the terror, but that of questioning it, that is, of *making it talk*. In other words, by means of image-building, representation, and language, to attempt to express the possible meanings it might contain, and, thereby, transform it without rejecting it.

The analyst's fright and the temptation to shy away is indeed due to the terrifying content of these images that spring from the underworld, but they have perhaps even more to do with the specific nature of the analyst's task—confront them, look at them, open them up, listen to them, feel them, touch them, taste what they are made of, and find the figurative and language-based means of metamorphosing them.

Lacan also makes use of the word "fright" at the very beginning of his chapter on "The function and field of speech and language in psychoanalysis":

> Such is the fright that seizes man when he discovers the true face of his power that he turns away from it in the very act—which is his act—of laying it bare. This is true in psychoanalysis. Freud's Promethean discovery was such an act, as his work attests; but that act is no less present in each psychoanalytic experience humbly conducted by any one of the workers trained in his school. (Lacan, 2006, p. 201)

I have drawn the reader's attention to the ambiguities and para-doxes that are linked to the idea of the power of the analyst. Misuse of power with respect to the analysand as a person is always a possibility and can be carried out by means of manipulating the trans-ference, so that the omnipotence of the parental imagos becomes embodied in the analyst as a person. It is that particular power that the analyst must at all times be prepared to put aside.

The idea of a power of transformation with the analyst as media-tor is, however, quite different; that element facilitates change in the patient's defensive structure and compulsion to repeat. That kind of power is of a different quality from that in which one person domi-nates another. Indeed, it becomes effective in the treatment only on condition that, in so far as is possible, the analytical relationship is free of any notion of ascendancy. Analysts cannot undertake any work of unbinding and rebinding that would constitute a liberating experience for the patient unless they acknowledge that they have no power over the rules that govern language, symbolic operations, and the pro-cesses that govern the transformation of affects. By allowing these ele-ments to operate inside themselves and in the analytical relationship with their patient, analysts can act so as not to thwart these various processes and let them play their part as much as possible in making use of their restructuring capacity. In so doing, the analyst enables the interpretational power of language and affects to come freely into play within the force-field created by the analytical situation.

The analyst who undertakes an analysis is, as it were, taking a gamble that he/she will be able to bring into play a capacity for inter-pretation that will make the whole undertaking meaningful. In the permanent temptation that the analyst might be faced with—that of turning aside from the task—lies a form of anxiety which he/she would prefer not to have: that of having the impression that the patient's freedom depends on the effects of the analyst's interpreta-tion, while thinking that any control he/she may have over the processing of that interpretation is, at the most, only relative.

The "fright" that analysts might feel when faced with the task of interpreting is due also to the tension that exists between their respon-sibility as interpreters and the temporality of the preconscious proces-sing of the interpretation, over which they have no control. Although responsible for their act of interpretation, analysts have no control over the moment at which they will have available to them an interpretation that might possess some *power of modification*. They cannot decide on that in advance—it is only in the deferred retroactive phase that they might perhaps be able to judge that. Nevertheless, every time analysts take the decision to say something other than make a rumbling noise or a mere interrogative repetition of a word uttered by the patient, this bears witness to the effects on them of their working through of the analytical process, and introduces a distance between the object of the transference and the subject of the enunciation, a distance that is conducive to opening up a path towards new meanings. In some cases, in an attempt to underline that distance, analysts will include in their formulation a reference to themselves in the third person: "You seem to think that your analyst . . .". Bringing the transference out into the open and highlighting it in an attempt to make it available for inter-pretation is also one way of letting the analysand understand that not all of the psychical phenomena that contribute to the analytical process can be reduced simply to that of the transference.

CHAPTER TWO

The repudiation of femininity in analytical listening

"So that what distinguishes a living machine is not the nature of its physico-chemical properties, complex as they may be, but rather the creation of the machine which develops under our eyes in conditions proper to itself and according to a definite idea which expresses the living being's nature and the very essence of life"

(Bernard, 1927, p. 93)

In Freud's life and in the development of psychoanalysis, the enigmatic obscurity of the dark continent played the part of a strange attractor, drawing thinking towards the umbilicus that links it to the unknown.

In Freud's writings, a secret thread connects the theme of the feminine element to that of the inexorability of time, the inflexibility of destiny, the inevitability of death, and the "unshakeable biological fact" (Freud 1933a, p. 95)—these topics themselves have a very close relationship to the conditions and unfolding of psychoanalytical treatment.

Freud did not like being the mother-figure in the transference because he felt himself to be too much of a man for that and, as is well

15

known, he fainted when the homosexual pressures of those close to him became too intense. Idealisation led him to theorise a mother–son relationship devoid of all ambivalence, since a mother's hatred for her son was, for Freud, even more unthinkable than a son's aggressiveness towards his mother; ambivalence, hate, and contempt could be part only of a mother–daughter relationship, as he wrote in a paper ("Femininity", 1933a) shortly after his mother, Amalie, died.

If we stay with the manifest content, Freud was indeed somewhat active and masculine in what he tells us, and in what we can surmise through his writings, of his manner of being a psychoanalyst. Yet, he left us a technique that, as far as possible, is free of any attempt at influencing, of suggestion, of manipulative domination, or the imposing of an alienating desire. The analyst must always refrain from being a Pygmalion.

> We refused most emphatically to turn a patient who puts himself into our hands in search of help into our private property, to decide his fate for him, to force our own ideals upon him, and with the pride of a Creator to form him in our own image and see that it is good. (Freud, 1919a, p. 164)

When Freud makes use of the aesthetic metaphor of the sculptor, he does so with the idea of helping us to feel and to touch the very substance of psychical material—soft clay or hard stone—with its inertia or its plasticity. How would it be possible to enable a lump of irritable matter to develop into a living form, with thoughts and desires, other than by kneading and moulding it directly with one's own hands?

"Je le pansai, Dieu le guérit" (1912e, p. 115). By attributing that comment to "a surgeon of earlier times" (see previous chapter), Freud, an atheist and a Jew, drew our attention to something that has to do with the principle of psychical change, something that lies beyond human willpower and brings about transformations beyond its control. In addition to warlike metaphors, with their idea of attacks undertaken in order to implement powerful strategies in the battle against resistance, Freud described, just as insistently, the conditions under which a process of transformation may develop, one that cannot come to fruition unless every intentionality and purposiveness involving a specific goal are put on hold. In his paper "Analysis terminable and interminable" (1937c), Freud writes of taming the drives and of the lion that only springs once, then goes on to discuss the question of the "natural end" to an analysis. In 1913, in his paper "On beginning the treatment", Freud insisted on the fact that the analyst's power had to be put into perspective and drew the reader/ trainee analyst's attention to a force that lies beyond his/her control, transcends technical devices, and emerges in terms of an irresistible momentum: "But on the whole, once begun, [the process] goes its own way and does not allow either the direction it takes or the order in which it picks up its points to be prescribed for it" (1913c, p. 130).

Perhaps God, too, together with the feminine element, time and death, is hidden somewhere in what Freud described as the conditions that facilitate the unfolding of psychoanalytical treatment. On the analyst's side, these include the psychical modifications brought about by the need for neutrality and free-floating attention. A God who is perhaps close to what Daniel Zaoui evoked,[7] a representation of Yahveh as "an idealized father but also someone who embodies an early maternal image—a scandalous and impure mixture, not representable by anyone other than the high priest, unmentionable by the faithful".

It would seem to be in order to question that feminine–maternal representation of God that the high priest ventures alone into the Holy of Holies on Yom Kippur. In the chapter of *Playing and Reality* entitled "Creativity and its origins", Winnicott says that

> in the evolution of Greek myth the first homosexuals were men who imitated women so as to get into as close as possible a relationship with the supreme goddess. This belonged to a matriarchal era out of which a patriarchal god system appeared with Zeus as head. (1999, pp. 78–79)

That hypothesis establishes the necessary link between his clinical observations on the splitting of the feminine element in male patients and the theory of object relations.

Long before its explicit appearance in that theory, the issue of refusal/acceptance of the feminine element was already contained and condensed in Freud's invention of the internal setting in the analyst's psyche, favourable to analytical listening, as defined by two concepts—neutrality and free-floating attention—which echo a third one—free association, the internal attitude that the analysand is required to adopt. Those two notions entail an acceptance of the feminine element that involves the acceptance of laws that define the Symbolic order and those that have to do with biology, that is, those which create possibilities for meaning and for life.

Disagreement with the ego

In "The theme of the three caskets", Freud (1913f) describes a feminine figure which, in the attractive guise of a goddess of love, represents the goddess of death. In mythical legends, as in Shakespeare's plays, the young woman whom the male character has to choose from three girls or three sisters always has the same typical characteristics: the dullness of lead, the dullness of silence (she is mute), and the dullness of her complexion; her paleness is striking, she tries to keep well out of the limelight, to stay in the background, to go unnoticed, and to remain unrecognisable. It is her total silence that enabled Freud, via the symbolism of dreams, to see in her a figure of death. Silence, withdrawal, neutrality, and self-effacing—those are the typical features of the analyst which we find in the attributes of that young woman: a representation of death, but also of one of the Fates and one of the two forms that the mother-figure takes on during a man's lifetime—the woman who destroys him, the mother-earth who takes him to her breast again. If we adopt Freud's metaphor of the pure gold of analysis as opposed to the copper of therapy, it would seem that we are some way away from any correspondence between that image of the young woman and psychoanalysis. On the other hand, if we apply to Freud's choice of gold his own method of interpretation via the opposite (a technique of which he makes significant use in "The theme of the three caskets"), then things do become clearer.

That figure appears in a different form in another paper that Freud wrote at about the same time as "The theme of the three caskets"— "On beginning the treatment" (Freud 1913c). It is through a kind of fable that Freud characterises the manner in which a lay person who knows nothing about the experience of psychoanalysis perceives neurosis: "Thanks to this ignorance, neurosis is looked on as a kind of 'maiden from afar'. 'None knew whence she came'; so they expected that one day she would vanish" (1913c, p. 129).

Yet, she is by no means ready to vanish. As in "The theme of the three caskets", she represents something inexorable, inevitable, inflexible: the inexorability of time as well as that of drive impulses, the inevitability of death, the inflexibility of fate.

The aim of the active technique is to diminish the length of time that a treatment lasts; it refuses to have anything to do with the passive attitude that consists in acknowledging and accepting the tempo that is specific to each analysis: "once begun, [the process] goes its own way". Neutrality must bring its passive aim actively into play upon the constantly repeated temptation to be "active". Freud puts this very clearly: "In males the striving to be masculine is completely ego-syntonic from the first" (Freud, 1937c, pp. 250–251). I shall try to show that, in fact, the topographical, economic, and dynamic modifications brought about in the analyst by neutrality and by free-floating attention are not in accordance with the ego.

Let us continue to follow in the steps of that maiden from afar, let us see just how far that process goes in its own way: it, too, is inexorable, inevitable, and inflexible, like the Fates, or perhaps like "the urge of what is living to return to an inanimate state", according to Freud's definition of the death drive in "Analysis terminable and interminable" (1937c, p. 246). The conservative nature of the drives means that they are always attempting to return to a previous state. It was on that basis that Freud conceived of the death drive as being an attempt to restore the primal inorganic state of inanimate matter; similarly for the drive towards recovery, which is responsible for our being able to convalesce and which borrows from embryology the capacity to regenerate lost organs ("Anxiety and instinctual life", in *New Introductory Lectures on Psycho-Analysis*, Freud, 1933a). Freud taught us that the arrival of anything new requires the expenditure of psychical energy, something that the psyche is loath to undertake. Psychical expenditure is, therefore, not at all "perfectly natural". To the extent to which that psychical expenditure can take place, in particular as far as the analyst is concerned, the psychoanalytical process cannot be superimposed on the unbinding effect of the death drive. Embryology is, in fact, completely in tune with that young maiden from afar in "On beginning the treatment":

The analyst's power over the symptoms of the disease may thus be compared to male sexual potency. A man can, it is true, beget a whole child, but even the strongest man cannot create in the female organism a head alone or an arm or a leg; he cannot even prescribe the child's sex. He, too, only sets in motion a highly complicated process, determined by events in the remote past, which ends with the severance of the child from its mother. A neurosis [i.e., the 'maiden from afar'] as well has the character of an organism. (1913c, p. 130)

Let us try to unfold the interlacing of those metaphors. The analyst's power applied to the neurosis, the maiden from afar, and also to the analysand's psyche, is comparable to the male sexual force which penetrates and impregnates: the analysand's neurosis and psyche are similar to a living female organism. The analytical act, sexual and virile, does not have any power of control; it gives an impulse to a momentum, an impetus, but the complex nature of the unfolding of the process is beyond its control; it impregnates, but the ensuing gestation is none of its business. The series of phenomena that characterise the unfolding of the analytical process does not range simply from impregnation to the creation of a child—which is not the main characteristic of the end/the aim of analysis. The outcome is not the birth of a baby, but separation, the separation of a child from his/her mother.

If we refer to the much later paper of Freud's, "Anxiety and instinctual life" (1933a), separation and the anxiety to which this gives rise are, for Freud, the prerogative of girls—their anxiety about losing love is the dominant one, compared to castration anxiety, which is the prerogative of boys. That trend in an analysis that goes "quite naturally" towards separation is, therefore, above all a feminine movement. In both the primary dimension (separation) and the secondary one (secondary sexual representations, both masculine and feminine), the gradual unfolding of the analysis, seen from the analysand's side, is, for Freud, feminine in nature. Freud appears to limit that feminine movement to what takes place in the analysand's psyche and to those extremely complex mechanisms and phenomena that are typical of the analytical process, the analyst having no control over them. It would even seem to be the case that this feminine aspect is "repudiated" with regard to the complexity of the processes that take place in the analyst. This dividing up, of course, plays a defensive role, all the more so in that it is in contradiction with what Freud invented—neutrality and free-floating attention—as being the psychical means to sustain the analyst's attentive listening.

That division, however, cannot stand up to a deeper analysis of the question: that is what I shall attempt to illustrate on the basis of a preliminary metapsychological study of neutrality and free-floating attention. Similarly, the very marked—and, indeed, "psychological"— distinction between what goes on in the analyst's mind and what is happening in that of the analysand does not account for the highly specific nature of the analytical process; it does not stand up to a crit- ical examination of what experience tells us. Once again, it is the metapsychological examination of the facts that can help us make some progress: an analysis from a topographical point of view, of course, because we are dealing with dividing and limits/frontiers, but also from an economic and a dynamic one, because it is also a matter of psychical intensity, therefore of energy, and of movement, and these elements tend to blur any attempt at clear and distinct topographical layouts. On that point, it is important to keep in mind two comments that Freud made: (1) repression is "a process that is neither conscious nor preconscious, taking place between quotas of energy in some unimaginable substratum" (1933a, p. 90), and (2), "If we advance a step further in our analytic experience, we come upon resistances of another kind, which we can no longer localize and which seem to depend on fundamental conditions in the mental apparatus" (1937c, p. 241). These two concepts—a describable psychical mechanism that applies to a non-representable substance, and resistances that can- not be localised in the mental apparatus or attributed to a specific agency—move us slightly further away from the positivist and realist point of view towards the domain of the negative, the potentialities of which have been studied by André Green.

> If, as Freud thought, negation does not exist in the unconscious, the question raised here is that of the relations between the language and the substitute (not subjected to the negative) for negation which corre- sponds to it in the unconscious. However, the category of the negative is not constituted and the hypothesis of the inexistence of 'no' in the unconscious is not thereby reduced to a pure and simple absence of negativity. (Green, 1999, p. 24)

If we try to bring these ideas into line with two other elements— on the one hand, a metapsychological description of neutrality and free-floating attention, and, on the other, a conception of the psychical

work carried out by the analyst in terms of an aptitude for and availability towards the implementation of psychical bisexuality—this
might help us to make some progress in our understanding of the
particular complexity that is brought into play through the psychoanalytical experience. We must not forget that Freud defined that
experience as "a state which never does arise spontaneously in the
ego" (1937c, p. 227), and that, in his "Observations on transference-
love" (1915a, p. 166), he commented, "The course the analyst must
pursue is . . . one for which there is no model in real life". The specific
element that has introduced itself into the ego of the person who has
had an experience of psychoanalysis cannot, therefore, be defined in
direct and immediate terms of some visible result or other: it is to be
expressed in terms of substantial changes in psychical material, the
consistency of the ego, the economy and dynamics of the relationships
between the various agencies. We must remember also that—and this,
too, was Freud's point of view—psychoanalytical therapy enables a
deferred and retroactive correction to be brought to bear on the
process of primary repression. No more than that—but no less!

Unbinding and reconstructing

It has often been said that the fundamental rule of free association is
impossible to follow to the letter. Similarly, the neutrality and free-
floating attention demanded of the analyst are only possible up to a
point. It would be a pity to see that limit as a superego bar placed too
high and, therefore, impossible to reach. The upper limit of the
demand made in this instance is the beginning of the switching-on of
the psychical apparatus within the dynamics set up by the indefinite
movement that tends asymptotically towards that limit. As long as it
is not dealt with from an ego-ideal perspective, that requirement
keeps permanently alive a to-and-fro movement that is not closed in
on itself but multi-directional, without any final resolution.

Neutrality and free-floating attention cannot be looked upon as if
they were independent of each other. In a dynamic field that is always
being renewed, the requirement of neutrality cannot be sustained
other than by means of free-floating attention. This, in turn, can sustain the indeterminate nature of its suspension only with active
neutrality as its background.

These two concepts gradually came to the fore when Freud's therapeutic experience—and, therefore, his attempt to theorise what was transpiring—began to disengage from hypnotism. It was through his attempt to think differently about the issue of influence in relation to psychical change that Freud came to the conclusion that neutrality (a word which he himself never used, in fact) and free-floating attention were the two specific factors that distinguished the psychoanalytical approach from other kinds of psychotherapy.

Recommending free-floating attention is something of a paradox because it implies the intention to break free of all intentionality, a willingness to suspend any cathexis of purposive ideas. That project makes it possible to loosen some connections and perhaps even to undo or dissolve them altogether. Free-floating attention has to do with *lysis*, with the activity of unbinding that is specific to psychoanalysis. It encourages discontinuity, disjunction, separation, division, decomposition, and breaking-up. Given that, it may easily—all too easily, perhaps—work hand in glove with the silent death drive.

Free-floating attention undoes ties within the overall coherence of secondary logic, it breaks up syntactic strings, it tends to dissociate word-presentations and thing-presentations, and to break the link between affect and representation, so that it liberates free energy and sets up a Brownian motion between all of these elementary particles which are, thereby, scattered everywhere. Whether we use a metaphor borrowed from physics, chemistry, or linguistics in our attempt to describe these effects, one particular aspect always predominates: unbinding. The consequence of this, from the point of view of psychical economy, is that the level of free energy in the system rises and things begin to move in the dynamic field.

Free-floating attention contributes to plunging the analyst into a kind of trance that comes close both to a dream-like state and to that of hypnosis; in this way, a reversal occurs with respect to the practice of hypnosis. However, the metapsychological description that can be made of the effects of free-floating attention depends on whether we look at them from the point of view of Freud's first (topographical) model of the mind or of his second (structural) model. For the moment, the manner in which I have described these is compatible with the topographical model. In that respect, free-floating attention comes into action mainly at the frontier between the Preconscious and Conscious systems, and with respect to the barrier formed by repression.

In this model, free-floating attention enables false connections to be modified; it comes into action with respect to concatenations and on what Lacan would later refer to as the signifying chain. It allows for formal regression of thinking, as in dreams. In spite of its economic and dynamic effects, it can be in harmony with an Unconscious conceived of in an essentially grammatical and rhetorical mode.

If, however, we look at the effects of free-floating attention with the structural model of the mind as our frame of reference, the description we make will be very different and, in the narrow sense of the term, will belong to quite another dimension. Free-floating attention does not simply impact in a linear fashion on repression or signifying chains. When the unconscious is seen as replete with drive impulses and when the personality is broken down into several agencies, this complicates the picture quite significantly. Free-floating attention has much more than a linear impact on binding and unbinding; it influences also the structure, the form, and the volume of the analyst's ego. From a two-dimensional picture, we move to a three-dimensional one—plus a fourth dimension in each case: that of time.

The structural distinctions between ego, id, superego, and reality become mobile and floating within the analyst's psyche, leading, for example, to the states of transitory depersonalisation described by de M'Uzan (1977) in his paper "The counter-transference and the paradoxical system", with their economic and dynamic consequences that give interpretation its mutative power.

In the topographical model of the mind, free-floating attention and neutrality are processes that have a passive aim: suspension, delay, holding back, and abstinence. In the structural model, what is added to these is the deployment of the analyst's interiority, the availability of his/her psychical space so that some mental operations concerning the patient can unfold and be played out there. The analyst's identifications and sense of identity are involved (the free-floating aspect is no longer aimed only at the signifiers or judgements being made, but also at the frontiers of the ego). Consequently, the requirement of free-floating attention and neutrality is not limited to ways of thinking; it involves mental functioning as a whole. It is only on that basis that the concept of containment becomes meaningful; indeed, it then becomes obvious that the containing function is, to some extent, defined by free-floating attention, which avoids any clear decisions, and even more so by neutrality, which actively maintains a kind of buffer zone that has many similarities with the protective shield against excitation. In that perspective, a welcoming attitude and receptiveness are some of the essential qualities of the being of the analyst, the feminine and maternal aspects of whom thus become obvious; this endows with deep meaningfulness concepts such as the mother's capacity for reverie, as described by Bion, and the primary maternal preoccupation, as explored by Winnicott. In the former, neutrality makes for processing rather than evacuating, while in the latter it promotes survival rather than retaliation.

The analyst's ego acquires the ability to tolerate some degree of distortion without falling to pieces; that ability can be kept in operation during a sufficient length of time to enable adaptation to transference demands, particularly those in the primary dimension. The analyst's ego agrees temporarily to be modified so as to avoid any traumatic repetition brought about by the transference. In that sense, the arrangement set up to facilitate the analyst's attentive listening enables a temporary suspension of the pleasure/unpleasure automatisms that usually trigger the requisite defensive operations. That renunciation, temporary but repeated, of the analyst's habitual defensive modalities will be tolerated differently by different analysts— from one patient to another, in any one patient depending on what is taking place at that particular time in the treatment, and according to the vagaries of the analyst's personal life. The psychical metabolisation of this required suspension of attention is more or less successful, and is not without its impact on the analyst's overall psychical economy. From this point of view, it could be worthwhile perhaps to look at the matter of the analyst's character.

In *Studies on Hysteria* (1895d), it was with a woman patient, Emmy von N—and partly thanks to her—that Freud was able to understand the negative impact, on the treatment, of his own enthusiasm (see Miller, 2012). After a session in which he promised her that she would be freed from any misfortunes and from the pains all over her body, he noted as an afterthought: "on this occasion my energy seems to have carried me too far" (1895d, p. 61, footnote). The patient rebelled at this, and Freud agreed to follow some of the specific indications that she gave him in a somewhat firm tone of voice. As a result, he gradually began to modify his technique. Putting aside the head-to-head confrontation—the counter-force of the will and suggestions of the physician opposing the force of the patient's resistance—Freud gradually developed a *laissez-faire* technique: let it go, let the patient think, speak . . . At the same time, hypnotic suggestion lost much of its former influence. That development of free-floating attention came to the fore in the encounter with Emmy and in his contact with her—contact in the literal sense of the word, because he massaged her on an almost daily basis. It was in that context, in which Freud found himself in the shoes of the original seductress who, while taking care of her infant, awakens the baby's eroticism, that he invented free-floating attention and realised the part that the auto-analysis of his own dreams could play in working out his theory. The progression of that dialogue between Freud and Emmy and between Freud and himself led to significant changes in technique:

1. Freud came to realise that Emmy's futile and disjointed conversation while he was massaging her had both meaning and purpose: "Nor is her conversation during the massage so aimless as would appear. . . . It is as though she . . . was making use of our conversation, apparently unconstrained and guided by chance, as a supplement to her hypnosis (p. 56)
2. The signifying interruption[8] is an avoidance. Freud realised this. His patient's words went their own way, at their own rhythm and tempo, and came to an end. It was up to him to wait for a favourable moment in which to make a comment. The analyst has to put up with any possible grip the patient comes to have on him/her, not the other way round: "I had interrupted her after her first story . . . I now saw that I . . . cannot evade listening to her stories in every detail to the very end" (p. 61).

    There are limits to enthusiasm and ardour. Something more important and more essential had to come to the fore, something that had its own internal logic, something of which neither Freud nor Emmy was in control.
3. The active technique is useless and suggestion is simply the illusion of controlling time, memory and death. It is a pity that, some twenty years later, the Wolf-Man was not as outspoken as Emmy, or was Freud's patient at a time when Freud was more involved in defending his method rather than inventing it, or, again, had, as a man, suffered from a somewhat pronounced "constitutional" bisexuality. "I requested her to remember by tomorrow. She then said in a definitely grumbling tone that I was not to keep on

asking her where this and that came from, but to let her tell me what she had to say" (p. 63). Here, we see that resistance is not always working against the general trend of an analysis.

4.   Emmy imposed on Freud her method and little by little relegated hypnosis to being something of merely secondary importance. "What she tells me before the hypnosis becomes more and more significant" (p. 64).

5.   Freud did not appear to feel any sexual excitement while massaging Emmy. The generative displacement from bottom to top increased the power of his thinking and enabled him to unleash the additional energy that was necessary for him to accept this new situation. While this was going on, Emmy did what she could to arouse his libido. "During massage . . . she told me a loosely connected string of anecdotes, which may have been true" (p. 66). We see from this that Freud was very interested in the negative side of things, and knew how to make something of it.

6.   Freud realised that what was going on deep inside him was sustaining advances in his theory and fuelling his understanding of what Emmy was saying to him. The analysis of his dreams enabled him to make a comparison between how the mind functions in dreams and in hysteria.

> I succeeded in tracing all these dreams back to two factors: (1) to the necessity for working out any ideas which I had only dwelt upon cursorily during the day—which had only been touched upon and not finally dealt with; and (2) to the compulsion to link together any ideas that might be present in the same state of consciousness. (p. 67, footnote)

Here, the idea of unbinding and rebinding is already present. It is easy enough to see in what way free-floating attention works in the direction of unbinding; what is not obvious is why that momentum of unbinding should come to a halt. There is always in the background the risk that Thanatos might grab hold of that unbinding function of free-floating attention and append it to its silent work of dissolution. Therefore, there has to be an abutment or a barrier to counter the movement towards unbinding. What, then, is the nature of the principle that sets up this brake and puts an end to unbinding? What drives it? Where does it get its energy from? Is it a "natural" principle, inherent in the mind and in the dynamics of the analytical process, or does it require the active intervention of the analyst? Does that intervention take the form of the analyst's direct influence or does it involve a mode of participation of a different kind, one that we do not usually encounter in "real life"? That was how Freud himself put the question in his paper "Lines of advance in psycho-analytic therapy" in 1918.

> The psycho-synthesis is thus achieved during analytic treatment without our intervention, automatically and inevitably. We have created the conditions for it by breaking up the symptoms into their elements and by removing the resistances. It is not true that something in the patient has been divided into its components and is now quietly waiting for us to put it somehow together again. (1919a, p. 161)

Automatically: Here again is the idea of a process, in this case one of recomposition, which takes place quite naturally, without any intervention by an external human being's will or desire; this comes close to the idea of an analysis which, once begun, goes its own way.

Inevitably: Here once more is the idea of something unavoidable, inflexible, irresistible—the trajectory of a force that has to accomplish its own destiny. Once false connections have been destroyed, the irresistible power of Eros will reconstruct the scattered elements and bring them together in their correct relationship to one another.

How, then, are we to reconcile what appears to be a complete elimination of any active intentionality on the analyst's part with the rest of the paper, in which Freud sees what the analyst does as "[opening up] a new field of analytic technique" (1919a, p. 162)?

The paradox that Freud invites us to reflect upon cannot bear any fruit unless we go deeper into the idea of neutrality. In order to do that, we will have to explore its metapsychological complexity, extricating it from a conception that undermines its meaningfulness and its significance through reducing it to merely abstaining from any kind of intervention or subjective manifestation on the analyst's part. Curiously enough, that would imply seeing neutrality as having a restrictive function, whereas, in fact, its aim is to preserve as much as possible the redeployment of all the potentialities and virtualities that are usually paralysed. Neutrality is not a behaviour-based instruction recommending phobic avoidance or obsessionalisation of attitudes. It is a subtle internal attitude, always on the alert, which not only feels at home with freedom of thought and the lively and spontaneous manifestations of the mind, but also, in principle, should guarantee that these will always be possible. It maintains internal mobility as opposed to the temptation to act which repeatedly finds in the drive for domination a faithful ally, leading to the fossilisation of the mind.

The attitude of neutrality, when faced with something obvious, a strongly held belief or a certainty, consists in letting the twofold question *Why?* and *Why not?* reverberate together for some length of time; this enables the object to be looked at simultaneously from different angles and points of view—changing the vertex, as Bion might have said. In Latin, *ne uter* means "not either", neither yes nor no, neither me nor the other person, neither masculine nor feminine. But it means also one and the other simultaneously in the possibility of being, in the same trend of thought, mixed together yet separate. Neutrality leads us towards the logic of primeval words and brings us near to primary processes.

Neutrality and primary creativity

It was the question of judgement that made Freud aware of the need to develop further his ideas on neutrality and free-floating attention. For free-floating attention, judgement as to reality has to be put on hold and for neutrality, moral judgement has to be withheld; this gives rise to an attitude of reserve, a delay before anything is said. Far from being a defensive manoeuvre, that attitude of withdrawal exposes the analyst's psyche while, at the same time, rejecting the comfort of explanatory findings and libidinal discharge. Delaying puts on hold any abrupt actualisation of possible meanings and affects via a concluding pronouncement. This, however, does not imply that neutrality leads to a neutralisation of the psyche. By doing without its usual defensive modalities, the psyche has to spend a great deal of mental energy in order to maintain that state of non-reactivity and non-enactment. The idea, in fact, is to set up a very specific state of dynamic mobility. Paradoxically, that required neutrality does not produce a state of lifelessness; it switches the psychical apparatus on and increases the level of free energy in the system—and this, contrary to the pleasure principle. Psychical intensity is maintained at a high level, without any discharge of cathexis. That psychical energy, in its unbound state, becomes available for facilitating simultaneous multi-directional movements along the various axes indicated by polysemy.

It will also enable a particular kind of treatment of the inflow of excitation by switching off the short circuit of co-excitation. Neutrality enables us not to respond to excitation by increasing that excitation (co-excitation), which sets up the short circuit of acting out as opposed to the longer circuit of working through. Neutrality introduces what could be called a re-routing of psychical economy by interrupting the cumulative logic of quantity. The traumatophile elements of excitation that seek the automatic functioning of repetition arrive via the transference path and make their way into a living environment that is able to take them in and contain them for a sufficient length of time until new pathways towards disengagement can be opened up. Neutrality enables the analyst's psyche to act as a mediator that, for the time being, puts on hold the enslavement of quantity[8] and its consequences (the compulsion to repeat) in order to find or to find again the road to what Winnicott called primary creativity. From then on, everything is ready for the emergence of psychosynthesis without any kind of stranglehold, takeover, or interventionist intention: a process can, thereupon, unfold freely, with access to the constraints of the symbolic and biological dimensions that enable transformation, metabolisation, metamorphosis, and mutation to take place: Eros and Thanatos, affect and representation, language and speech, masculine and feminine—not in opposition to each other or intertwined, but linked together in an unending, process-related conflict.

Neutrality enables the setting-up of temporary conditions that are related to the possibility of finding/refinding a sufficient feeling of continuity of being described by Winnicott (1975, p. 303) as "uncut by reactions to impingements". For that feeling to be sufficient, the mother has to be able to let herself go entirely into that normal illness that Winnicott called the "primary maternal preoccupation"; "she must be able to reach this state of heightened sensitivity, almost an illness, and to recover from it" (1975, p. 302) "which enables [her] to adapt delicately and sensitively to the infant's needs at the very beginning" (1975, p. 302).

Elsewhere, I have described the analyst's mental activity during a session as a temporary normal illness. Through some of its aspects, if neutrality is indeed in place, it corresponds to that particular state of mind: the primary maternal preoccupation.

This will help us to see how we can differentiate more clearly between therapy and psychoanalysis, and, at the same time, take us back to the idea of the repudiation of the feminine dimension.

Winnicott talks of women who missed the boat initially because, for various reasons, they were unable to offer their infant that "illness", the availability that allows them to adapt to the baby's needs. It should be noted that this "inability" implies that those women actively struggled against an availability which was quite naturally present in them, but which they rejected. In order to compensate for that missed opportunity and for the subtle consequences that this will entail for their infant's future development, these women put an incredible amount of effort, an enormous activity, into their attempts to put things right and to adapt to the situation. In so doing, says Winnicott, they act as though they were therapists, not the child's parent: "Instead of taking for granted the good effect of an early and temporary preoccupation they are caught up in the child's need for therapy, that is to say, for a prolonged period of adaptation to need, or spoiling" (1975, pp. 302–303).

In this light, it is easier to understand that the temptation of reparatory activism which might take hold of the analyst, in the sudden grip of a burning desire to be a "good therapist", is the sign that he/she finds it difficult to remain in that particular "ill" state of psychical availability brought about by neutrality and free-floating attention. We could say that that represents the "positive" aspect of the countertransference, the negative one being exemplified by destructive acting out. The countertransference is, therefore, both a struggle against accepting and sustaining the mental dynamics specific to the analyst's attentive listening, and a refusal of the internal modifications that this attitude entails. In its dimension as a counter-resistance, the countertransference has always to do with narcissistic reassurance and the affirmation of self-identity. The other aspect of the countertransference is what could be called its heuristic dimension, which is an integral part of its encounter in the analytical situation with the transference.

We are beginning to see more clearly how that refusal comes close to that of the feminine element in its aspect as a fundamental resistance to psychoanalysis. This is how Winnicott analyses why some women refuse to let themselves be taken over by their primary maternal preoccupation: "When a woman has a strong male identification she finds this part of her mothering function most difficult to achieve, and repressed penis envy leaves but little room for primary maternal preoccupation" (1975, p. 302).

Perhaps, however, the main element does not lie in repression of the wish for a penis. The threat of absolute dependence is even more fundamental in the repudiation of the feminine dimension, in the difficulty that may be experienced in agreeing to remain within the parameters of psychoanalytical attentive listening, with all that that implies with regard to depersonalisation and passivity.

> Indeed a recognition of absolute dependence on the mother and of her capacity for primary maternal preoccupation, or whatever it is called, is something which belongs to *extreme sophistication*, and to a stage not always reached by adults. The general failure of recognition of absolute dependence at the start contributes to the fear of WOMAN that is the lot of both men and women. (Winnicott, 1975, p. 304)

Winnicott has often been criticised for never speaking of the father. It is not quite true to say that he never mentioned the father, but he did so only rarely. In my opinion, when Winnicott was writing, thinking, and theorising, *he*, in the overall movement of his thoughts, was the father looking at the mother and the infant. That is perhaps a fantasy interpretation on my part, but I would say that it is not only that. From the "vertex" of the primary maternal preoccupation, what is the father? The father is what enables the mother to let herself slip into that temporary but necessary state of madness; in order to do this, the father can identify with the mother, without any desire to replace her, and identify with the infant without entering into rivalry with him/her. The father can "hold" mother and baby in his thoughts and maintain his cathexis of reality so that the mother can temporarily not concern herself with that. From that point of view, in his/her mental functioning, the analyst identifies with both the mother and the father.

Biology, femininity, and the death drive

At the end of his paper "Analysis terminable and interminable" (1937c), Freud writes, "The repudiation of femininity can be nothing else than a biological fact" (p. 252). In a footnote on the same page, he adds, "What they [i.e. men] reject is not passivity in general, but passivity towards a male".

If that were indeed the case, it is difficult to understand why Freud went as far as to link the enigma of resistance to recovery with the relationship between bisexuality and the death drive. Defending oneself against recovery implies defending oneself against death—or, more precisely, against the death drive as the impulse of the living to return to a state of non-life. Over and beyond the horror of castration, it is also a matter of horror of dissolving, of going back to a primitive kind of mental functioning, of returning to the maternal breast experienced as equivalent to being abandoned in the arms of death. Beyond the forms in which that force is bound in the guise of destruction, such as in a guilty conscience and the need to be punished, "other quotas of the same force, whether bound or free, may be at work in other, unspecified places" (Freud, 1937c, pp. 242–243).

That silent stranger of no fixed abode resembles the maiden from afar, pale-faced and unobtrusive—the disturbing face of psychoanalysis, the deadly hostess who just might drag us far beyond the limits of what is thinkable, towards formlessness, vagueness, and lack of differentiation. In that sense, the repudiation of femininity is the refusal to follow that deadly seductress in the inexorable logic of the pleasure principle. Repudiation of femininity bears witness to Eros's struggle against Thanatos.

As a counterpoint to what has been called Freud's pessimism, abundantly illustrated by the intertwining of femininity and the death drive, and which appears to dominate his thinking, there is his assertion of life's unremitting stubbornness in maintaining its existence; that idea is related to concepts such as traces, facilitation, memory, the intemporality of the unconscious, and the immortality of the repressed, as well as to that of phylogenetic transmission: "What has once come to life clings tenaciously to its existence" (1937c, p. 229), he writes imperturbably in "Analysis terminable and interminable". We have all seen clinical situations in which representations of the drive to dominate have pushed their way into the very idea of life as a constraint by Eros to create more and more links, which, thereafter, are seen only as the chains of the worst possible kind of alienation: "Condemned to cathect", as Piera Aulagnier put it.

One of my patients, a highly qualified researcher in biology and physiology who specialised in oncogenesis, told me about the petrifying horror she felt every spring when she saw grass beginning to grow. Her most powerful ally in her attempt to reconquer the short-lived fragments of a feeling of liberty was, in fact, the death drive, since the logic of life was nothing but a spreading of tentacles representing a fantasy of primary maternal omnipotence. If we were to go a step further, we would no longer be able to locate that fantasy, in its function as structuring the architectonics of mental space. How, then, are we to understand, following the separate causalities of mental determinism on the one hand and biological determinism on the other, an illness as eloquent as autoimmune disease? (See Chapter Thirteen, 'A thirst from so long ago".)

To what degree of topographical, formal, and dynamic regression must the analyst's psyche be subjected for it to be able to navigate around those regions in which some meaningfulness is preserved (but in what form?) when the barrier between the psychical and biological dimensions appears to have been abolished? If psychoanalysis is something more than the simple application of scientific knowledge to mental phenomena in order to explain them, no reductive theory, mathematical, linguistic, or cybernetic, could account for its specific nature. Psychoanalysis is, of course, one of the human sciences, and it shares with biology the difficulty of having to work out a theory of living beings via the importing of explanatory models from other fields of thought that threaten it with reductionism. What Alain Prochiantz (1995) wrote about Claude Bernard could also apply to Freud:

> Although his intelligence was rigorous, he was methodical in his observation and he constructed his experiments in the form of traps for live beings, Claude Bernard did not make a religion of method or false precision; he knew, as he himself put it, when to leave the furrow and rush across the fields. And it was across the fields, in that indecisive locus where science comes close to literature, in that indistinct area not yet lit up by the brightness of pure logic yet already separate from the spheres of darkness, that, like so many others—not all of them biologists—he made the most beautiful of his discoveries.

Biology, the bedrock of resistance and the frontier of psychoanalysis, lay always on the horizon of Freud's thinking—indeed, he often presented it as being the future of psychoanalysis. Perhaps some metabiology is at work in metapsychology. When we talk of mental life, what are we really talking about?

As far as I am aware, Freud mentions Claude Bernard only once—but in a very prominent place: Chapter 7 of his *Traumdeutung*, in which he describes how difficult it is to get hold of "involuntary ideas".

> Anyone who seeks to do so must familiarize himself with the expectations raised in the present volume and must, in accordance with the rules laid down in it, endeavour during the work to refrain from any criticism, any *parti pris*, and any emotional or intellectual bias. He must bear in mind Claude Bernard's advice to experimenters in a physiological laboratory: 'travailler comme une bête'—he must work, that is, with as much persistence as an animal and with as much disregard of the result. If this advice is followed, the task will no longer be a hard one. (1900a, p. 523)

It is, in fact, surprising that Freud did not make more explicit any interest that he might have had in the scientist who discovered/invented the concept of internal milieu and of the regulative mechanisms that ensure its constancy. Piera Aulagnier, who trained as a biologist and who intended initially to undertake fundamental research in that field, gave the concept of metabolisation a pivotal place in her theorization of metapsychology. (See Chapter Eight "Psychical metabolisations of the body in Piera Aulagnier's theory".) A metaphorical use, no doubt, of a term borrowed from physiology—but in the transportation that it brings about, where does the metaphor stop? That question concerns psychoanalytical interpretation, produced by neutrality and free-floating attention, and it comes to the fore in that internal milieu: psychoanalytic listening.

CHAPTER THREE

The psychoanalyst and his/her discontents

"It is my belief that, however strange it may sound, we must reckon with the possibility that something in the nature of the sexual instinct itself is unfavourable to the realization of complete satisfaction"

(Freud, 1912d, pp. 188–189)

"The relationship between the amount of sublimation possible and the amount of sexual activity necessary naturally varies very much from person to person and even from one calling to another."

(Freud, 1908d, p. 197)

Sublimation is a term surrounded by a twilight zone of chemical and religious associations; as a concept, it is open to criticism and is perhaps inadequate—we would like to be able to do without it—but it does attempt to designate, at least approximately, an undeniable psychical reality.

If we hold the view that the quality of the analyst's psychical work during the session and the conditions under which that work is initiated are not incidental as far as the deployment and quality of the analytical process are concerned, we would tend, therefore, to see the analyst's capacity for sublimation and the sublimating dimension of the analytical setting as significant factors with respect to sublimation for the patient *in the course of the treatment*. That is the point of view that I shall adopt in order to explore this delicate issue.

Sublimation is more of a movement than an outcome—one of transformation, of a change of state—and perhaps even the movement of drive transformation itself. I think it better to define sublimation as a process rather than as a product, although it is true that Freud always highlighted the production of cultural objects that can be shared—mainly intellectual or artistic creations.

In that sense, sublimation is one of the aspects—perhaps the most high-ranking?—of what defines psychical outcome as a transformation of excitation from its biological roots.[9] That model of a transformation movement towards an ever higher degree of mentalization does not apply only to psychical growth in human beings—it concerns also the evolution of the treatment and of civilisation, and the development of psychoanalysis.

Sublimation and creativity

Freud constantly emphasised the fact that the capacity for sublimation varies greatly from one individual to another and depends on several factors:

> The original strength of the sexual instinct probably varies in each individual; certainly the proportion of it which is suitable for sublimation varies. It seems to us that it is the innate constitution of each individual which decides in the first instance how large a part of his sexual instinct it will be possible to sublimate and make use of. In addition to this, the effects of experience and the intellectual influences upon his mental apparatus succeed in bringing about the sublimation of a further portion of it. (Freud, 1908d, p. 187–188)

At that time, the issue of sublimation involved the complex problem of the neuroses, the mechanisms of displacement and repression, and was part of the processes of permutation and transformation made possible through access to symbolic equivalence. It had to do with the sexual drive in its perverse or pre-genital elements. What could stand in the way of sublimation was essentially a matter of psychical economics. The development of drive theory and the shift towards the structural model of the mind, together with the difficult issues brought up by narcissism, the death drive, and some ego defence mechanisms (above all, splitting) brought to light other complicating elements that could hinder the individual's capacity for sublimation. It was no longer possible to consider sublimation simply from the standpoint of the avatars of the sexual drive. It was in the disturbances brought about in the initial stages of the functioning of the mind by early anxieties that the premises of what might later make sublimation more difficult were sought. More specifically, the quality of introjection, projection, and projective identification is what impacts upon the possibility of sublimation.

After the turning point of 1920, Freud saw sublimation as involving mainly the superego and ideals. One aspect did not change, however: he continued to see sublimation as being linked to that part of the psychical apparatus that is socially usable and able to be shared, to what belongs to the work of culture and the process of civilisation. The concept of sublimation is intrinsically linked to that of the discontents of civilisation. "This may help us to understand better also why, very often, *the achievements due to sublimation do not in any way satisfy their originators*, and why they may be concomitant with minor or major psychopathological distortions" (David, 1985, p. 221).

It could be pointed out that that concomitance makes a connection between splitting and sublimation. Sublimation may turn out to be possible only in a split-off part of the personality. It is possible also that sublimation might not always go in the direction of sexuality and the life drive; its antisexual dimension, with its antilibidinal impact, might also be at work on the side of death narcissism and lethal unbinding.

When we ask ourselves what might facilitate sublimation in psychoanalytical treatment, we must, of necessity, take another look at what lies beneath the principle of change in an analysis. Freud went as far as to argue that it is impossible to speak of the mutative effect of psychoanalytical treatment if nothing to do with primary repression has been brought up and modified. What he meant by that was that the effectiveness of psychoanalytical treatment depends on the possibility of reorganising the earliest psychical impulses, thereby enabling the individual to give up those primary defensive modalities that hindered the deployment of other organising potentialities.

An improvement in access to the possibility of sublimation should, therefore, be on a par with the capacity for regression in the treatment, especially for formal regression, not only on the patient's side but also—and in some cases, above all—on that of the analyst.

Even if verbal interpretations communicated to the patient are fundamental in every case and undoubtedly contribute to the work of mentalization (of which sublimation is one aspect), we must not disregard the importance of the preconscious work of processing, at the frontiers of primary and secondary processes, in the attempt to recapture capacities for sublimation that are clearly distinct from reaction formations and counter-cathexes. Paradoxically, the manner in which the analyst's intelligence manifests itself in brilliant interpretations might actually hinder the patient's sublimation by preventing any regressive movement and potentiality for re-libidinalisation and by reinforcing the ideality of intellectual processes and the ideology of sublimation.

Winnicott was the first to explore those paradoxes of analytical technique when he spoke of interpretation as retaliation, a tendency towards envy and possessiveness in the analyst that deprives the patient of the emergence of psychical creativity. In that perspective, access to sublimation has to do with creativity, seen as a process inherent in the fact of living, of feeling oneself to be alive and real, and clearly distinguished from the idea of creation, which refers to an object, something that is produced:

> ... the link can be made, and usefully made, between creative living and living itself, and the reasons can be studied why it is that creative living can be lost and why the individual's feeling that life is real or meaningful can disappear. (Winnicott, 1999, p. 69)

In order to understand what then might be at stake in an analysis, we have to call upon notions such as chaos, integration, disintegration, and non-integration. The hiatus that exists between the fact of being alive and that of feeling alive and real is all the more important—and palpable in the course of the treatment—when early disturbances have hampered the structuring of the ego. In such cases (borderline patients for the most part), the analyst has to let the patient have the experience, during the session, of tolerating a phase of non-integration without

immediately feeling threatened by disintegration. The possibility of
having that experience, discovered in the course of the treatment
thanks to a specific kind of psychical availability in the analyst, which
Winnicott called a capacity for adaptation, will be the starting-point
(Winnicott called it "a kind of primary repression") that will form the
basis upon which ego-relatedness and the drive-based relationship
with the object will be able to be processed differently:

> There is now for the first time in the patient's life an opportunity for
> the development of an ego, for its integration from ego nuclei, for its
> establishment as a body ego, and also for its repudiation of an exter-
> nal environment with the initiation of a relatedness to objects. For the
> first time the ego can experience id impulses, and can feel real in so
> doing, and also in resting from experiencing. (Winnicott, 1975, p. 298)

As in every analysis, but even more so in this case, where the analyst's
regressive capacities are severely put to the test, the conception of the
analytical setting, the metapsychological implications of its various
parameters, and the manner in which the analyst's psyche is able to
take part in it so as to make it function and be usable—all of these
elements are fundamental for the unfolding of the analytical process.

Several aspects of that complex set-up which is specific to the
analytical situation are conceived of with the idea of sublimation as a
goal; the demands that the analytical situation makes on the analyst's
psychical work in the session are like a paradigm of the "pressure
towards sublimation" that civilisation imposes on the mental development of human beings. It could be said that the analytical situation
represents one of the most demanding degrees of civilised morality in
the relationship between two persons who are present together. Of
course, there are, in addition, all the unknown factors linked to the
consequences of drive renunciation on the process of civilisation as
such. In this way, the analyst's superego, in its relationship to the aim
of sublimation in the treatment, comes into the picture.

Kulturversagung

Civilization and its Discontents gave Freud another opportunity of
exploring "the similarity between the process of civilization and the
libidinal development of the individual" (1930a, p. 97) to demonstrate

that sublimation is one of the most prominent features of cultural development, and to draw the conclusion that the structure of civilisation is built on drive renunciation and the non-gratification of powerful instincts. He defined this as *Kulturversagung*: the refusal laid down by civilisation to satisfy the drives, making renunciation necessary.

If we think about the immense power of the drives (Freud spoke of their excessiveness) brought into play in the transference by the analytical situation and about the draconian conditions of giving up all direct satisfaction that the analyst has to impose on his/her psyche in order to use that energy as a lever for psychical change, it becomes clear that the analytical situation is a kind of experimental paradigm of that *Kulturversagung*.

The analytical situation is a *locus* in which the life of the drives is intensified and exacerbated, given the frustration imposed by the analytical setting in which there is some renewed speculation that tensions can be processed and resolved by means other than sexual satisfaction. The trilogy of renunciation on the analyst's part—abstinence, neutrality, and free-floating attention—takes its dynamic power from the considerable degree of economic pressure created by frustration in the analysand, as well as in the analyst.

The most obvious aspect of that renunciation on the analyst's part, which Freud explored more specifically in "Observations on transference-love" (1915a), concerns genital desires and their satisfaction with patients. That renunciation in the sphere of object libido is backed up by a renunciation in that of narcissistic libido, and this has dynamic and economic consequences—which, in the dynamics of the analytical process and the transference–countertransference interplay, are just as important and sometimes even more important.

Freud himself pointed out—though without going into any detail—the narcissistic aspects of the impact of transference love on the analyst. Naturally enough, for reasons of medical deontology, the analyst must not give in to these—and, even more so, because this would amount to nullifying the real meaning of the transference: do not be flattered, you are not the actual object of this passion, stand back and let the transference figures come into the picture, you are simply a medium.

While a session is ongoing, analysts—it is part of their work—must prepare themselves for self-forgetfulness, for a kind of self-detachment that lies close to a kind of temporary self-mourning.[10] Detachment, renunciation, mourning, separation—these appear to be the elements of sublimation that we find in the analyst's asceticism during the session. What is specific to the analytical situation, however, is the fact that, unlike the anchorite who is alone in the presence of God, the analyst is alone in the presence of another human being. In addition, detachment and renunciation do not, in this case, lead to an absence of affects or representations—they go hand-in-hand with an intensification of drive-related impulses, both narcissistic and object-related, and an increase in word-presentations and thing-presentations: *Kulturarbeit und Kulturversagung*!

Let us take a closer look at the various elements of that renunciation, particularly as to its narcissistic aspect, which, more often than not, is left in the background.

I mentioned earlier the self-effacing that follows on from dispelling the illusion of being the object of transference love: this amounts to giving up any increase in narcissistic pleasure which, in principle, should, for the analyst, be sought elsewhere and differently. In that same idea of giving up narcissistic satisfaction, the analyst accepts the fact that the patient will show no appreciation or gratitude (and, indeed, hopes that this will be the case)—"After all, I knew that all along, there's nothing new in that" is what the patient thinks after repression has been lifted. The analyst makes no claim as to his/her role in the successful outcome of the treatment, and agrees not to have any more news of the patient and to be forgotten. Placed in a position of omnipotence by the strength of the transference, the analyst keeps his/her distance and rejects any relationship of domination or possession—consciously and, as far as is possible, through the analysis of what might be the result, indirectly and symptomatically, of the unconscious dimension of the countertransference.

That list, which is not exhaustive, could give the impression that this renunciation and detachment has to do with what Judaeo-Christian ethics has taught us to acknowledge in terms of self-denial. At first sight, the austerity of the analytical rule applied to the analyst would seem to bracket together psychoanalysis and puritanism—and even then, all I have discussed until now concerns positive narcissism, life narcissism. The requirement of neutral processing, of maintaining enough free-floating attention, and of abstaining from any acting out (here, from any reaction) becomes much more of a problem when what is at stake is negative narcissism and the patient's attempts, by whatever means at his/her disposal, to inflict narcissistic wounds and pain on the analyst's psyche. Freud obviously had something of this in mind when he justified his instruction that the patient lie on the couch by saying that he personally was incapable of putting up with people looking at him ten hours a day. In what is felt as unbearable, the dimension of erotic seduction that has to be resisted is, no doubt, the most superficial and harmless of all. What can go all the way to the very limits of what is tolerable are projections full of hate that are directly expressed (or, even worse, not expressed), pathological projective identifications which interfere with mental functioning, paralysis brought about by a kind of staring that seeks to gain control and is reinforced by total silence, and the persecutory dimension of that terebrating stare which awakens the cruellest aspects of the superego.

The analyst must really feel these attacks, otherwise he/she will be in a manic-defensive denial, but without making any backlash reaction. The analyst's psyche has to be prepared to put up with these attacks, to contain them (i.e., to allow them to stay inside for as long as necessary), to process them, and to reconstruct them in a form that is thinkable and, therefore, conducive to introjection. According to Winnicott, in certain clinical moments like these, all that the analyst can do to further the analytical process is to survive, that is, to refrain from retaliating. It is not simply the content of an interpretation that will enable working through to be maintained throughout the treatment; the very quality of the analyst's psychical texture plays a major role in this. That is why, in such clinical contexts, Winnicott wrote of the possibility—and even, at times, of the necessity—of breaking the barriers of a professional attitude, with the patient thereby obtaining a "real" part of the analyst's ego, one that will enable him/her to feel real.

These are borderline situations in which the protective shield function of the analyst's psyche has to be subjected to reality testing in such a way as to enable the introjection of the experience of an internal environment, which Winnicott saw as different from the introjection of an internal object. I shall return to this point later, when I discuss the capacity to be alone, receptiveness, and the capacity for internalisation in the analyst.

In discussing the issues surrounding the processing in the session of mental pain and the damaging attacks against life narcissism, we find ourselves at the outer limits of the analyst's capacity for sublimation: that is, at the limits of what lends itself to analysis; these, in the actual situation, vary a great deal from one analyst to another, and even, for any one analyst, from one patient to another and from one day to another. Given the topic under discussion, sublimation in psychoanalytical treatment, it is impossible to avoid the question of the analyst's masochism. Faced with mental suffering, pain, and destructive attacks, what role will mental processing (in the direction of sublimation) play, and what will be given over to substitute gratification in masochistic terms?

That is, perhaps, one of the most delicate aspects of the analysis of the countertransference, because everything depends on limits and thresholds. To what extent does tolerating psychical destructiveness bear witness to the analyst's capacity to survive hatred? At what point does that same tolerance become an indication of a countertransference enactment in which the pain endured by the analyst becomes a masochistic substitute gratification that creates a link marked by domination, in which the analyst denies his/her own hatred and rushes headlong into a reparatory kind of activism that deprives the patient of all possibility of discovering his/her own capacity for reparation in order to find some way out of the turmoil of the depressive position?

The issue here is that of the analyst's capacity to be sufficiently attentive towards whatever may, in a subtle way, prevent the emergence of a negative transference or towards any tendency to avoidance whenever negativity makes its appearance in the transference. Over and beyond the analysis of the countertransference, the question of masochism remains in its primary form with regard to any mental activity aimed at representation and the capacity to think. From that point of view, some degree of masochism comes inevitably into the treatment; all we can hope for is that it remains fairly mild and that it lies in the direction of temporisation.

> Masochism makes for duration, for internal continuity; it is the bridge that links the a-temporality of the id to the specific temporality of the Preconscious–Conscious system or, as it is described in the structural model, of the conscious and unconscious ego. ... Masochism is the condition of psychical processing and plays a part in the analytical process given that this process does unfold, i.e. that the patient

succeeds in tolerating the session, does not put an end to the treatment or, on the contrary, turn the analysis into an interminable one. . . . The primary masochistic nucleus operates in the background and ensures the continuity of the analytical process and, within that process, of working-through. (Rosenberg, 1990, p. 67, translated for this edition)

That part of masochism which involves the mental activity of the analyst in the session, which is constitutive of the work of processing (*durcharbeit*) and which is not a symptomatic aspect of the counter-transference, has to do with the part played by the primary object in facilitating the binding of the drives: "It is the mother who takes on the task of binding the death drive by libido for as long as her infant cannot do so by him/herself" (Rosenberg, 1990, p. 67, translated for this edition).

There could, therefore, be, in the analyst's mental functioning, something that has to do with that kind of masochism—the guardian of life—and which facilitates the rebinding of the drives. That appears to me to be close to what Bion theorised in terms of the mother's capacity for reverie and to what troubled Ferenczi in his discussion of the unwelcome child and his/her death drive.

That renewed opportunity for the analyst to forget him/herself and to stay in the background *qua* person amounts to some degree of depersonalisation; its aim is to make available the analyst's mental space, not simply as a surface, but also in terms of an interior, so that the other person can make use of it to his/her own ends, the outcome never fully attained of an internal processing that is based mainly on drive renunciation. That libidinal renunciation, characterised by its twofold aspect, narcissistic and object-related, implies putting a stop to erotic satisfaction and repressing aggressiveness, in particular the kind of aggressiveness that may emerge in reaction to narcissistic attacks. Here, we are at the very heart of the issues raised by Freud in *Civilization and its Discontents* concerning unconscious guilt feelings and the construction of the superego. The conditions that make psychoanalysis possible confront the analyst, in a very acute way, with the paradoxes of civilisation described by Freud.

[Conscience] (or more correctly, the anxiety which later becomes conscience) is indeed the cause of instinctual renunciation to begin with, but later the relationship is reversed. Every renunciation of instinct now becomes a dynamic source of conscience and every fresh renunciation increases the latter's severity and intolerance. (1930a, p. 128)

If the analyst is not careful, the odds are that respecting the ethical demands which underlie all possibility of analytical work will strengthen his/her unconscious guilt feelings, the fierceness of what we are accustomed to call the analytical superego, and also the manifestations of his/her unconscious aggressiveness in the countertransference. The pressure on the analyst towards sublimation in the treatment creates these difficulties, which, in turn, require out of the ordinary means of sublimation in order to be processed. The issue here is nothing less than the sublimation not only of aggressiveness, but also of destructiveness in so far as it is a manifestation of the death drive. In a rather splendid flight of speculation, Freud writes,

> But even where it [i.e., the death instinct] emerges without any sexual purpose, in the blindest fury of destructiveness, we cannot fail to recognize that the satisfaction of the instinct is accompanied by an extraordinarily high degree of narcissistic enjoyment, owing to its presenting the ego with a fulfilment of the latter's old wishes for omnipotence. The instinct of destruction, moderated and tamed, and, as it were, inhibited in its aim, must, when it is directed towards objects, provide the ego with the satisfaction of its vital needs and with control over nature. (1930a, p. 121)

Part of the analyst's sublimated sadism is, no doubt, present in the acuteness of his/her intuitions and sharpness of thinking, as well as in his/her writings and verbal communications. But, as we have seen, the analyst has to keep an eye on them during the treatment, in case they tend to turn into a kind of retaliation. Failures in this aspect of sublimation in the analyst can take on several forms. We can easily see them at work, in the shape of hatred of the analysis, either in destructive transgressions, erotic or violent, of the analytical setting, or in the reinforcing of a negative therapeutic reaction, or, again, in the interminability of some analyses. When these failures are neutralised in the treatment, they often reappear in the shape of temperamental manifestations or narcissism of small differences, not only in psychoanalytical Societies but also in everyday life. It was perhaps for all of those reasons that Jacques Lacan was in the habit of saying that the analyst is horrified by what he/she does.

Being alone in the presence of another person

In spite of these pessimistic considerations, and without forgetting that Freud was proud of the fact that he could be blamed for not giving his patients any consolation, it is, all the same, probably the case that psychoanalysts do take pleasure in their work—and not only masochistic pleasure—and that that pleasure contributes to a significant degree to the progress of the treatment. From what I have discussed beforehand, we know that the economic aspect of that pleasure has, above all, to do with sublimation. That brings to mind epistemophilia and everything which, in terms of narcissistic and object-related economics, may be attracted to this and take nourishment from it. There is no doubt that analysts do find satisfaction in the exercise of their profession; this fuels their drive for new discoveries and their thirst for knowledge, and enables them to develop further their theories as to how the mind works. However, all of these achievements that the experience of analytical treatment makes possible are reached outside of the analytical situation itself. Can it really be argued that *during the session* an analyst satisfies his/her epistemophilic drives? And that it is this activity of sublimation, based on the scoptophilic and auditory component drives, which contributes to sublimation in the course of the treatment? A typical feature of any session of analysis is the mental activity that is occurring in the presence of, and with, the other person, the word "with" often implying a temporary obliteration of the frontiers of each one's sense of identity. That being the case, perhaps the pleasure has more to do with the very particular nature of the link that, in this context, might perhaps exist between two minds.

Some phases of analytical treatment—often mutative ones—make the analyst experience a quality of affect which the term "pleasure" cannot adequately describe. That pleasure has a particular quality about it that the word "joy" would express better. In order to differentiate between pleasure and joy in this particular context, we could perhaps say to start off with that pleasure has to do with something gained, while joy involves something lost.

Analysts can take pleasure in observing that at least some of their hypotheses seem to be correct, that the material which emerges confirms the validity of an interpretation, and that there exists some agreement between metapsychological theorisations and the clinical work of the analysis: all of this constitutes a narcissistic plus in the field of their knowledge. The quality of the affect that I am discussing here is of a different nature, and corresponds to an experience that the analyst has during a session. I shall try to outline it more clearly via a series of somewhat vague statements. The particular moment that may give rise to this "joy" is contemporaneous with an opening-up to the experience of the unconscious in the treatment; this occurs, for both analyst and analysand, in proximity with primary processes and thing-presentations, in the enduring capacity to break free of the tyranny of a linear narrative imposed by secondary processes and turn towards (and take on board) whatever might spring from the heterogeneity of the different psychical dimensions, in which several temporal levels can coexist and the various elements of a condensation can be kept in a de-condensed state. This, in other words, is the outcome of a process of preconscious working through punctuated by various interpretative moments that had no immediately perceptible impact. It is the point at which repression is lifted, and some loosening takes place, as does the kind of reconstitution that follows on from a phase of unbinding. The analytical risk of unbinding (*analysis*: from the Greek verb: *analuein*, meaning to undo, to untie) has been taken on board, with the anxiety about death and disappearing to which it gives rise; what is now taking place shows that that danger has been overcome, thereby bearing witness to the power of Eros.

The affect "joy", however, is not related to the strengthening of the erotic link between the two individuals present in the consulting-room. On the contrary, it has to do with a moment of separation and detachment that takes place simultaneously with a movement towards introjection, in which the analysand distances him/herself from any relationship of anaclisis with respect to the other person's psyche. The analyst, at that point, has the impression that the mental structuring that is about to emerge has, henceforth, not much to do with him/her. The impetus was given by the analyst, but the rest takes place of its own volition. Far from making the analyst feel depressed, he/she is delighted, while, at the same time, becoming conscious of his/her mortality, of the illusion of omnipotence, of castration, and of the loneliness that he/she must accept. While acknowledging some responsibility in the triggering of that process, the analyst acknowledges also that it goes far beyond anything he/she could do. The analyst is not in control either of life and death or of the processes of symbolisation.

Distancing and renouncing go hand-in-hand here with an acceptance which is, perhaps, in the end, the acceptance of the dissatisfaction that lies at the very heart of satisfaction, the acceptance of the limited and limiting nature of satisfaction, which runs counter to the demand for unlimited satisfaction made by the id, one that, because of its rejection of mental life, is very close to the death drive. Paradoxically, narcissistic distancing and loss here contribute to the enhancement of life narcissism, while, at the same time, following paths that move away from the significance of any one person or persons and draw close to the domain of the superpersonal. The transpersonal and transnarcissistic dimension is the characteristic feature of the joy that the analyst may experience at certain rare mutative moments. It is that dimension which enables the patient's tendency towards sublimation to be reinforced, and this all the more so in that the internal attitude of the analyst, governed by the rule of abstinence, neutrality, and free-floating attention, implicitly signifies, all the way through the treatment process, that the analyst's narcissistic needs and sexual desires are satisfied by means of objects situated elsewhere.

It could also be said that analysts will be in a better position to take on board the demands that the analytical setting imposes on their psychical activity if they have solidly built up within themselves that internal environment which gives them the capacity to be alone. That ego-relatedness lies at the very heart of the possibility "to feel *satisfied with the game*, without feeling threatened by a physical orgasm of local excitement" (Winnicott 1965, p. 35). It was in that way that Winnicott made a connection between sublimation and cultural experience.[11] Starting with the difference between the fact of being alive and the experience of feeling oneself to be a living human being, he encourages us to move towards another space, a transitional one, a potential space in which, in the interplay of psychoanalytical treatment, psychical virtualities can be deployed once more. The illusion of which Winnicott speaks is a cornerstone of a quite different quality from that of which Freud wrote in *The Future of an Illusion* (1927c).

By basing the development of the individual and the process of civilisation on the struggle between Eros and the death instinct, Freud argued that they "are also vital processes—which is to say that they must share in the most general characteristic of life" (1930a, p. 139), adding that "under the influence of cultural urges, some civilizations, or some epochs of civilization—possibly the whole of mankind—have become 'neurotic'" (p. 144). If the experience of analysis in the treat-ment situation is a theatre in which are played out the real issues of the process of civilisation, psychoanalysis has more to fear for its future from an internal threat than from an external danger.

CHAPTER FOUR

The paradoxes of neutrality

According to Freud, what two human beings communicate to each other in the context of an analytical session has no equivalent in real life. It is true that there are certain similarities in what is at stake, but the way in which they are treated and made use of—outside of any alienating attempt to take control in a relationship in which the effects of alienation are potentially at their highest level—depends on the conditions under which the analytical encounter takes place. The issue is directly and simultaneously both ethical and scientific. Hence, the importance of thinking constantly, in the here-and-now of the actual session, about the method and the setting; such questions have to be kept alive, but they are no more than a sustained attempt at reflecting upon what is at stake in psychoanalysis, grafted as it is on to theoretical assumptions which, if psychoanalysis can claim to have its place in the scientific domain, must always be capable of being revised in the light of actual experience. There is always the risk that technique for technique's sake might take over from a theoretical processing *in vivo* of what is actually being experienced, with its vicissitudes, its unexpectedness, and its absurdities. Theorisation is always one step behind an analysis: the one that will begin with the very next patient.

The work of neutrality

What, in my view, lies at the very heart of the practice of psycho-analysis is the idea of work, of labour, from odd jobs to parturition: working on psycho-corporeal reality *by means of* psycho-corporeal reality. As for Freud's masterful metaphors for gaining ground, for example, about draining the Zuider Zee, I would see them as applying to the constant effort by both analyst and analysand, as constant as the pressure of the drives: an effort to put into words, to represent, to imagine . . . an effort that brings in its wake changes to one's psycho-corporeal organisation. The model for that work—a work of transformation that comes up against resistance of many kinds—is the theoretical model of the drives in which Freud described in a dynamic way both the relationship of continuity between the somatic and mental spheres and the differentiation between them. Dream-work is seen as following a similar model (between the somatic dimension of sleep and its psychical counterpart of desire), and the analytical session as invented by Freud is conceived of as being in the same vein.

It is, therefore, starting from the concept of the drives that I understand the work of analysis and try to explore the question of its mutative impact. Lacan argued in favour of a kind of psychoanalysis that would not be simply a semblance of analysis. The question is indeed a fundamental one: more than any other discipline in the human sciences, psychoanalysis may give rise to imposture and sham, to a discourse on discourse in a solipsistic sterility.

Some attempt has to be made at identifying more precisely under what conditions a work of real transformation can be undertaken. What seems to me to be fundamental is the way in which the analyst agrees to subject his/her psychical reality to certain topographical, dynamic and economic modifications. Fundamental in the way that the analyst makes him/herself available to the analysand, to be made use of in whatever manner the latter wishes. From a psychoanalytical point of view, all clinical work must take into account the way in which the analyst's mind functions. Although the clinical functioning of analyst and analysand are indissociable, they are by no means symmetrical or similar. If the analysand is truly to agree to follow the rule of free association, the analyst must undertake to try (i) to be as much as possible in a complex state that brings about a change in consciousness and a topographical regression—free-floating attention—

and (ii) to adopt an internal attitude which, while being complex and paradoxical, does not limit itself to the intellectual sphere—neutrality, the fundamental component of abstinence. These three elements—free association, free-floating attention, and neutrality—make up a dynamic whole, if not a system, in which each element draws its heuristic, dynamic, and economic effectiveness from the existence of the other two and from the relationships of equilibrium and disequilibrium between all three. That rather brief description highlights, *inter alia*, the trans-subjective nature of the experience that is thereby "set up".

Here is a brief clinical illustration that gives some idea of the psychical effort that an analyst must make in order to preserve the possibility of neutrality when confronted with the patient's narcissistic attacks. What is at stake here is, in fact, the work of neutrality. It concerns the early phase of the treatment of a very respectable young man, immaculately dressed, who presented some elements of what could be called an illness of ideality. Not long into the treatment, narcissistic or mirror aspects of the transference began to appear. There was nothing he was not prepared to sacrifice in the name of psychoanalysis, which he wanted to see placed "above everything else".

He hesitated for some time before undertaking analysis with me, on the pretext that I did not live in a very "stylish" district and that the entrance hall to my building left much to be desired. He himself preferred to live in a tiny attic room in one of the more bourgeois districts of Paris, rather than in a comfortable flat in the outskirts. He told me that in the posh part of Paris, where he lived, people threw quite a lot of things away, so that he had got into the habit of looking through their dustbins. The previous day, he found a table and took it up to his room. Just when he was looking at the table, a man walked past and looked at him. The patient felt like addressing him sharply and asking him what business it was of his. Then he told me that he had been looking for a book I had written (he had searched on the Internet for information about me), and that he had managed to find it in a bookshop. He wondered if he had done the right thing. He had flipped through it, but he did not want to read it in case he found something that might jeopardise the continuation of his analysis. So, all he read was the contents page and the dedication. That surprised me, because I had not written a dedication. I asked him what he meant by dedication. "Well, the facsimile of your writing and your signature, and the name of the person to whom the book is dedicated, it's all written on the flyleaf." I still could not understand, and asked him if he was sure that it was my book. "Oh yes, no doubt about that, and it's printed, it's your writing." That was when my temporary denial, protecting my narcissism, came to an end, so that I was able to perceive the reality in all of its comic cruelty: he was informing me that somebody to whom I had sent a dedicated copy of my book had already got rid of it by having it sold second-hand in the Gibert bookshop! I hardly need say that I felt overwhelmed by some not very pleasant thoughts. Once the reality of the situation had become "clear", I pointed out to the patient that he had wanted to hang on to a mistaken perception (the printed facsimile), perhaps in order not to think of the book as having been thrown out, as just a second-hand book. I linked this to what he had said about the table, a reject from some rich person living in his part of Paris. He then began to praise highly my skills as a psychoanalyst. I said that perhaps he was trying to reassure me and to calm me down after having spoken of my book as though it were rubbish, perhaps even a piece of crap. He demurred, and then said that he had always been ashamed of his father.

It was important that, for a brief moment, I was able to share his tendency to deny the situation. It was the work of neutrality that enabled me to overcome that denial by accepting the narcissistic wound and by taking it on board without counter-reacting. Holding back any discharge via acting out, processing the narcissistic wound via a temporary fantasy of retaliation, and getting back in touch with the capacity to interpret—these were the elements that made it possible to stand back from a kind of persecutory way of thinking. The psychical work of disengagement is part of the process of breaking free of denial and is, in itself, a victory for the psyche.

Do we still need to refer to neutrality? If the same gesture, the same attitude, can, in one particular analytical context, bear witness to a profound understanding and, thus, enable free associations and processing to continue because it strengthens basic confidence and the possibility of communication, we could well imagine that, in another analytical context, it might well prove exciting because it is experienced as seductive or intrusive, thus becoming a destructive element with respect to any possible processing. It could also be said, of course, that abstaining from making any gesture or from saying anything—supposed to embody the very notion of analytical neutrality—might bring about a negative kind of excitation or constitute an enactment that has the same effect as a traumatic repetition. If neutrality is still meaningful, it is because it has nothing to do with the casuistry of behaviour.

Could we argue that neutrality is part of the analytical method? That it is a fundamental rule in the same way as free association and free-floating attention are? Or is it enough to point out that Freud never himself used the word neutrality in order to invalidate it as a concept and its existence in the analytical method as invented by Freud? Does the fact that the word as such is not present in Freud's original texts mean that neutrality is a notion that cannot be found? Or should we not rather think that we do not, for the moment, have an appropriate term for defining what is, in fact, a dimension of analytical experience which is indispensable if we are to characterise the specificity of the practice of psychoanalysis, but which is difficult to put into words because we find it hard to describe its constituent elements, its essence, and its finality?

Simply as an anecdote, I would point out that the word "neutrality" appears in a somewhat tendentious translation by James Strachey of the word that Freud actually used-*Indifferenz*—in his paper "Observations on transference-love" (1915a); "neutrality" probably appeared to him to be more acceptable from a scientific point of view. In the context of Freud's paper, *Indifferenz* relates simply to the point-blank refusal with which the analyst must meet the erotic components of transference seduction. It should be emphasised that Freud was not taking a moral stance here, but one that had to do specifically with the psychoanalytical method: in order to maintain the effectiveness of psychoanalytical treatment, one must not give in. That scientific point of view does, all the same, correspond to what the tendentious translator was aiming at. The psychical reality that we are trying to define via the questionable term "neutrality" goes beyond the seductive impact of the erotic transference on the analyst and the requirement not to respond to this. The word "neutrality" should, for the moment, be employed as a kind of variable—"x"—in the same way as Bion decided to designate via letters of the alphabet certain functions that he defined succinctly in order to prevent any name given to them from restricting the complexity of the psychical events that he was attempting to describe. One of the difficulties with the word "neutrality" is precisely the fact that it is not neutral. And it is not easy to drain it of its associative penumbra in order to continue to designate, in as "neutral" a way as possible, a domain of experience that remains open.

The body disappears

Faced with these difficulties, analysts have adopted several attitudes, thereby showing that the question is by no means neutral: it brings into play the way in which we think of the various issues that arise in analytical treatment. One tendency is that of reifying the idea of neutrality. That tendency is not particularly characteristic of any one school of psychoanalytical thinking; it implies a "belief" in neutrality in terms of reaching a state of mind that might possibly eliminate all subjectivity. One of the starting-points for that ideologising drift is the metaphor of the mirror (I shall come back to this later) or the telephone receiver: the analyst is transformed into an instrument or a machine that is supposed to reproduce an image, acoustic or visual, without in any way modifying the original. We all know of analysts whose idea of neutrality involved the sterilisation of their actual consulting-room: no photos, no books, no paintings on the walls, certainly no flowers, no personal objects, so-called "neutral" colours, beige or grey, no expression on their face, no hand-shaking, no good-day, no goodbye . . . Gradually, this puritanical minimalism was applied also to their voice and to the words they pronounced, which became fewer and fewer, for fear of encouraging substitute satisfaction.

A friend of mine from New York told me about the analysis that he had had with a famous Central European "dinosaur", an adept of ego psychology. The patient would enter the empty consulting-room, lie down on the couch, and wait. He would hear a door opening out of his line of sight, then the sound of heavy emphysematous breathing and arthritic movements, mingled with the creaking of an armchair. Once silence was restored, the patient would talk until the same noises—in reverse order, as it were—informed him that the session was over. He never saw the analyst or heard him say anything. That theatricality, farcical and pernicious in its effects, was, I suppose, one way in which that generation of psychoanalysts attempted to put an end to the harmfulness of the seduction, transgression, and incestuousness typical of the first generation—including Freud—whose analysands they had been. I have chosen that somewhat grotesque but, none the less, authentic illustration, because, in its very exaggeration, it allows us to see in a dramatic way one aspect of the question which I shall explore more fully: the temptation and the attempt to make the analyst's body disappear (although in the example I have just given, the analyst's body is very much present, and in a highly somatic manner).

Lacan also was very much involved in that attempt at elimination, especially in his definition of the signifier—that which represents the subject for another signifier. The increasing formalisation of the theorisation of the subject ran parallel, in the actual treatment, not only to a growing tendency to say less and less, but also to a reduction in the length of the sessions, to the point, indeed, where the time of the session became virtual; this was accompanied by what, in Lacanian terminology, we could call the return into the Real of the body excluded in the actual session.

As a reaction against excessive sterilisation of the setting and desubjectification of the analyst, there has been some degree of rejection not only of that particular expression of neutrality, but also of any attempt at neutrality, because it was seen to be something impossible that might even lead to deadlock. Ferenczi was the first to initiate that controversy with his idea of professional hypocrisy; he went on to introduce some methodological experiments aimed at establishing a kind of symmetry between analyst and analysand in what he called "mutual analysis". The motive behind these technical modifications seems to have been the fact that some analyses were at a dead end. They were, in fact, strongly over-determined by the reproaches addressed by Ferenczi to Freud concerning the fact that he had not been allowed to analyse his negative transference. Freud's reply, in "Analysis terminable and interminable" (1937c), published after Ferenczi's death, was that he could not analyse something of which there was no sign. This shows how a certain conception of neutrality can be used to hide countertransference rationalisations. In such cases, what is claimed to be neutrality has, in fact, to do with avoidance. In some situations, neutrality does not consist in withdrawing into the background and putting on hold any involvement. Here, I would argue that neutrality implies searching for the negative transference, that is, offering it the possibility of emerging and becoming interpretable. That does not mean that it should be provoked into appearing or created out of nothing by some kind of active method or other; the analyst should not defend him/herself against its possible emergence or feel relieved that it is not present, but, on the contrary, attempt to imagine it. In that sense, neutrality is quite the opposite of diplomacy: instead of avoiding conflicts, one must feel surprised that there do not appear to be any even though everything points to their existence, although sometimes this is only perceptible through fairly subdued signs of reaction formation in the countertransference. Freud pointed out that in addition to "medicina", there will always be room for the "ferrum" and the "ignis":

> No; in medical practice there will always be room for the "*ferrum*" and the "*ignis*" side-by-side with the "*medicina*" and in the same way we shall never be able to do without a strictly a regular, undiluted psycho-analysis which is not afraid to handle the most dangerous mental impulses and to obtain mastery over them for the benefit of the patient. (Freud, 1915a, p. 171)

In some analytical contexts, in an apparently paradoxical fashion, the ferrum and the ignis are the instruments of neutrality.

The contemporary version of Ferenczi's revolt can be found in some representatives of intersubjectivism or interrelation who make use of the argument concerning professional hypocrisy in order to justify their practice of "self-disclosure", in which the analyst communicates to the patient, during the session, some elements of his/her personal life, past history, and present-day preoccupations. Those analysts, in the USA, have become sickened by all the *diktats* concerning the asepsis of the setting, and have therefore decided to put an end to any reference to neutrality. In so doing, they adopt an attitude condemned by Freud as that of "young and eager psycho-analysts" who are tempted to let the patient look inside them, and to "afford him a glimpse of [their] own mental defects and conflicts and, by giving him information about [their] own life, enable him to put himself on an equal footing" (Freud, 1912e, pp. 117–118). It is worth underlining the fact that what is to be avoided is letting the patient look *inside* the analyst. It is also the fact that, whether it be a matter of the idealisation or of the rejection of neutrality, the underlying idea is that the question can be resolved via intentional attitudes and behaviour. But it is well beyond conscious intentionality that the question of neutrality arises in its most complex, most paradoxical, and most instructive form, one that helps us think about what is psychically at stake in an analysis, following Freud's idea according to which there is no model in real life.

Psychical penetrability

Over and beyond what they might say or not say in the psychical privacy of the analytical encounter, psychoanalysts do communicate a great deal about their psycho-corporeal being in a preconscious and infra-verbal way; the patient takes this in pre-consciously and some aspects of it will be reprocessed, through dream-work, for example. I have elsewhere described the example of a patient who had very clearly, in a dream, diagnosed in his analyst a very severe heart condition. That piece of information, picked up subliminally in a way that would be well worth examining in detail, played the part, in the dream, of a diurnal residue participating in the construction of a transference dream that was both rich and complex. The fact that that secret element of the analyst's psycho-corporeal reality passed into the analysand's preconscious processes does not run counter to that "x" element that we still call neutrality. On the other hand, the analyst's reaction when he heard that dream did shatter that necessary "x" element. The patient was about to associate to the transference aspects of the dream, when the analyst abruptly interrupted him and asked him to stand up—and this barely ten minutes after the beginning of the session, in spite of the fact that the sessions were of fixed length. The analyst said that he had recently been diagnosed as being seriously ill, that he was going to have an operation, and that he would have to stop working for an as yet unknown length of time. Later, when the analysis began again and the patient wanted to talk about the dream and the way in which the session had been ended, the analyst flew into a rage, yelling that the patient was obviously proud of his intuition and that he (the analyst) would not put up with anyone threatening him in his own home; he told the patient in no uncertain terms to get out of his sight.

That somewhat extreme example—but, in fact, more frequent than one might imagine—is a very eloquent one, because it arose in an analytical situation usually described as the classical setting: a neurotic patient, lying on the couch, with several sessions per week.

Overstepping the limits of psycho-corporeal space, which in this example seems even greater as though seen through a magnifying glass, given the intensity of what was at stake with respect to the analyst's narcissism, is something that always occurs, in a more temperate way all the same, in analytical sessions—and not only with borderline or psychotic patients. Most of the time, we pay little attention to it, but it is no less the case that openings and closings of psychical permeability occur frequently and have an impact on the dynamics of the process. A certain kind of self-cathexis by the analyst may (or may not) hinder the patient's analytical process. The psychical effort required to put temporarily on hold the analyst's habitual narcissistic defensive modalities is part of what I am trying to define in terms of neutrality; there is also the case of the capacity to tolerate the use, in the patient's psychical economy and for the purposes of the treatment, of an element of the analyst's psychical reality of which he/she agrees temporarily to be dispossessed. An element of the analyst's psycho-corporeal intimacy is, for the time being, used in a more or less depersonalised way to support representation and processing in the psychical economy of the treatment.

Let us take a look at some of Freud's metaphorical representations that have contributed to the construction of the idea of neutrality, without naming it as such. They have all to do with bodily representations and are echoed in the bodily metaphors that Freud used in his attempt to give weight to his theory of mental functioning. First, that of the mirror, in "Recommendations to physicians practising psycho-analysis" (1912e, p. 118): "The doctor should be opaque to his patients and, like a mirror, should show them nothing but what is shown to him". In that representation, the analyst's psyche is a surface, which must reflect what comes from the patient's unconscious and show it to him/her; this is consistent with the representation of the analyst as decipherer who throws light on what was encrypted and shows it to the other person. The analyst's psyche seen as a surface has one very important function: that of not allowing itself to be penetrated. Ideas such as psychical permeability and penetrability are excluded from such representations of how a psychoanalyst listens to his/her patients. That said, in another paper, written at about the same time, Freud makes use of representations that seem to me to be of a quite different nature, in so far as they evoke a complex mechanism of interiority. In "On beginning the treatment" (1913c), Freud suggests one possible way of helping the patient to understand the fundamental rule of free association:

> So say whatever goes through your mind. Act as though, for instance, you were a traveller sitting next to the window of a railway carriage and describing to someone inside the carriage the changing views which you see outside. (p. 135)

In this representation, analyst and analysand are both in movement and inside a railway carriage. We could say that they are both taking part in the same journey and that they are looking at the analysand's psyche from the inside of that enclosed space which contains both of them. Knowing the importance of trains and travelling in Freud's unconscious dynamics, we might well feel that choosing the metaphor of a railway carriage, although it may not be intentional, is by no means neutral. The analysand is a traveller invited inside the analyst's psychical reality, inside a body in movement marked by representations of bisexuality; that interior is a point of view from which the analysand can look at and talk about him/herself. By means of these representations, we enter into a world that is no longer that of surfaces that reflect.

It must not, however, be forgotten that, in Freud's theorisations, the interplay of representations between surface and interior in order to give substance to a representation of the development and functioning of the psychical apparatus is part of a complex relationship based on a figurativeness borrowed from embryological development; in this metaphor of psychical development and recovery, what was most external becomes deeply internal and *vice versa*, with the ectoderm becoming the central nervous system, which is thus connected to the bodily envelope, the skin. Lacan would later attempt to formalise the complex relationship between external and internal, outside and inside, via the mathematics of toruses and Borromean knots. When, in the course of his seminars, he manipulated those Borromean knots, the pieces of string always ended up by getting all mixed up, falling apart, and becoming like entrails in his fingers.[12] It was Lacan who called Melanie Klein an "inspired tripe-butcher" (Lacan, 2006, p. 632). Let us go back to Freud.

The metaphor of the mirror as a reflecting and impenetrable surface may, when we first consider it, seem to be similar to his theorisation of the protective shield against stimuli. The surface of the ball of irritable matter, a schematic and simplified image of the organism, becomes differentiated through its contact with the external world and develops an intermediate layer; the most external part of this does away with its nature as living matter. That physiological bodily model describes a defensive modality against the destructive irruption of external excitation through the setting-up of a filter. The filter lets some quantity of excitation travel inside, modifying it in such a way that the stimuli can be taken in and accepted. The surface of the protective shield, unlike that of the mirror, neither deflects nor reflects what impinges upon it. It lets stimuli in, transforming the outer layer, which loses its attribute as living matter.

I would like to illustrate this idea of psychical penetrability and its connection with the "x" function we call neutrality through two very brief extracts from analytical treatments. They both show how, after much difficulty, it becomes possible to process the ruthless power of the fundamental need and desire to enter into the object's psychical body in order to trigger, or perhaps to re-launch, mental growth.

The incident, in itself, was in no way out of the ordinary: the door that I open via the entry-phone was not working properly, but I was not aware of this. I thought that I had opened the door as usual. She thought that I did not want to hear her call, that I was leaving her on the other side of the door and that she was obviously prohibited from entering into my consulting-room. It was like a verdict that simply confirmed the most negative of representations that she had of herself: a monster of intrusive avidity against which all one could do was try to protect oneself. Everything in her froze again under the impact of that verdict, and she stood there, petrified, dumbfounded. She had discovered that way of hiding herself a long time ago: paralysing her thinking and her feelings, rigidifying her body and its movements, becoming a kind of puzzled robot cut off from any liveliness. When at last she reached my consulting-room—someone had opened the door for her—she was distraught, locked into the internal catastrophe that she was experiencing. When she sat down opposite me, she gradually began to pull herself together as she became able to experience and express the anger with me that she felt rising inside her. The scenario of the closed door, the analyst's face and body shut like the door of a prison cell, enabled us, in a deferred and retroactive representation, to understand at last what, deep down, the various psychical processes that we had experienced in the course of the treatment really meant for her. The way in which she had thrown herself at me in a highly eroticised transference love had simply been a distorted representation of the frenzied impetus of her maternal transference in order to get inside me, and from which she protected me. I began to understand the way in which I had experienced those moments of hate in the face of all the confusion, chaos, and feeling that I was going mad that she provoked in me at times—I felt that she was forcing me to destroy the analytical relationship: don't think about it any more, that's enough, silence, not able to be analysed. How many times had I almost agreed to her interrupting the analysis in order to have some peace? I think it is in that "I almost", at the very limits of internal tolerance breaking down, that it became possible to recapture the space for thinking that enables a little more room to be made for analysability, a word impossible to pronounce.

The second patient, on the other hand, had a very good brain and was very level-headed. An intellectual of some considerable standing—had we met in other circumstances, I would have been delighted to have intellectual discussions with him. That is one element of the work of neutrality, which is by no means insignificant. He had his own way of keeping me at a distance through his over-zealous free associations that confused me so much that I had no idea what to think; I felt completely stupid. Masses of dreams, four or five per session, swarming with details, digressions, people in his life with complicated biographies, extremely precise indications of topographical patterns which I experienced as sadistic constraints. I had the impression that my head was too small to contain the immensity of his mind. I thought a lot about the film director Peter Greenaway and his first film, *The Draughtsman's Contract*. Then, as I began to sink under the sheer flood of dreams and resigned myself to never understanding anything, I thought of *Drowning by Numbers* at each session. Unable to let myself go in well-constructed interpretations, I did, nevertheless, manage to find the opportunity from time to time to tell him of these associations when they came into my mind. There was something else that I noticed: in the midst of the intellectual drowning that I very often experienced in the course of the sessions, I began to hear, faintly at first, but then more clearly and insistently, some songs. They ranged from the Beatles' "Yellow Submarine" to Ariel's song in Shakespeare's *The Tempest*: "Full fathom five thy father lies . . .". That, too, I managed sometimes to communicate to him, in the form of an enigma: look at what comes into my mind when I am drowning while listening to you. It was only later that I realised that the songs were lullabies.

Never missed a session, never a minute late. As the years went by in this appetite of a very ambivalent father, in the terrible fear of an emotional coming-together in the maternal transference that risked feminising him, I at last managed to hear an infantile distress, the emotional expression of which in the sessions was consistent with the prematurity of the wise baby's ego, and to see emerge, in fragments of his dreams and fantasies, representations of terrifying sadism: the transference substitutes were tortured, skinned alive, plunged into vats of sulphuric acid, eviscerated, and decerebrated. With respect to those acts of physical cruelty, the cotton wool of mental confusion is a protective balm, but the cutting-edge of interpretative intelligence is retaliation, a tooth for a tooth. The bite of an interpretation on the razor's edge of thinking, how exciting!

It might not seem much, but, as the months rolled by, little by little and step by step, we came to the conclusion that this was a matter of ferocious anger and destructive envy related to the storm of affects aroused by the primal scene, the wish to eat up the mother's fertile interior, to swallow the father-and-mother's penis, to get inside the analyst's head and empty it of all its contents, and to refuse to tolerate the idea that the analyst–analysand pairing might produce beautiful babies.

Then came a dream. There were gangsters, shootings. The patient did not know how, but, while he was up against a wall and in defiance of all the laws of ballistics, a stray bullet entered into the base of his skull and ended up in his nose, creating a swelling that could be seen from the outside. I had the feeling that the bullet entering from behind came from my side, but we studied the turgescence of his nose. The patient knew already—we both tacitly understood—that, given the way in which he spoke of the trajectory of the bullet from behind towards the swelling of his nose, he was putting into effect in the transference the anal-sadistic castration of his father; we had heard that before. But why the nose? A nose that swelled up: strange, muck-raker, head-searcher, homing device, head that sniffs.

His associations were many in number, they came and went in the analytical dialogue; I was no longer in the cotton-wool of confusion, I could think with him—but how far could I go without becoming myself too intrusive? It was a Friday, just before the weekend, a well-earned rest of the kind that might set on fire the imagination of baby analysands with their homing devices.

The following Monday (the fallout from Friday's interpretations gave him a splitting headache that, in spite of everything, lasted three full days) with in mind the idea of penetration by an interpretation, wished-for but unbearable, we took another look at the trajectory of the elements of Friday's interpretation. The physical conversion symptom represented a compromise but bore witness also to the transformation of the processes of working through that were part of that particular patient. That temporary hystericisation displayed the ambivalent conflict as it was structured in a confrontation with the experience of an emotional encounter that might become a factor of psychical growth.

A temporary normal illness

In one passage—as dense as it is enigmatic—of *The Ego and the Id* (1923b), Freud says that the ego is first and foremost a bodily ego, or a body-ego. He never later came back directly to that idea, but it did come into his structural description of the psychical apparatus, in which mental functioning is increasingly seen as having to do with the body and the drives.

"The ego is first and foremost a bodily ego; it is not merely a surface entity, but is itself the projection of a surface" (1923b, p. 26). The following footnote was added in 1927 to the English translation; it does not appear in the German editions:

> The ego is ultimately derived from bodily sensations, chiefly from those springing from the surface of the body. It may thus be regarded as a mental projection of the surface of the body, besides, as we have seen above, representing the superficies of the mental apparatus. (1923b, p. 26)

It was Winnicott who raised the question of the implication and utilisation of the analyst's body-ego in the analytical process when, in his 1960 paper "Counter-transference", he wrote, ". . . I personally do my work very much from the body-ego, so to speak" (Winnicott, 1965, p. 161).

In order to reach a better understanding of that somewhat isolated remark upon which he made no further comment, we shall have to take into consideration a whole series of notions which, although based on situations of regression in psychoanalytical treatment, concern also the less turbulent waters of the classical form of treatment. It is thanks to the analyst's capacity for psyche–soma integration that phases of emotional and affect-related turbulence in an analysis can be brought into the service of psychical processing.

In "The location of cultural experience", Winnicott writes, "What I say does affect our view of the question: what is life about? You may cure your patient and not know what it is that makes him or her go on living" (1967, p. 370).

It is on that basis that we can have some idea of how he saw the implication of the analyst's bodily ego in the treatment process.

It seems to me that the most fundamental aspect of what I am trying above all to identify in the idea of neutrality has something to do with those areas of the analyst's life cathexes in their relationship with the choice of that profession and with the way in which the analyst looks with a critical eye on his/her use of the analytical method in each encounter with a new patient.

Neutrality is not there to protect the analyst—on the contrary: it commits the analyst to working constantly in such a way as to avoid responding as a person, while at the same time communicating what is most alive in his/her own self. It is the analyst's narcissistic economy that is involved here, as well as the equilibrium of his/her defence mechanisms. Neutrality—that "x" function so difficult to define— exposes the analyst to what Freud (1915a) called the absolute intensity of the transference, at the same time prohibiting the usual recourse to interacting and reacting; it exposes the analyst in a way for which truly there is no model in real life. Neutrality has just as excessive an aspect as does the transference; it is in contradiction with the ego's usual functioning, and it is a temporary normal illness. It cannot be isolated in its functioning, because it is part of a system that includes the two fundamental aspects of the psychoanalytical method: free association for the patient, and free-floating attention for the analyst. The structure that these three dimensions set up has its own dynamics and economics; none of them is operational or comprehensible unless in terms of its relationship to the other two. That structure goes to make up a living system with its own dynamics and economics.

Looking inside oneself in order to get in touch with the possibility for free association or free-floating attention is a conscious approach that attempts to bring about some modification in mental functioning in both analysand and analyst, the effects of which are no longer conscious or intentional. Free-floating attention does not lead to any given state of mind, but to a series of oscillations between various states of consciousness and modalities of psychical functioning, to some extent dependent on the patient's capacity for free association and regression. When free-floating attention can be sustained, it has an impact on several dimensions: the relative suspending of the predominance of secondary processes and judgements, putting enacting and reacting on hold, and the capacity to have access to what, in metapsychological terms, we call formal regression. This draws mental functioning in the direction of the hallucinatory dimension and tends to mobilise affects, emotions, and feelings. Free-floating attention leads to more bodily availability and permeability.

This, in turn, facilitates the expression and actualisation of certain psychical forces which, in order to be adequately processed, require not a surface, but a container, an inside that can bear to take them in and contain them for as long as is required for them to be transformed. These psychical forces are the phenomena that Melanie Klein discovered and described in terms of projective identification; Winnicott and, above all, Bion went on to develop these further. They bear witness to a primitive and complex intersubjective link, at the heart of every possibility for mental development and growth, in which representations are still very close to bodily experiences—indeed, they are hardly distinguishable from such sensations. When they emerge in the course of an analysis, they involve in the analyst a kind of mental functioning that is very close to the bodily dimension—sometimes they give rise to temporary psychical experiences that are on the verge of hallucination, enactment, or somatisation.

In order to become active, these phenomena follow a different path from what we usually call transference projections. Their intensity and modes of expression in the analyst's psyche are extremely variable; they are not the prerogative of borderline or psychotic patients, even though, in the treatment of such patients, they may be manifested in a more boisterous and eloquent manner; they can be expressed more silently in the treatment of neurotic patients, and, in such cases, they may well go unrecognised, so that the opportunity for making use of their mutative resources is lost. These psychical occurrences, different though they are in intensity, do share some common characteristics: like foreign bodies, they must make their way into the analyst's psyche and make it experience situations in which affects and bodily sensations are very much present; given the intensity of that presence in real-time, they might pose a threat to the analyst's professional attitude and the internal distance that is required of the analyst in order to maintain the analytical setting.

The temptation to neutralise these manifestations, or to pretend that they do not exist, is a powerful one—treating them as if they had to do with resistance, the analysand's and the analyst's, and denying them any role other than negative with regard to the process of working through. Contrary to neutralisation, neutrality consists in the first place in attempting not to prevent the emergence of these phenomena—in agreeing to allow them to follow the path to formal regression in the analyst so as to make contact with some possibility of representation. In addition, neutrality implies the capacity to agree to take on board these phenomena, to identify their strangeness, to tolerate them for some length of time before reattributing them, to be able to conceive of them, not simply in terms of pathological phenomena, but as an attempt, however desperate, to find some way towards a less defensive redeployment of mental functioning. The analyst might experience them as persecutory, perceive them as parasitical, and decide to attribute them to some kind of inflexible resistance.

We often find it difficult to accept the idea that the patient's resistance corresponds to an expectation that internal modifications in the analyst will enable the analysand to be in a position in which he/she can let go of these defences. The work of psychical growth implied in psychoanalytical treatment, which often gives rise to an experience of internal catastrophe, is not limited to the analysand. We do not willingly accept the idea that, with each of our patients, we shall have to go through such a process. We do not like having to face up to any representation of the excessiveness to which the practice of psychoanalysis commits us, in the most intimate part of our being.

Essentially, the issue of neutrality echoes another one: what does an analysand need in order to put up with the analytical situation and succeed in making use of it to further his/her mental growth? The answer to that question, of course, varies enormously depending on the patient, on his/her need to regress, and on the early failures of the environment to which he/she may have been subjected. Another way of putting the question would be to ask how one makes contact with a patient. How can some kind of psychical "touching" take place without its being too exciting, intrusive, eroticised, or captivating? It is the quality of that touching, of that contact, which gives a profound feeling of being safe, thanks to which every kind of transference turmoil can, thereafter, be experienced and analysed. Who could claim that any true psychoanalytical process could develop if the conditions for that basic sense of security did not exist? Neutrality has to do with that fundamental sense of security, as well as with the idea that the analyst must adapt to the patient's needs. Our representation of that adaptation and, therefore, of neutrality, is, to a great extent, obfuscated by the contrast between gratification/frustration of needs which, via abstinence, is supposed to set up the dynamic conditions under which the treatment can proceed. Adapting to someone's needs as a basic condition for psychical development is not the same thing as satisfying eroticised needs derived from the erotogenic zones. The needs that are involved here are the basic conditions, the stimuli towards life that enable mental life to emerge. That, in my view, is why Winnicott called for a scientific study of the environment, and also why he wondered whether it is possible to have analysis with a potentially suicidal analyst.

> What would be said of an analyst's inability to reassure? If an analyst were himself suicidal? A belief in human nature and in the developmental process exists in the analyst if work is to be done at all, and this is quickly sensed by the patient. (Winnicott, 1954, p. 25)

It is in that area of the basic conditions that favour the development of mental life that I would situate neutrality. I think that it is essential for the implementation, as non-alienating as possible, of the deepest of inter-human relationships, as it unfolds, in all of its nakedness, at the heart of the psychoanalytical relationship.

CHAPTER FIVE

The being of the analyst

The question of the analyst's being lay at the heart of the impassioned controversies that took place when the first schism in psychoanalysis occurred in France, in 1953. Although we might perhaps have forgotten how it came about, it will have had a long-lasting influence on psychoanalytical thinking in France, right up to the present day in fact.

A French controversy

In the context of the conflict that arose concerning the founding of an Institute for training future psychoanalysts distinct from the psychoanalytical Society itself, Sacha Nacht edited a two-volume collection of articles, written by several analysts, under the title *La psychanalyse d'aujourd'hui* (*Psychoanalysis of Today*, Nacht, 1959); this book was intended to be a testimony to the state psychoanalysis found itself in at that time, as well as to the theoretical and technical developments that were taking place. Nacht himself wrote a chapter, entitled "Psychoanalytical therapeutics" ("La thérapeutique psychanalytique"), which gave Lacan the opportunity of criticising him viciously and repeatedly—Lacan took one sentence out of context and made fun of it because of its conceptual flimsiness. To have some idea of this, it is enough to quote the following extract, which cannot fail to surprise anyone who claims to be a follower of Freud; after all, Freud did say that the analysis of dreams is the royal road that leads to a knowledge of the unconscious.

> A dream, after all, is never more than just that—a dream: the psychical reality that it contains, even when it is correctly analysed, will still have the meaning of a second-degree reality; it will never be felt by the patient to be the equal of an experience that has really been lived through. (Nacht, 1956, p. 149)

By raising the issue of the analyst's being, Nacht posed a fundamental question, but did not go into it in any detail; in addition, he made use of it in a way similar to throwing a stone into an "enemy's" garden. In a polemical context, thoughts lose their value when they are used as weapons. Lacan himself launched a crusade against the reference to "the analyst's being" in the manner in which Nacht wrote of it, although it is obvious that that particular issue was of great concern to Lacan himself (in the depths of his own being, in all probability).

I shall begin by quoting Nacht's short sentence, but, to do him justice, I shall quote it in context. In that part of his paper, he illustrates the complexity of the relationships between the constancy of the analyst's "professional attitude", the unconscious dimensions of the countertransference, and the analyst's person and personality; he then goes on to show how all of these factors, depending on how the analyst deals with them, can either facilitate or prevent the development of the treatment process. He then writes (I have italicised the part which Lacan took out of context and criticised): "I often think that *what matters in psycho-analysis is not so much what the analyst says as what he is*" (Nacht, 1956, p. 135).

Taken like that, it does sound somewhat provocative (and it was probably intended to be, at least to some extent); it is difficult to understand why and how what the analyst says or does is not also part of what he/she is. All the more so, in fact, since, in that same paper, Nacht argues that, whatever the analyst's desire to have control over things, the patient can perceive his/her unconscious reactions and underlying attitudes "so that, behind this seeming neutrality, the patient finds in the analyst's unconscious attitudes a response to his demands—a response which is not always the one that the analyst would consciously have chosen to give" (Nacht, 1956, pp. 134–135).

The wider debate of which these ideas are part is that of the factors which, in the psychoanalytical process, lead to recovery. The elements that interested Nacht in that debate were historical, technical, methodological, and metapsychological. As always, these questions spring from a confrontation between, on the one hand, the purified and perhaps even idealised model of analysis and, on the other, the difficulties and perhaps even failures encountered in the actual practice of analysis. While agreeing that Freud had to set up in no uncertain terms a model of treatment that stressed above all the transference and resistance, and of psychoanalytical research based on the psychical phenomena that helped to draw up his successive models of the psychical apparatus, Nacht showed how important it is to think about other aspects of the psychical phenomena at work in an analysis and about their contribution to recovery, elements to which Freud paid little attention. This led Nacht to turn the spotlight, perhaps somewhat schematically, on the phenomena that bear witness to the analyst's subjective commitment to the treatment and on the dimension of intersubjectivity:

> Radical change can be brought about only through the participation of both analyst and analysed in the process outlined above: a mode of exchange, based on the relation, is created between them and constitutes a second element of therapeutic action, which reinforces the one that already exists simply because of the analytical situation. (Nacht, 1956)

In his paper on "The direction of the treatment", Lacan is aiming directly at Nacht when he writes,

> For it is at the heart of their claim to be satisfied with effectiveness that a statement like "the analyst cures not so much by what he says and does as by what he is" can be made. . . . Yet being is being, regardless of who invokes it, and we have the right to ask what it is doing here. So I shall cross-examine the analyst again, insofar as I myself am one, in order to note that *the more his being is involved, the less sure he is of his action*. (Lacan, 2006, p. 491, my italics)

On the same page, Lacan shows clearly—and even more emphatically than Nacht—that the analyst in his being is interested by the action of the analysis; indeed, he emphasises the fact that there is a domain of experience that is shared by both analyst and patient. At first sight, this is something of a surprise, coming as it does from someone who never stopped sharply criticising what he called the "two-body ego-psychology". Lacan writes, "Let us say that in the capital outlay involved in the common enterprise, the patient is not alone in finding it difficult to pay his share. The analyst too must pay" (p. 490).

The analyst's investment in that common enterprise involves what is most intimate: his/her words, being [*sic*], and judgement:

- pay with words no doubt, if the transmutation they undergo due to the analytic operation raises them to the level of their effect as interpretation;

- but also pay with his person, in that, whether he likes it or not, he lends it as a prop for the singular phenomena analysis discovered in transference;

- can anyone forget that he must pay for becoming enmeshed in an action that goes right to the core of being (*Kern unseres Wesens* as Freud put it) with what is essential in his most intimate judgment: could he alone remain on the sidelines? (pp. 490–491)

One of Lacan's main concerns at that time was the devaluation and what he called the "abrading" of psychoanalytical technique. He always drew a parallel between shifts in technique and the refusal to think about how and by what means psychoanalysis produced a particular effect. The tendency to replace interpretation in the psychoanalytical sense with the exercise of power, that is, an acting out, follows on from that:

What I want to convey is that the more impasses researchers and groups encounter in conceptualizing their action in its authenticity, the more they end up forcing their action into the direction of the exercise of power. They substitute this power for the relation to being where their action takes place, making its means—especially those of speech—fall from their veridical eminence. (Lacan, 2006, p. 511)

How are we to understand the path that leads from the "heart" of the relation to being (*Kern unseres Wesens*) and the consideration of every acting as an exercise of power to a psychoanalytical technique that brings acting more and more into its very principle and claims that "unbeing" (*le désêtre*) is the ultimate goal of the treatment?

Maternal omnipotence and negative mysticism

At the time of the 1953 schism, Lacan was already being criticised (and probably envied) because he was overwhelmed by the sheer number of analyses requested of him—training analyses especially—and because, unwilling to say no to anybody (*quid*, then, of the non-response to a request?), he was gradually having to diminish the length of sessions. These contingent factors undoubtedly played a part in the modifications to the setting and to technique that became more pronounced and manifest in Lacan's practice of analysis as the years went by. Their role, however, was almost certainly simply one of facilitating these changes, because the underlying reasons for them had to do with the "being" of their inventor, in his relationship with psychoanalysis, in his personality, in the history of his own personal analysis, in the intellectual and cultural influences that had an impact on him and in his firmly held beliefs as to the nature of the human psyche and intersubjectivity. Each of these factors, of course, deserves much closer scrutiny, but this might not be really possible until more time has passed and the passionate atmosphere which continues to surround the "phenomenon" of Lacan has cleared away somewhat. For the moment, I shall simply make a few brief comments.

As a good Freudian, Lacan was particularly sensitive to, and attentive towards, the negative dimension. There is nothing surprising in that for anyone who has thought about the fundamental part played, in the positive construction of the psyche, by negative or negativising factors—first and foremost primary repression, secondary repression, and negation. When Lacan writes of the relation to being, he is, of course, much more in a metaphysical perspective, as he himself points out, than in a metapsychological one; that perspective has more to do with the "lack of being" than with the fullness of being.

Much of what he writes in "The direction of the treatment and the principles of its power" (1958, in Lacan, 1966) is indicative of that:

from "the subject's want-to-be ('manque à être') to simply be recognized as the heart of the analytic experience" (1966, p. 512) to "What silence must the analyst now impose upon himself if he is to make out, rising above this bog, the raised finger of Leonardo's 'St. John the Baptist', if interpretation is to find anew the forsaken horizon of being in which its allusive virtue must be deployed?" (p. 536).

Note that the negative sign that attaches to the being in question concerns also what is love, good, and desire. For Lacan, who as a young man spent a lot of time with the Dadaists and the Surrealists, whose heroines were the murderesses Violette Nozière and the Papin sisters,[13] the obscene and ferocious figure of power is to do good: "It is the power to do good—no power has any other end—and that is why power has no end" (1966, p. 535).

Another undoubtedly major influence on Lacan—one that, as far as I am aware, is not often mentioned in reviews of Lacan's work—was his somewhat complex friendship with Georges Bataille,[14] whose impressive work is like a black sun, the negative mysticism of an anti-theology. *Inner Experience* (*L'expérience intérieure*) (Bataille 1988) is a glorification of Nothingness at the heart of Being, a Night of the Soul that sanctifies dereliction, a bitter combat with God, in which the Antichrist is fascinated by St John of the Cross, St Theresa of Avila and St Angela of Foligno.

> The summit of joy is not joy, for, in joy, I sense the moment coming when it will end, while, in despair I sense only death coming: I have of it only an anguished desire, but a desire and no other desire. Despair is simple: it is the absence of hope, of all *enticement*. It is the state of deserted expanses and—I can imagine—of the sun. (1988, p. 38)

The book carries as an epigraph this quote from Nietzsche's *Also Sprach Zarathustra*: "Night is also a sun".

At that same period, there was another decisive influence: Alexandre Kojève's interpretation of Hegel. Lacan was a student of Kojève's and he was struck by the question of recognition through the dialectics of Master and Slave, in which he encountered the figure of the Absolute Master: Death. Death and God were probably the main interlocutors of that thwarted mystic for whom the Spiritual Exercises of St Ignatius of Loyola and the poems of St John of the Cross are, perhaps, the secret model of psychoanalytical asceticism (Lacan writes of "psychoanalytical transmutation").

According to his now-famous expression, love is defined only by the paradox of its absence, which is part of the dialectics of being and having.

> For if love is giving what you don't have, it is certainly true that the subject can wait to be given it, since the psychoanalyst has nothing else to give him. But he does not even give him this nothing, and it is better that way—which is why he is paid for this nothing, preferably well paid, in order to show that otherwise it would not be worth much. (Lacan, 1966, p. 516)

A little further on in that chapter, Lacan discusses the impact of that conception on theorisation and technique. In his discussion of demand, desire, regression, and identification in psychoanalytical treatment, Lacan returns to the question of transference and suggestion, and to that of the transference as suggestion: ". . . transference is also a suggestion, but a suggestion that operates only on the basis of the demand for love, which is not a demand based on any need" (p. 530).

That statement has serious repercussions, because it calls into question not only Freud's whole idea of the anaclisis of desire with respect to needs, but also the theory of the drives. Desire and love acquire some degree of autonomy by means of a kind of functional splitting, in which the function of the signifier comes into play:

> The fact that this demand is constituted as such only insofar as the subject is the subject of the signifier is what allows it to be misused by reducing it to the needs from which these signifiers have been borrowed—which is what psychoanalysts, as we see, do not fail to do. (Lacan, 2006, p. 530)

This implies that regression is conceived of in a very specific manner, one which has an impact on technique. Regression, according to Lacan, is important only in its temporal dimension—and even then limited to "the time of remembering" (2006, p. 530)—leaving in the background the other two aspects of regression that Freud emphasised: topographical regression and formal regression.

The regression people foreground in analysis (temporal regression, no doubt, providing one specifies that it has to do with the time of remembering) concerns only the (oral, anal, etc.) signifiers of demand, and involves the corresponding drive only through them. (2006, p. 530)

In that case, why waste time in allowing the analysand, by means of formal and topographical regression, to get back in contact with the experience, lived through during the session, of coming close to a revival of the affects linked to early experiences of having his/her needs satisfied? Not only is it not desirable, it would be much better to put a swift end to all that.

As for desire, Lacan illustrates this via a brilliant analysis of the dream reported by the "butcher's witty wife" and included in Freud's *The Interpretation of Dreams*. Why choose that dream? The reason would seem to be that it has to do with the desire to have an unsatisfied desire; once again in a negative definition, it becomes a very model of desire.

A figure of maternal omnipotence becomes more and more salient in Lacan's writings which, by satisfying need, prevents any access to desire:

Furthermore, the satisfaction of need appears here only as a lure in which the demand for love is crushed, throwing the subject back into a kind of sleep in which he haunts the limbo realm of being, letting it speak in him. (p. 524)

In the whole of that paper, there is only one—more colourful—representation of the primary relationship, a picture of stuffing food into the infant in a way that threatens to suffocate him:

But the child does not always fall asleep in this way in the bosom of being, especially if the Other, which has its own ideas about his needs, interferes and, instead of what it does not have, stuffs him with the smothering baby food it does have, that is, confuses the care it provides with the gift of its love. It is the child who is the most lovingly fed who refuses food and employs his refusal as if it were a desire (anorexia nervosa). (p. 524)

That scenario is not presented as being one example among many other possible scenarios; it functions rather as a kind of prototype of the primary relationship and, consequently, of what can develop in the analytical relationship.

That distrust, that suspicion concerning the maternal preoccupation of satisfying her infant's needs—at first thought of as the basic support necessary for the construction of the mind, including the acquisition of speech—means that it now comes to be seen as the most formidable instrument of alienation; this cannot but leave us puzzled.

It is easy to understand that, in that kind of fantasy scenario, every exchange, every sharing and every relationship runs the risk of being poisoned; if the refusal of all food is seen as the only way of disengaging and heading towards freedom of thought and desire, any tendency towards incorporation, introjection, and identification becomes especially difficult and dangerous.

If we transpose that scenario into the analytical situation, we can see that the analyst is always in danger of finding him/herself in that all-powerful maternal imago's shoes, stifling her infant's desire by the excessiveness of her love that fills up any "lack of being". It is also the case that the analyst might be in the infant's shoes, in so far as that cardinal attitude of refusing to satisfy demand—which should be that *par excellence* of the analyst—might be attributed to the infant.

A mother who refrains from giving anything to her infant in case she deprives him/her of a vital lack—her wish to be an ideal mother is so powerful—or the anorexic child who, in refusing to swallow the *flatus vocis* of a word supposed to be empty, signifies to the mother (i.e., the analysand, according to this scenario) that his/her desire is elsewhere and that the truth of what he/she says lies only where it is just about to fall into a void, so that nothing can be held in common or in the communion of shared pleasure.

> But what, in fact, was the appeal the subject was making beyond the emptiness of his words [*dire*]? It was an appeal to truth at its very core, through which the calls of humbler needs vacillate. But first and from the outset it was the call of emptiness itself, in the ambiguous gap of an attempted seduction of the other by means in which the subject manifests indulgence, and on which he stakes the monument of his narcissism" (Lacan, 2006, p. 206)

This leads to a paradox: the analyst who has instructed the analysand to speak freely will have to tell him/her that the content of what is said will interest the analyst only if it reaches that limit, the point where it tips over towards the emptiness that marks the incompatibility between desire and speech. Lacanian theorisation which, quite rightly, gives such an important role to language will end up by considering that, in its practical and technical work, the productions of speech—always under suspicion of involving "the monument of narcissism" and the illusions of the imaginary—will be interrupted as soon as they emerge. Only scansion and punctuation, which put an end to the session, deserve the value of interpretation, since any more articulate statement, marked by the seal of the analyst's subjectivity, can only alienate the pure subject of desire. The rationalisation of this technique leads to a levelling-out[15] of the various dimensions and of all the nuances of speech and words; it prevents any emergence of affects, emotions, or feelings bound, and able to be bound, to thought associations that might accompany some production of language in the session if it were to continue. The theory, however, states that that part of psychoanalytical work must continue—but above all *in the absence of the analyst*.

In any case, going on with the session would only encourage regression, but

> [that] regression *is not real*; even in language it manifests itself only by inflections, turns of phrase, and 'stumblings so slight' that even in the extreme case they cannot go beyond the artifice of 'baby talk' engaged in by adults. Imputing to regression the reality of a current relation to the object amounts to projecting the subject into an alienating illusion that merely echoes one of the analyst's own alibis. (Lacan, 2006, p. 210, my italics)

When Lacan's derision concerning regression in psychoanalysis is not making a mockery of "baby talk", it sees the analysand as "acting like a child": "That no doubt happens, and such playacting does not bode very well" (2006, p. 516) The grandiose contempt of the wise baby for any expression of infantile distress is a good indication of what at all costs must be prevented from emerging during the session and in the presence of the analyst.

The countertransference is mocked, too, particularly that part of it which concerns what the analyst is feeling, that is, his/her affects:

> But it is rather the facile excitement of their gesture in dumping feelings, which they class under the heading of their counter-transference,

onto one side of the scales—the situation balancing out due to the weight of those feelings—that to me is evidence of a troubled conscience corresponding to a failure to conceptualize the true nature of transference. (2006, p. 492)

Somewhat strangely, it is at that point in the analyst's feelings that the image of death re-emerges:

But what is certain is that the analyst's feelings have only one possible place in the game, that of the dummy (*mort*);[16] and that if the dummy is revived the game will proceed without anyone knowing who is leading it. (p. 493).

From that perspective, the analyst's neutrality is seen as a form of mortification. A little further on in that paper, Lacan writes of the self-denial imposed on the analyst by what is at stake in an analysis.[17]

What is primarily at stake in this conception of the analyst's technique has to do with the role of affects, emotions, and feelings in the psychoanalytical process—on the analysand's side, but even more so on the analyst's—in the way that the analyst responds to the patient's emotional expressions during the session and—above all—to the emergence of his/her own affects in the presence of the patient. That is indeed a very complex question, given that, over and beyond the characteristics specific to any particular human being, it pertains to the theorisation of affects in their relationship with representation, language, speech, and capacity for symbolisation. Affect is the conscious perception of something that tells us about the state in which the organism finds itself; it is part of the psychical domain, but, at the same time, it bears witness to the indisputable link between mind and body. Depending on the theoretical representation that we have of the affects, they will have different—and perhaps even contradictory—functions and values. Some will see affects as being opposed to thoughts, to the capacity for representation and to symbolisation. Others—and this, of course, is my point of view—would see in them an elementary and fundamental expression of the psyche, the complexity of which is far from having been sufficiently explored; affects in themselves are a form of representation that takes its elements and its characteristics from sensations and sensoriality and which, through the ability to distinguish between pleasure and unpleasure, sets up an initial value system within the psyche and the basic modalities of intersubjective relationships.

Shutting out the body

Starting with a completely justifiable criticism of the reductionistic and psychologising tendency at work in psychoanalytical thinking, Lacan gradually reinforced his idea of *shutting out the body*—in the way it is presented in analytical treatment via those psychical phenomena that are at the very limits of the somatic dimension: affects and emotions—from his thinking and from the analytical scene in the way that it is experienced (a word banished from Lacanian vocabulary!) *in vivo* on the analytical stage. Behind that way of dealing with the situation, there is, so it seems, a kind of anorexic theory of psychoanalysis—a kind of disavowal of the body; it is a theorisation which is not so much cerebral as cortical.

In one session of his 1953–1954 Seminar devoted to Freud's Papers on Technique, a young and somewhat brilliant hospital doctor, one of the "master's" favourite "pupils", asked a question about the nature of the transference, at the same time daring—but choosing his words with great care—to add a comment about affect. He was at that time in analysis with Lacan (in general, the term "pupil" designates those who attended his seminars and were having their training analysis with him), and it is obvious that he was attempting to obtain from his analyst, outside of the analytical setting, what he was not getting from him in the actual analysis. At the beginning of that seminar session—the last one of the year, entitled "The concept of analysis", Lacan said to his analysand, ". . . surely you must also have things to ask. Last time after the session you said to me something remarkably like a question—*I would have really liked you to have talked about transference, even so*". Since we know that the person concerned was one of Lacan's analysands—and by no means the least of them—what follows is something of a surprise: "They are tough, those *even so's*—I do nothing but talk to them about it and they're still not satisfied. There are profound reasons why the subject of transference always leaves you craving for more." (Lacan, 1991, p. 273) Profound reasons, indeed! In the end, the analysand did manage to explain what left him hungry for more:

> When one looks at what is written on transference, one always gets the impression that the phenomenon of transference falls in the category of manifestations of an affective order, of emotions, in contrast with

other manifestations, of an intellectual order, such as procedures aimed at understanding, for instance. Hence one always finds it a bit difficult to give an account of your view of the transference in the current, ordinary terminology. (Lacan, 1991, p. 274)

After listening to some developments on the progress of the symbolic order and mathematics, together with a very pertinent comment on the lack of any foundation for opposing the affective and intellectual domains, the analysand, as Lacan was mentioning his paper delivered at the Rome Congress (i.e., "The function and field of speech and language in psychoanalysis"), came back to the point that he was making, saying "Exactly, both this silence, and these direct attacks on the term affective did have an effect" (Lacan, 1991, p. 275). That insistence brought him an unequivocal retort, which is a clear indication of the foundation of Lacan's project as to theory: "I believe that is a term which one must completely expunge from our papers".

The name of that young doctor? Serge Leclaire.

The impassioned debates that have surrounded Lacan's developments, the passionate reactions that he himself aroused—hate or veneration—and the Passion that he put on show every week during his seminar clearly bear witness to the fact that it was powerful affects which pushed him into the path of purging . . . all affects. But whatever is rejected in any theorisation and split off from experience always comes back on to the stage of reality. The anecdote that I have just reported is a moving example of that. In Lacan's theory, putting affects aside more or less came to mean a prohibition against thinking, which, as a result, led to acting in the treatment and ended up in the institutionalisation of acting in his technique of psychoanalysis. Acting in the form of all kinds of acting-out in the encounters with patients outside of the analytical setting itself (the result of the refusal to process and work through the affects arising in the treatment), acting-out promoted to the rank of a cornerstone of the technique, via short and variable-length sessions, and the scansion that interrupted a session at the precise moment when an important psychical event was about to occur, all of these are examples of hateful retaliation: responses in the form of actings to the rigours of a kind of mortification that the analyst cannot tolerate and with respect to which he/she takes revenge on the patient while at the same time rationalising that revenge—"It's for your own good".

Given Lacan's intellectual background, he brought into his own practice of psychoanalysis, and into that of many of his followers, some abuses—abuses of power identical to those against which he rebelled in his diagnosis of the deep-rooted reasons for certain "abradings" in psychoanalytical technique. The paradoxical effect of the traumatic seduction entailed by those ways of operating was such that, by that very means, they were passed on to his followers. In the name of being, of course.

It would, all the same, be too simple and simplifying to restrict the potentiality and effectiveness of these abuses to Lacan and some of his epigones. That would really amount to doing a favour to those kind souls who see everything in black and white, and I would tend to agree completely with Lacan's distrust of those who proclaim what is good. Unfortunately, "Lacanians" do not have the exclusive right to abuse of all kinds, learnedly rationalised under the guise of "technique". Even though they might take on different forms—perhaps less blatant—they may concern all analysts, whatever the school of thought to which they belong. Rather than put them carefully into the category of "stumblings so slight" or justify them in a way that declares the analyst "innocent" and in no way responsible for the transgressive act, "clinical" justification being with reference to "fate neurosis", "negative therapeutic reaction", or "projective identification", it would be better for psychoanalysts to think more deeply about the possible negative potentialities of their discipline and the actualisation of those potentialities, always a possibility, in the course of psychoanalytical treatment.

CHAPTER SIX

The presence of the analyst

L et us stay for a little while longer on our road towards the being, because the question of presence has always been in its immediate surroundings.

As we have just seen, it was with respect to action that the issue of being came to Lacan's attention, and for the *infans* with respect to what will enable a disengagement from the maternal omnipotence that assigns to him/her the role of being the phallus, in the place of the object of the satisfaction of need. The fourth section of Lacan's paper on "The direction of the treatment" is headed "How to act with one's being". It deals immediately with issues involving introjection and identification, questions that enable Lacan, from a psychoanalytical point of view, to explore the metaphysical issue of being, because it indicates the movement of appropriation to *become* the object in order to *be* that object. That movement aimed at the object's being is indeed a mental action. Lacan's intention is to decide whether that action is *real*, because, on the one hand, the fundamental reason behind his criticism of Nacht's idea of the relationship to being is that it is not a fact of the Real, and, on the other, "it is ruled out that anything real should be consummated in analysis" (Lacan, 2006, p. 508). That point will be one of the major axes of my exploration of the issues involving the presence of the analyst.

Before taking another look at this via introjection and the scathing derision with which Lacan treated Ferenczi, let us first of all go back to Winnicott, to whom Lacan paid tribute in no uncertain terms. Lacan agreed that observation of the mother–infant relationship, when it is subsequently thought about and theorised by a psychoanalytical mind, may well give rise to some interesting ideas:

> Geneticism-based research and direct observation are far from having cut themselves off from a properly analytic spirit. When I discussed object-relation themes one year in my seminar, I showed the value of a conception in which child observation is nourished by the most accurate reconsideration of the function of mothering in the genesis of the object: I mean the notion of the transitional object, introduced by D. W. Winnicott, which is key in explaining the genesis of fetishism. (Lacan, 2006, p. 511)

In passing, let me pay tribute to Lacan for having shown some interest in the thinking of someone so different from him, a psychoanalyst whose writings very few French analysts at that time (1958) had read, far less commented upon. The opposite was also true, because very early on Winnicott had acknowledged the significance of Lacan's paper on "The mirror stage" (Lacan, 2006[1966]). But even then the gap between their ways of thinking was widening and their approach to those issues became more and more opposed to each other. For Winnicott, the mother's body was from the outset the *locus* of the mirror; her face and the subtleties of the emotional responses that she feels inside herself are what act as a mirror for her infant.

The depth and the subtlety of Winnicott's thinking led him to explore further the paradoxes of reality and illusion and to put the experience of play and illusion at the very heart of identity, identification, and the ability to access reality. I do not know whether Lacan was still reading Winnicott in 1971, when *Playing and Reality* was published, but I think it hardly likely. He would, all the same, have discovered, as he read through that book (but would he have been able to realise it at the time?), one way of thinking about the question of reality and of the relationship to being which neither he nor Nacht were able to do at the time of their controversial discussion:

In the growth of the human baby, as the ego begins to organize, this
that I am calling the object-relating of the pure female element establishes what is perhaps the simplest of all experiences, the experience
of *being*. . . . But I find that it is here, in the absolute dependence on
maternal provision of that special quality by which the mother meets
or fails to meet the earliest functioning of the female element, that we
may seek the foundation for the experience of being. . . . Now I want
to say: 'After being – doing and being done to. But first, being.'
(Winnicott, 1999[1971], pp. 80, 84–85)

I do not doubt the fact that Lacan would have been interested, in
his being, by Winnicott's remarks. However, to take them into consideration rather than throw them away immediately, in a gesture of
contempt and derision, would have demanded of him a profound
review of his relationship to psychical reality and passivity: being is
not dying.

Lacan bullied by Loewenstein, his analyst

It would be a mistake to say that Lacan did not take to heart the experience of his own personal analysis with Loewenstein. At that time, six
years of analysis represented quite a considerable duration—it could
even be described as exceptional—especially for a so-called training
analysis. Most of those analyses lasted just a few months. We could,
therefore, imagine that Lacan, more than any other analyst of his
generation, was profoundly interested in exploring his unconscious
conflicts via the experience of psychoanalysis, something that was
completely different from subjecting himself to a mere formal requirement. Some commentators have not hesitated to call upon the most
distasteful of arguments: Lacan was too ill; he was impossible
to analyse. With that way of handling things, there is nothing more to
say and everything gets back to normal! It is not hard to imagine that
Jacques Lacan might not have been an "easy" analysand (but then
who anyway is an easy analysand, and who could claim that analysis
is easy?). This is because, no doubt, of the complex nature of his personality, but also—and above all, I would say—because of the sheer
quality of his gifted nature, his intelligence, his intellectual and social
life, and his love affairs, which might well have given rise, in his
analyst, to countertransference difficulties, particularly with regard to

envy. From that point of view, who could really have taken on the task of being Lacan's analyst and of continuing to do so in France in 1932? Why did Lacan not go to Vienna to consult Freud?[18] Was Loewenstein competent enough as an analyst to take on Lacan? We may well have serious doubts about that, particularly perhaps when we look at the scandalous circumstances that brought Lacan's analysis to a hurried end.[19] As the time drew near for the members of the Paris Psychoanalytical Society to vote on Lacan's election to full membership (which would have allowed him to become a training analyst), Loewenstein offered him a fool's bargain: Lacan would agree to continue his analysis with Loewenstein while, on his part, Loewenstein would ensure that Lacan got the required number of "yes" votes.[20] That really is an example of a major transgression of the analytical setting and of all the ethical and technical principles on which it is based; it is quite definitely a misuse of power. It is, of course, a traumatic event, the fundamental aspect of which is the violent irruption of reality into the analytical process—and this at the analyst's own behest—which leads to the collapse of all the conditions that govern every possibility of enabling psychical reality to emerge and be interpreted. It is an example of a behaviour, on the part of the analyst, full of hatred towards the analysand. Lacan pretended to agree to this, but, as soon as he was elected, he decided to put an end to his analysis. Given the circumstances, it was probably the best thing he could do in order to protect himself. But what terrible damage. Lacan was suddenly faced with a twofold dispossession. The destructiveness inherent in what Loewenstein did is a retrospective attack on the whole credibility of the analytical process that Lacan had undertaken and was still continuing with him; in addition, it takes all credibility away from Lacan's election to full membership, because he was elected apparently "thanks to" pressure being brought to bear, not because he was acknowledged as being worthy of the position.

For the rest of his life, Lacan was to pay a heavy price for that act full of hatred, and he himself constantly made Loewenstein, ego psychology, the Paris Psychoanalytical Society, and a significant part of the international psychoanalytical establishment pay for it, too. The traumatic aspect of the end of that analysis led to a kind of functioning enacted via repetition. The way that Lacan always spoke, in his writings, of the issue of reality is an example of the ghostly presence of that event in his theorising and thinking—often marked as they are by a counter/contrary element. Another example, concerning this time the practice of analysis, is that of his repeated actings with respect to his patients, setting up some degree of collusion between psychical reality in the treatment and social reality, and rationalised in his theory as being the only way of not exercising any alienating power against the analysand. We see here how a *traumatogenic acting-out is presented, under the cover of technique, as being the only way of breaking free of the consequences of the trauma.* That destructive paradox continues to be handed down from one generation of analysts to the next.

Why did Lacan not undertake further analysis after this? In the absence of any clear reply, we can simply put together a few hypotheses. The events that I have just reported took place in 1938. It would have been even more difficult to find an analyst available at that time, given the approaching war and the exodus of most analysts other than a few who were particularly close to him. After the war, he was one of the few eminent training analysts in the Society; he had in training several young analysts, and he rapidly found himself the intellectual leader of a whole generation. In such circumstances, all that he could have done would have been to look to the other side of the English Channel. We could now perhaps indulge in a construction game of psychoanalysis-fiction, imagining the outcome of the transference depending on whether Lacan had contacted Melanie Klein, whom he once called "an inspired tripe butcher" (Lacan, 2006, p. 632), Winnicott, the author of "Hate in the counter-transference", or perhaps Bion, the theorist of the transformation of affects and Beckett's analyst. So, here I am, finding myself with the extremely difficult (as always) task of referring Lacan to an analyst for re-analysis, and measuring the weight of my responsibility. Difficult to decide whether any one of those three, each in his/her own way, would have helped Lacan to process his affects and his negative transference through dealing with the actual experience of the treatment. Winnicott, no matter how much he placed hate at the centre of countertransference issues, never really managed to cope with Masud Kahn's grandiosity—and that is the least we can say—so I would rule him out. I would be afraid that Bion and Lacan, although at two opposite ends of the spectrum of analytical thinking and practice, might eventually enter a zone of collusion and blindspots in the area of their mutual potentials for mysticism. I think Lacan might have needed a woman analyst, a woman with guts, not easily deterred by threats, no matter how seductive, and capable of working with the regressed psychotic parts of a wise baby. I definitely believe that the inspired tripe butcher would have done the job. But, come to think of it: buckle up, it's going be a bumpy ride!

Nevertheless, it is likely that the very nature of that traumatic act, in the way that it resonated with his own character traits, would have made the option of re-analysis relatively unthinkable. The die was already cast, and the dramatisation of what was at stake in the reality scenario in the period preceding the 1953 schism was an opportunity for building up once and for all, as the destiny of a grandiose victim of exclusion, what might just as well have been processed differently with an analyst who would not have put it all down to the pathetic reality of a very small world. It is impossible not to have that idea in mind when we read these lines:

> But who will say what the analyst is there, and what remains of him when he is up against the wall of the task of interpreting? . . . Thus he prefers to fall back on his ego, and on the reality about which he knows a thing or two. But here he is, then, at the level of "I" and "me" with his patient. How can he manage it if they're at each other's throats? It is here that we astutely count on the secret contacts we must have on the inside—named, in this case, the healthy part *of the ego*, the part that thinks like us. (Lacan, 2006, p. 494)

In those sentences about theoretical controversy, every single word refers back to the history of an abortive analysis and its violent outcome. It is really to be regretted that Loewenstein wriggled out of the task of challenging Lacan's spirits as they rose from the under-world. Several generations later, they still haunt us, waiting as they are to be listened to, heard, and dispersed; since they are by now exhausted by their fruitless knocking on the door, they can speak only in hackneyed phrases, ever more rudimentary as time goes by, which each day take them further away from the living origins of a suffering that henceforth is unthinkable. Over and beyond all the images of heroic and grandiose characters that Lacan delighted in portraying and feeling victimised by (and which his admirers clearly contributed to by erecting statues to them and singing their praises), it is per-haps interesting to see therein, and to listen to, a child—gifted, disappointed, ill-treated, and wounded.

Lacan derides Ferenczi

The mention of a child brings us back to Ferenczi, ill-treated and made to look ridiculous by Lacan because of what he said about introjection. Lacan argues that the question of being is a very old one in psychoanalysis and that it was Ferenczi—he who was "the most tormented by the problem of analytic action" (Lacan, 2006, p. 512)—who first spoke of it in "Introjection and transference" in 1909. Lacan does not make it clear that at the time when Ferenczi wrote that paper, barely two years had gone by since he first became acquainted with Freud's articles on psychoanalysis and that he had been part of the circle of psychoanalysts for only about a year then. That makes even more remarkable the exceptional quality of that paper, written by a young physician who had barely been in contact with psychoanalysis and who at the time had had no personal experience of analysis; it bears witness to Ferenczi's capacity for an introjective processing that was both creative and anticipatory, no doubt buttressed by a keenly developed capacity for identification combined with certain aspects of precociousness and prematurity from which Ferenczi suffered all his life—a suffering that his analysis with Freud did not enable him to overcome—quite the contrary, in fact. That brief evocation of Ferenczi's early genius might lead to the conclusion that Lacan could, perhaps, see something of himself in that picture—but of a "himself" that set off in a completely different direction, that of an excess of cathexis of primary suffering, not its counter-cathexis. As Lacan puts it (2006, p. 512): "Ferenczi conceives of transference as the introjection of the doctor's person into the patient's subjective economy" and "what he means is the absorption into the subject's economy of everything the psychoanalyst makes present in the duo as the here and now of an incarnated problematic" (2006, p. 512). Reducing a complex paper of that kind to those few sentences is undoubtedly tendentious, but it remains part of a debate on ideas, and it exemplifies in a very precise way what, for Lacan, was inadmissible with regard to the theory of psychoanalysis. However, what does give rise to feelings of unacceptability and to a scathing response full of contempt, which bursts forth from the bastion of narcissistic megalomania, is the idea, expressed by Ferenczi, that the psychoanalyst might be hurt, as the analysis draws to a close, by the departure of his/her analysand and say so in so many words. "Must one pay this comical price for the subject's want-to-be to simply be recognized as the heart of analytic experience . . .?" (2006, p. 512).

It is now easier to understand why Lacan preferred to place the figure of the dummy (see note 16) where the analyst's feelings are, in particular, those that have to do with suffering and separation.

An attempt at theorisation is not necessarily defensive, and Ferenczi gives us an insight into the more primitive and crude aspects of introjection and the ferociously cannibalistic aspects of incorporation—those on which the "inspired tripe butcher", his former analysand, laid particular emphasis. But the deep-rooted movement towards de-corporisation at work in Lacan's thinking and theorisation meant that it was impossible to see the "highest" degree of symbolic functioning as issuing from those primitive psychical mechanisms. Any discussion of the idea of the analyst's presence based on introjection thus opens on to a debate about two diametrically opposed conceptions of symbolisation and the symbolic dimension. And since separation anxiety has just been mentioned, it might be worthwhile pointing out that the representation of a symbol is linked to that of separation: the separated-off part of the whole enabling recognition and reunification when the two parts are brought together again.

I shall follow two paths in my exploration of the presence of the analyst, one with the idea of contact, the other with that of the substance of the object.

Tact and contact derided and vilified

Among the ideas vilified by Lacan, tactility and contact are very much in the foreground, not only because of their reference to "the current relation to the object" (Lacan, 2006, p. 210) but also to sensoriality and, therefore, to the body:

> Nothing could be more misleading for the analyst than to seek to guide himself by some supposed "contact" he experiences with the subject's reality. . . . But its obsessive value becomes flagrant when it is recommended in a relationship which, according to its very rules, excludes all real contact. (2006, p. 210)

On first reading those words, we feel compelled to share in that noble indignation: it is quite true, contact is something very primary and pre-analytical, it runs contrary to the rules that define the setting, with their implication that we do not touch each other. But let us think about this for a moment. Lacan uses the words "real contact" as if this were self-evident. But what, then, *is* real contact? In the context of that sentence, with its reference to the rules of analysis, the contact that is prohibited is the direct contact between two bodies, skin touching skin. Did Lacan not have any other representation of the reality of the contact between two people? This would imply that, in his view, reality can be attributed only to the here-and-now body, a "carnal envelope", yet he spends a lot of counter-cathexis energy in denying this in his theory. It would imply also that he brushes aside one of the very cornerstones of Freud's theory: the concept of psychical reality, which, via the idea of the drives, is always defined as lying at the frontier between mind and body.

The prohibition against any erotic contact in the analytical setting enables the presence of psychical reality in both protagonists to be intensified, and some modification of the way of being and appearing of these psychical realities so that they come into contact with each other and penetrate into each other, thereby creating in the session areas where exchanges can take place and the frontiers between the two participants can become more blurred.[21] These phases of relative vagueness, non-differentiation, and non-integration (Winnicott) bring into play the capacity for topographical and formal regression, which constitute an approximation to the primitive psychical movements which exist between the *infans* and his/her human environment and which are made use of experimentally in the session. This deployment is neither the transference nor the countertransference. It is a kind of psychical work that enables us to reach certain mental states that have their own capacities for processing; because of that, the psychical work involved is not simply absorbed by the dimension of the compulsion to repeat. Thanks to that psychical work, there begin to emerge—above all in a way that makes them interpretable and able to be processed—transference figures and various forms of defence mechanism that are there to hinder, each in its own way, that work of the psyche.

That "supposed 'contact' [the analyst] experiences" (Lacan, 2006, p. 210), which Lacan in another of his defensive rejections expresses in derogatory and derisive terms, "trashing"[22] it as a "vacuous buzzword of intuitionist . . . psychology" (2006, p. 210), is much less "primary" than he would have us believe.

The contact that is set up or felt to be a refusal of contact is never a hard fact, even though it might appear to be direct. In addition, even though it might be presented as lying "beyond discourse",[23] it is not split off in the interpretation that the analyst may give of it (even though splitting may, at that point, exist in the patient's psychical reality). There is often a hiatus, which might be something like isolation, dissociation, difference, or splitting between what is experienced in "contact" on the one hand and in "discourse" on the other. In itself, that hiatus always has a discriminating and interpretative significance.

Experiencing contact is not a first-degree reality as Nacht seemed to think and as Lacan criticised it. It is one level—in itself highly complex—of perception of the other person's somato–psychical reality. Although it passes via sensoriality, proprioception, and the affects, as they are structured in a value system that determines how reality is perceived, it is refracted and metabolised in the more secondary process psychical elements that structure it in terms of preconscious and conscious representations. That work of processing corresponds, for example, to what Bion described in terms of the capacity for reverie.

Contact bears witness to the capacity for tolerating the presence of someone unfamiliar. Very primitive reactions of rejection may sometimes be set up in a very brutal way whenever two people find themselves in each other's presence. Given the rapidity and the force with which those reactions are set up, they are more like immunological reactions than the mentally processed strategy of psychical defence mechanisms, which the analyst might experience as a temporary tendency towards phobic avoidance, disgust, inhibition, anxious obnubilation, etc. In order to facilitate permeability, receptiveness, and porosity, which are part of the quality of the analyst's presence and enable the analysand's psychical reality to be received and taken in, the analyst must put on hold his/her usual system of defences and perhaps even what might appear to be immunological reactions of reject. It is possible to do this only up to a certain extent, variable from one patient to another—and even with regard to the same patient, depending on the particular phase of the treatment. It is the quality of this mental work by the analyst that will determine and facilitate the processing of the patient's resistance, just as much as the correctness of the interpretations that punctuate the analytical process. Neither can function properly without the other, especially since the relevance of the preconscious processing of an interpretation is highly dependent upon the analyst's capacity to put on hold any sophisticated form—that is, judgemental—of his/her reactions of reject.

All this is an outline, admittedly somewhat perfunctory, of what might be occurring in the analyst. As far as the analysand is concerned, there is one difficult question that cannot be evaded: is everything that the analysand feels in the contact with the analyst a matter of transference projections? Does one part of it have to do with the perception of certain aspects of the analyst's psychical reality? Everything that the analyst, without realising it, communicates about him/herself, contributes to the "atmosphere" of the encounter and quietly influences the analytical relationship. We can decide to leave that question to one side as being irrelevant from a psychoanalytical point of view and argue that, whatever the situation, everything must be interpreted in terms of the transference. It is true that some of what is perceived will be the object of transference projections, and that certain aspects of the analyst's psychical reality might be activated by a patient who unconsciously tries to bring about some repetition of traumatic factors. The fact remains that the question still arises when those elements, although perceived and in action, are not identified for what they really are. In such cases, transference interpretations which fail to take into account some of the elements that have been perceived (they may remain unconscious, but it is also possible for them to be consciously felt by the patient) might amount to a denial of perception: No, you did not perceive what you perceived. In every case that denial is harmful—but it is particularly so when the analysand had already, in childhood, been the object of such a denial, leading to the decathexis of his/her own capacity for thought, judgement, and intuition.

In order to illustrate these remarks, let me give a few brief examples. Imagine some unobtrusive melancholic elements in an analyst towards which the analysand, given his/her own past history, is particularly sensitive and receptive. In a very subtle and almost imperceptible way, they instigate in the analysand a continuous wish to repair, thereby repeating an unconscious infantile tendency, which prevents any unconscious aggressiveness being brought into the transference. This is indeed a "beyond discourse": a simple change in the tone of voice, a sigh, a movement unusually slow, a particular state of stillness of the body, the rhythm of a sentence, the tonality of silence: in short, the emotional colouring of the presence, perceived and unconsciously deciphered as "depressive elements", which set up a defence mechanism similar to reparation. If all of these elements remain unacknowledged, the analysand will be a "good" analysand who will do a "good" analysis—which, indeed, will have no reason to be brought to an end since it is doing so much "good" to the analyst. In the course of all this, analytical material will have been produced and interpreted in the most analytically correct way possible. The analysand may well become an analyst at the end of all this, an excellent theoretician, and there you have it! It is precisely those unobtrusive and unrecognised elements that are the object of the most stubborn of "identifications with the analyst". Fortunately, often a slip of the tongue, a dream or a bungled action (either by the analysand or by the analyst) will highlight what is hampering the analytical process. If, in interpreting this compromise formation, the analyst cannot discover the means to pick up and clarify the part that his/her subjective implication might have played "well short of discourse", the opportunity will have been lost, the interpretation will be incomplete and will not go to the roots of the unconscious complex or, therefore, to the compulsion to repeat. Let us suppose (I am deliberately simplifying) that this analysand perceives a conscious feeling that makes him/her say to the analyst: "Well, today I felt that you looked sad, and I said to myself that there must be something wrong." The analyst, if he/she does say something at this point, may simply interpret the projective dimension, and there would be no mistake in that. However, with respect to what is really at stake on this particular analytical stage, things would be completely different if the analyst could say: "It is quite possible that you did perceive that, but . . ." with several possibilities to choose from in continuing his/her intervention. The simplest—but which may well contain a maximum of potentialities—would be: ". . . but we could perhaps try to understand why you are so concerned with how I am feeling that you seem to find it hard to think about anything else." That intervention acknowledges the transference dimension *because* it is able also to acknowledge the reality of the perception. It enables the analysand to disengage from that and to take an interest in his/her own psychical reality. That standpoint is, of course, very different from a puritanical concern for transparency based on guilt feelings—which puts an obligation on the analyst to inform the analysand of what he/she is feeling in order to hide nothing, thereby reducing the analysis to a series of mutual relation-based transactions.[24]

Another example, even more complex: a patient has a splendid transference dream in which the analyst is clearly represented. It has to do with the analyst's car, certain parts of the engine of which are in very bad shape; these will have to be changed as a matter of urgency, otherwise the analyst is in danger of having a fatal accident. In the dream, the patient is a motor mechanic. In reality, the analyst recently learnt that he is suffering from a serious illness that affects certain vital internal organs and that he will have to have surgery very soon. The dream is a transference dream, in all probability an important one, and it should be perceived and analysed as such. But it is not *only* a transference dream, and the complex nature of the psychical impulses that led to its construction deserve to be taken into account if the analysand is to be able to make use of all of the processing potentialities that it contains.

In this case, too, the analysand perceived (but how?) something very precise concerning the reality of the analyst's internal state. It is a diagnostic dream that involves the diagnosis of an illness beginning to take root not in the body of the dreamer, as Freud defined it, but in that of another person representing the primary object. If the analyst does not wish to include in his interpretation that dimension of the process of constructing the dream of *that* patient in *those* particular circumstances, he will destroy the possibility of enabling part of the patient's mental functioning to emerge. That blunt refusal might begin to function as a prohibition against thinking that will coincide with the despair of never being able to make himself heard for himself, but always for the other person.

This is where we reach some very interesting frontiers, the frontiers of what is thinkable in and through our theory—and, moreover, of what is bearable, thinkable, and able to be processed by the analyst in the analytical situation. In the example I have just mentioned, we can imagine how difficult it is for the analyst, at that point when his life is in danger—and he, therefore, is in a kind of narcissistic withdrawal—to continue being his patient's analyst, that is, able to put his own worries about himself to one side to a degree that will enable the analysand to grasp the instruments of the interpretation in order to process what is vital for him. The analyst will certainly need to have an unusually strong capacity to tolerate having been "seen right through" and to envisage his own death, accepting the fact that the other person will live longer but without hating him for that—a capacity that requires a fundamental degree of respect for the other person. We could, perhaps, say that an analyst treats the patient also via *who* he/she (the analyst) is—but may also destroy, if too much importance is given to that element.

The analyst will never be a pure subject, as Lacan would have wished. He/she will always have to come to terms with those irreducible rests of an elusive subjectivity that may, of course, be consistent with the alienation of the subject in analysis, but may also contribute to keeping the analytical process alive. It is not a matter of eradicating the subjective data of the analyst's psychical reality, but, rather, of how he/she puts them to the analysand. In the best of cases, the analyst will succeed in doing this in such a way that the particularities of his/her psyche will have served simply as a provisional support that facilitates access to the universality of the rules that govern mental functioning in order to help the patient make use of them to his/her own ends so as to reorganise his/her mind.

From a psychoanalytical point of view, understanding and intelligibility can never come from outside and simply be applied to a material that has to be deciphered and translated. First of all, there must be set up an experience of the other person; this requires a psychical "touching"/contact that derives from a vital link. That psychical touching is an analogon in the analytical relationship of what in early relationships is called *holding*; it has the twofold valency of that concept, bodily and mental. In my opinion, setting up that link, via a series of subtle exchanges between analyst and analysand, creates the conditions for a feeling of basic security that in itself enables the subsequent analysis of the dimension of transference repetition, putting aside as much as possible the effects of inducing repetition. Setting up that basic psychical touching is probably the most profound degree of what we call the analyst's neutrality (see Chapter Four "The paradoxes of neutrality"). The following anecdote is an illustration of what I have just said. It was told to me by a psychoanalyst (Jose-Luis Goyena) who was in supervision with Herbert Rosenfeld. One day, Rosenfeld asked him point-blank if he had a basin in his consulting-room. The analyst was somewhat surprised at this, and Rosenfeld went on, saying that if he really wanted to analyse psychotic patients, he had to be prepared for their being unable to express their impulses towards projective identification other than by vomiting it all up—and in such a case, the only analytically thinkable gesture was to hold a basin out to them.

The substance of the object

If we agree that the *infans* is not a monad, we cannot deny that the presence of the primary environment is important. The quality of that presence, through the way in which it offers its services and gives of itself when faced with the infant's basic needs, will play an important role in shaping the potentiality for development present in that infant, whatever the weight we might give to constitutional factors. Transformative and integrative processing thus becomes possible; particularly in the earliest period of life, these are of a somato–psychical nature, and are very *real*.[25] Primary identification is the first way of appropriating the components of the mind, the form of psychical tendencies and their qualities. Among those basic components is primal repression, which, in Freud's sense, is an attempt to represent for the self a very primitive mode of acquiring and maintaining a potential space into which will come a psyche in its representational form. Freud argued that an analysis can make for some rearrangements of the modalities of primal repression; this was because he assumed that the transformations made possible by psychoanalytical treatment are real and correspond to actual modifications in the structure of the very fabric of psychical reality.[26] We could add, as a hypothesis, even though these are not part of the object of study specific to psychoanalysis, the rearrangements that take place in neurobiological, neurophysiological, neuro-immunological, and neuro-humoral reality, if we accept the idea of an indissociable somato–psychical structure.

It would, therefore, seem difficult to claim, as Lacan does, that "it is ruled out that anything real should be consummated in analysis" (Lacan, 2006, p. 508). If nothing real were consummated, it would be difficult to understand how some real changes could occur. There remains to be shown—and this, of course, is the most difficult part—by what means that reality comes about and what theoretical representations of its effectiveness we can imagine.

Lacan, quite correctly, refuses to accept the idea of a *direct* effectiveness of the presence, of the reality of what is experienced, and of the affects—in other words, any cathartic resolving by emotional discharge in analytical treatment. He does, however, emphasise the fundamental character of intersubjectivity in the constitution of the individual and in the process of the treatment, but in a context in which he sees love, desire, and the body only in terms of alienation:

> The nature of the desire is expressed in a sort of bodily agglutinating of freedom. We want to become for the other an object that has the same limiting value for him as does, in relation to his freedom, his own body. ... In so far as we remain within the register of analysis, we will be obliged to admit an original intersubjectivity. (Lacan, 1991, p. 217)

Similarly, the issue of the presence of the analyst is a recurrent theme in Lacan's writings, as we see in the following extract:

> Although primary transference most often remains little more than a shadow, that doesn't stop this shadow from dreaming and reproducing its demand when there is nothing left to demand. This demand will simply be all the purer since it is empty. It may be objected that the analyst nevertheless gives his presence, but I believe that his presence is initially implied simply by his listening, and that this listening is simply the condition of speech. (Lacan, 2006, p. 516)

That restrictive "but", coming after the affirmation of the gift of presence, has, in my view, to do with what I earlier called the rejection of the body and of affects; presence is implied simply by listening which, in order for it to be the condition of speech, must be disembodied. Thus, in that form of thinking. which ends up being close to nominalism, the concept becomes the thing in itself: "It comes down to this, that speech has a creative function, and that it brings into being the very thing, which is none other than the concept" (Lacan, 1991, p. 242).

It is with regard to the idea of identification, incorporation, and introjection that Lacan wants to stay as far away as possible from any consideration of the substance of the object; he contrasts the representation of a "real consummation" with that of a symbolic assumption. But to what reality is he referring here? Symbolic operations become able to generate symbols only if the individual already has the capacity to symbolise. That capacity to symbolise has its origins and its roots in the earliest and most primitive experiences in mental life; it is not a given, it is conquered through repeated experiences of encounters and separations between the body-mind and the outside world. That primal test is a crucible for transformations in which the intrapsychical dimension takes shape in the deployment of intersubjectivity as more and more complex connections are set up between the psychical *loci* (topography), psychical impulses (dynamics), and psychical energy (economy).

These primal issues arise to a variable extent in the course of every psychoanalysis that proves able to bring about certain mutative effects in psychical economy. They are played out again in the encounter between analysand and analyst, whose potentiality for qualifying them is real enough, even though, as Freud put it, "there is no model in real life" (1915a, p. 166). Replaying is not simply repeating; it involves starting the game over again in order to play it again with someone who is, perhaps, nobody, but who, knowing how to sidestep, also knows how to answer: "present".

CHAPTER SEVEN

The early shapings of sexuality

One of Freud's major discoveries was the fundamental role of infantile sexuality in the shaping of the human mind. This chapter deals with the relationship between the very early aspects of psychical life and the ways in which a human being experiences his/her sexuality in adolescence and adulthood. The ideas that I am attempting to formulate here are the result of my analytical experience with patients, male and female, who suffered severe disturbances in the course of their sexual relationships: frigidity in women, an incapacity to experience sexual intimacy with a partner, or even with themselves during masturbation, impotence in men, from premature ejaculation or anorgasmia to a total lack of erection, even during masturbation, where the penis would remain flaccid and ejaculation happen without the experiencing of orgasm, as just a kind of "flowing out of a liquid" with no sense of any projective force from inside heading outwards into the object.

Looking back, I realise that, in most cases, the outcome of analysis significantly transformed not only their capacity for love, but also the intensity of enjoyment of their sexuality. Hence, the question: what aspects of the analytical process seem to have been more effective and transformative in that respect?

As sometimes happens in the ordinary life of an analyst, I received a letter from a former patient. When I opened the envelope, what first emerged was the photo of a beautiful newborn baby's face, then a note that read,

> Here is our son, Julien. When I look at him I fully realise the long road I have travelled thanks to you, during those nine years of analysis. When I first came to see you I was light-years away from fatherhood. Claire and I have recently decided to marry, on an impulse. In short, we are very happy.

I must say I read this with some emotion.

This young man had come to analysis when he was thirty, his love life and sexual life desert-like and deserted; he felt totally impotent, even when trying to masturbate, and also emotionally impotent. He seemed to present a severe failure neurosis with moral masochism, a very hostile superego in both its maternal and paternal aspects, and what I sensed as an unfortunate potential for negative therapeutic reaction. The figure of a "hard-headed intellectual woman" gradually appeared in the maternal transference, along with an over-protective and protected paternal figure. The hard-headed mother, a scientist, was lost in her epistemophilia, forgetful of her child, not only because she was absorbed by her sexual object, causing oedipal rage in the child, but more primarily because she seemed inaccessible to any emotional sharing and communication. Nesting into her head seemed to be barred, access was denied, hence an accumulation of protracted rage, resentment, and despair turning sour into feelings of persecution and self-destructiveness. The issue of analytical change lay, of course, in the interpretation during the analysis of the various oedipal aspects of the transference, of castration anxiety relating to separation anxieties, in the "slow demolition of the hostile superego", as Freud (1940a), p. 180) put it. But how could these interpretations become meaningful if they came from a hard-headed mother before the infant could experience the capacity to break in, penetrate, and explore his mother's psychical space?

Penetrability, permeability, receptivity

The early forms of communication seem to lie at the heart of sexual dysfunctioning in adults.[27] Their unfolding in the course of an analysis, in the subtle, unconscious interplay of transference and countertransference, enables their slow working through, the analyst becoming gradually aware of their specificities, very often through the occurrence of his own enactments, parapraxes, and "slips" of all sorts. Most of the time, we are dealing with issues of *penetrability, permeability, and receptivity*. These very early forms of interplay contribute to the construction of the psychical apparatus, but they are also experienced at a stage where the bodily aspects of the ego are prevalent. Their modalities have to do with all kinds of different forms of interpenetration of the infant's and the mother's psychical spaces, experienced as pleasurable or unpleasurable sensations shaped by all aspects of sensoriality.

Here is a simplified way of describing the idea I would like to explore, based on a modelisation that Winnicott developed in his 1956 seminal paper, "Primary maternal preoccupation". In the first weeks of the infant's existence, the mother can surrender to what Winnicott described as a normal kind of madness. In such a state she can, for instance, wake up just seconds before her baby starts crying. This psychosomatic continuity between infant and mother's bodily ego tends to reduce the frequency and intensity of disruptions by internal traumatic quantitative discharges. I suggest that this repeated experience of an adaptive psychical and bodily response to need can potentially lay a foundation, in particular for the way in which sexual intercourse will be experienced by the adult. I am not talking about a direct causality, but a potentiality. I think, for instance, that it can lay a foundation for the capacity of letting oneself merge with the other person in the experience of intercourse and orgasm and feel less threatened by the loss of boundaries that that implies.

An infant whose mother could not allow herself to enter this state of transitory madness might, in later life, have more difficulty in submitting to the experience of merging with his/her partner in the course of sexual intercourse. It could be anticipated as potentially violent and shattering, defences will be put in place to prevent it from happening, resulting, for instance, in premature ejaculation or anorgasmia. Once again, I am aware that I am isolating just one aspect, rooted in a very primitive experience, and that the construction of the capacity to experience sexual drive intensity together with object love depends on a multiplicity of factors, each over-determined by the others, in a long, multi-layered history.

I shall now present a short clinical narrative. I was waiting for a woman coming for her first appointment. When I opened the door she was standing there, motionless, clad in a long black leather coat, a young woman in her twenties. My first thought was "She has just stepped out of a film by Almodovar". Her face was completely immobile, white and made up in such a way as to make it appear like a mask. A fearful mask indeed, inducing a cold sense of being rejected and judged. Her gaze was black and still. She was hard and impenetrable, so much so that I failed to realise that she was very pretty. Once seated, she began talking relentlessly, in a sharp voice, each word very clear and detached. Her discourse was becoming increasingly aggressive, the usual negative thoughts one can hear about psychoanalysis and psychoanalysts, and, of course, she could already sense that I was going to be one of those cold, remote, totally silent analysts. It was amazing to witness the growing intensity of her hostility. After a while, I ventured to say that I noticed how angry and increasingly aggressive she was becoming, and that I was wondering why this was the case; I asked her if she was aware of it and had any idea where it came from.

She paused, and then sighed, as if breathing for the first time. Her stiff body mellowed and something quite difficult to describe changed in her eyes. I had been confronted by two small, hard, black buttons with an icy glaze on them shooting arrows at me. Suddenly it was as if they were opening up, the pupils dilating into a shadowy space inviting and absorbing, as if she was calling me in, turning her gaze into herself; for the first time I had the feeling that she was looking at me. In a hesitant and affect-laden voice she said, "I think it's because I'm scared."

After a few years of analysis, the patient reported a dream: she was in bed with a woman making love to her. In the dream, the patient had a penis and would eventually penetrate deeply into this woman and have a very pleasurable intercourse with her.

At this stage in her analysis, change was occurring in her inner world and in her life. She was moving away from a very glossy, glamorous, high-speed show-business world full of phallic narcissistic challenges, fierce oedipal battles, and dreadful separation anxiety to a more subdued environment where privacy, intimacy, and emotional encounters were discovered and valued, where, for the first time, she was looking for a man who would be not only an exciting lover, but who could also become a father to the children she might have with him.

That dream formation uses openly sexual elements, undoubtedly leading to ideas of homosexual desire and penis envy. But these elements, in the context of the maternal transference, were retroactively used to give form and meaning to an evolving psychical intercourse between infant and mother, between analysand and analyst. Beyond penis envy, the image of the penis is used in the dream in a figurative way to depict the capacity to penetrate the mother's psyche and to enter into an active and pleasurable intercourse with her. Thus, it is also depicting the transformation occurring within the analytical process from an excess of projective identification, desperately trying to break into the mother's psyche in an overload of angry excitation, to a pleasurable psychical interpenetration.

The early forms of psychical interplay are laden with sexual anticipation; the construction of infantile sexuality and the expressions of sexuality in adults are determined and shaped by the qualities of early bodily interpsychical experiencing.

My patient thought that boys were better equipped to explore their mother and to be understood by her because they possess a specially designed contraption which enables them to do so. How does a girl manage to communicate with mother if she does not have a penis, or if she has lost it? Such were some of the predicaments my patient had tried to come to terms with in her infantile sexual theories. Analysts grapple with the same questions in their attempts to construct sexual theories of the mind, or theories of the mind that shed light on sexuality.

If we take Bion's concept of normal projective identification (Bion, 1962, 1963) as one possible model of the early development of mental life and of the psychical apparatus, we see that the first stage takes the form of a penetration *into* the maternal psychical space, that penetration being either facilitated or made difficult (and sometimes impossible) by the disposition of the maternal mind. This model lends itself to being retroactively illustrated through masculine, phallic representations. This is quite consistent with Freud's theory of the libido being essentially masculine.

The bodily psychical action of evacuation of beta elements into the container (the mother's psyche) in the process of what is called projective identification is actively experienced by male and female infants.

Does this constitute a nuclear form of masculine sexuality in both sexes? In other words, and to follow my Almodovarian patient's pre-occupations (shared by many women), how does a woman experience her vagina as actively sexual? And how does it relate, if it does, to projective identification? In other words, is there an active vaginal sexual orgasmic pleasure that is not related to penis envy, aggressive castration drives, oral cannibalism, or anal retention? What is actively passive in sexual pleasure for both sexes?

In order to explore this question in terms of early mental develop-ment, I would argue that we must turn to the second phase of projec-tive identification: the (re)introjection, constitutive of the growing mind, of elements metabolised by the mother's psyche. This process of introjection is also active, but more likely to be depicted as an invagination. It takes in not only metabolised elements but also the process of metabolisation itself. I think that the "fundamental" vaginal orgasm has to do with this introjection of the metabolising process. In that respect it would be *a nuclear form of feminine sexuality in both sexes*. The quality of introjection (and, sometimes, the mere possibility of introjection) is totally dependent on the quality of the metabolisation taking place in the primary object's psyche. If mecha-nisms of pathological projective identification are prevalent in the primary object's psyche, the process of introjection, depending on the quality of metabolisation, is injured and sometimes destroyed. This is particularly true of the pleasurable experience associated with it, which contributes greatly to the processing and construction of psychical growth. In that respect, sexual pleasure, and, in particular, the sexual pleasure called "passive"—which, in fact, is always *actively* passive—is related to early introjective capacities, and, hence, to a capacity for emotional growth and psychical development, together with a progressive linking and unification of the erotogenic zones. In the case of an excess of projective identification from the mother *into* the infant's psychical space, there occurs a deadly passivisation of the infant's psyche: injection instead of introjection.

Another young woman came to analysis because she felt suicidal and her capacity for work seemed to be collapsing. She thought of herself as a lesbian, although she said that she did not like being touched by anyone, including herself. Her sexual life consisted of giving pleasure to her partners, either manually or with a dildo. She had quite extraordinary intellectual capacities, developed certainly to a great extent as a defence against a very mad, borderline mother who made her live in an environment of constantly eroticised excitation, not buffered in any way by the father, and who used her daughter's mind to evacuate into it her own raw elements. It was very difficult for the analytical process to develop into one of psychical growth. I was subjected to an inflation of intellectualised material flooding my ears and my mind; above all, it prevented any access, so that I could not "penetrate" or "touch" her. She hardly stopped talking, her material was kept under control, already "processed" and "analysed" so as to make my interventions useless, there was no representation of a possible working together; interplay and intercourse were denied.

Some time into the analysis, in a Monday session, she reported that the previous Saturday she had gone for a stroll and was walking along a street where shop after shop was selling all sorts of plants—they were, in fact, nurseries. It was a very sunny day, there were lots of people, and in this very animated crowd she heard a voice that instantly gave her pleasure and made her feel good. Then she felt that the voice was familiar, it was a man's voice, her analyst's voice. She turned round and saw me: I was talking to a shopkeeper about something concerning plants. (This was not a delusion on the patient's part.) She felt overwhelmed by happiness. All of a sudden, she realised that I was a living creature interested in life and in helping plants to grow. This marked a turning point in the analysis and her growing capacity to relate to me as an object whom she could trust enough to bully, but also to listen to.

Masculine and feminine qualities of the psychical apparatus

The polarities of masculinity and femininity and the notion of a primal or original scene (*Urszene*) are always present in the different models of the origins of psychical life at a time when *representations* of sexual difference are not meaningful as such for the infant, but are very present and meaningful in the mental lives of his/her parents. In the analyst's attentive listening, bisexuality appears in the form of different psychical forms such as fantasies, dreams, or identification, as well as through the different transference positions that we, as analysts, are required to take on. These psychical elements are very elaborate representational forms of the individual's psychosexual structuring. Behind these complex representations, more elementary psychical movements are at work in the analyst's listening; these could be seen as forerunners of sexual difference.

I shall now explore some modelisations of the beginnings of psychical life, in particular those of Bion, together with some links to Winnicott's. In subsequent chapters, I shall examine Piera Aulagnier's concepts and their similarities and differences with respect to those of Bion.

As a backdrop to different modelisations of the origins of the psyche are Freud's models of the emergence of psychical life, in particular the notions of the mental apparatus and of psychical drive derivatives. The mind is the *locus* in which somatic quantities and energies are transformed into representations and thoughts endowed with psychical qualities. This apparatus carries out a task, and it is also the end result of the work that it is performing. It is governed by a paradox: it is fabricated out of the living phenomena of the organism that, at the same time, it is required to process and metabolise.

When Bion broadens the notion of projective identification first described by Klein, what he describes is not a pathological phenomenon, but one that lies at the very foundation of the psyche. In order to become humanised and to develop a mind, not just a brain, the infant needs to propel the raw elements of somatic experience, sensory perceptions, into a human mind that is able to transform them into elements which can be mentally processed. There is an innate expectancy (see Chapter Thirteen, "A thirst from so long ago") that the environment will perform this task in such a way that the need will be met. In order to describe this phenomenon, Bion uses the notions of content entering into a container in order to be contained. One very specific aspect of Bion's approach is that the container is modified in the process of containment. In my reading, this notion of expectancy implies a certain complementarity between container and contained for the process of containment to be achieved. The idea of complementarity is very important in Piera Aulagnier's theorising of what she calls *l'originaire* (the primal), the encounter between a "zone" and its complementary object; also, her concept of pictograms (Bion talked of ideograms) refers at the same time to the representation of the affect and to the affect of the representation. At the origin of mental life there is the notion of an encounter, a kind of primal scene that takes place both intrapsychically and intersubjectively.

According to Bion (1962, p. 90), "both container and contained are models of abstract representations of psycho-analytic realizations". With the need for a greater degree of abstraction in order to designate container and contained, he leaps to an amazing decision: "I shall use the sign ♀ for the abstraction representing the container and ♂ for the contained" (1962, p. 90). He adds that both signs (which are actually pictograms) "denote and represent". I hope that what I am in the process of writing will manifest some of the powerfully evocative aspects of Bion's abstraction, which, in fact, in a kind of formal regression, place us as we read and listen in a peculiar kind of experience. We cannot read the pictograms, we have to point at them to make them seen. Any form of words would miss the complexity of what is being designated and conveyed: for ♀, feminine, woman, vagina, or matrix would not suffice, and, similarly, for ♂, masculine, penis, or man would not do.

Something is represented which cannot be put into words and yet brings words and thoughts to our mind, something at the dawn of psychical activity which has to do with femininity and masculinity but which, in itself, does not yet pertain to the sexual attributes of man and woman. At this stage, the only difference that is about to take place is between self and non-self. Bion's abstraction, however, links this initial differentiation to sexual difference.

Let me explore further Bion's bold decision. There exists a dynamic circulation between ♂ and ♀ which Bion represents thus: ♂↔♀, a relation he calls "commensal":

> By commensal I mean ♂ and ♀ are dependent on each other for mutual benefit and without harm to either. In terms of a model the mother derives benefit and achieves mental growth from the experience: the infant likewise abstracts benefit and achieves growth. (Bion, 1962, p. 91)

This is a description of a productive primal scene giving birth to mental life. In order to emphasise this idea of copulation and primal scene, I shall again quote Bion: "a pre-conception mates with the appropriate sense impressions" (1962, p. 91).

The activity ♂↔♀ which is described as being shared by two minds is introjected by the infant. Bion describes this first introject as an apparatus, the apparatus ♂♀. This apparatus is installed in the infant's mind and will function as part of the alpha function apparatus.

This apparatus ♂♀ is the embryo of psychical development. Emotion penetrates the elements ♂ and ♀ and either joins them together or disjoins them. Here, I would like to underline the proximity of this model with Piera Aulagnier's concepts of a pictogram of junction and a pictogram of rejection, as forming the two possible activities of the mind initially. Emotion allows the two elements ♂ and ♀ to function as an apparatus. In fact, the *qualities* of the emotions involved will determine the modalities in which this apparatus functions. Emotion is a variable that joins together or disjoins ♂ and ♀. The capacity for reshaping of ♀, which is also its capacity for *receptivity*, depends on the replacement of one emotion by another, just as the capacity for penetration of the ♂ elements will depend on the value of the emotion.

The development of ♂ and ♀ has to do with the capacity to take sensory impressions into the self. This capacity develops in parallel with the capacity to become aware of sensory data. The activity between ♂ and ♀ allows for an initial self-perception of oneself in the act of perceiving.

In *An Outline of Psycho-Analysis*, Freud (1940a, p. 197) reminds us that "the core of our being . . . is formed by the obscure *id*", adding that "the id knows no solicitude about ensuring survival and no anxiety" (p. 198). And then, as often happens when he writes, in a sort of internal dialogue with himself, another thought comes into his mind: "or it would perhaps be more correct to say that, though it can generate the sensory elements of anxiety, *it cannot make use of them*" (my italics). These self-perceptions within the id are coenaesthetic feelings and feelings of pleasure–unpleasure, and they rule with a despotic force without any consideration for self-preservation. The latter will be the task of the ego.

To use Bion's vocabulary, we could say that ♂ does not encounter ♀. When ♂ starts to encounter ♀, and if an apparatus ♂♀ begins to exist allowing ♂ ↔ ♀, then the emergence of a drive representative becomes possible.

This task of self-preservation is seen in Bion's model in the trajectory of projective identification when the "fear of dying" (1962, p. 96) is metabolised by the active receptivity of ♀. If the metabolisation (reverie) is successful, the infant will introject a part of the personality which has become more tolerable and which, through this very process of becoming more tolerable, stimulates growth. If this fails, "the infant who started with a fear he was dying ends up by containing a nameless dread" (1962, p. 96). When Bion uses the expression "fear of dying", he is, in fact, describing what the infant is experiencing in a way that already implies a mental apparatus capable of creating representations linked together by the activity of thought. What the infant is experiencing is more likely to be a kind of organismic helplessness implying a threat of extinction biologically triggered. This takes on a psychical significance through the mother's fear of seeing her child die (if such is the case).

In some patients the prospect of a sexual encounter awakens the shadow of this "nameless dread" and compels them to give up. Giving up might also be the outcome of a dreadful superego, or accomplished in the name of castration anxiety.

A mailbox

The process of change in the course of an analysis implies finding a capacity for change and growth in both partners. Penetrability and permeability are enabled by plasticity. One of the major discoveries of contemporary neurobiology is the formidable plasticity of the human brain throughout life. An analogon of what has been described by Bion's abstractions, at the dawn of psychical activity, is likely to happen in the course of treatment. It is a daily source of puzzlement in our psychoanalytical practice when we realise the extent to which we are tempted to resist our capacity for plasticity. I am not talking here about the "elasticity of technique", as Ferenczi put it, but the elasticity of our minds as they are put to work with another individual's mind in a specific work setting.

It has become a habit to say that the analytical pair is a couple. If such is the case, we need to further our understanding of the kind of copulation that is taking place, the different aspects of the intercourse, and how it ends up being either sterile or procreative.

Some years ago, in a foreign country, I was having lunch with a dear friend who is also a colleague. We always speak English together, because she does not speak French. At one point in our conversation, she said that she was very preoccupied by an analysis that she was carrying out and wanted to take this opportunity of discussing the case with me, an "extra-territorial" listener. She had in analysis for many years a very gifted young woman. A great deal of analysis had been done, and the analyst even thought that it might be time to put an end to the treatment, but she had a feeling of failure, she feared an interminable analysis or a negative therapeutic reaction. She felt that the analysand did not really accept her interpretations and could not make use of them for herself. As I listened, I formed the overall idea that the patient could not experience pleasure, that she could not metabolise what the analyst—or, indeed, men in her life—was giving her into food for mental growth. She might defensively be refusing satisfaction in order to avoid the pain of separation, but it seemed also that she did not know what maturing and developing meant and that, each time her analyst attempted to give her an interpretation, she had the feeling that the analyst was taking something away from her. I communicated this to my friend, and then I felt like asking her if any elements having to do with bisexuality had appeared in the course of the analysis. She immediately answered: "Well, of course, fantasies", but she seemed to be thinking about something completely different. After a pause, she said, "It's really amazing. When you asked your question, a moment of her analysis suddenly came back into my mind; I had completely forgotten about it. It was the end of the month and the patient had to pay for her sessions, but somehow it seemed difficult. During the session she thought she would come back with a check and put it in the mailbox. Then she said, 'No, that's impossible; I can't put a check in the mailbox.'"

My friend went on: "It's strange, I had heard 'male' when she said mailbox, and I remember immediately repeating: 'a male box?' with my intonation underlining the word 'male'. But I had not linked it to projective identification and to my countertransference, so we couldn't do anything with it."

We can think about this vignette of analytical work from many angles. I shall start with one aspect that I will call the tyranny of significance[28] and the need to understand it in terms of resistance, expressed in secondary thought processes, to letting ♂ and ♀ freely copulate together in a fertile relationship producing mental growth.

Let us single out the patient's sentence, "I cannot put a check in the mailbox", and see it as a manifestation of both transference and countertransference. Let us now examine the three main elements that make up this sentence: "I cannot put . . .in", "check", and "mailbox".

"I cannot put . . . in" seems to indicate that the movement of normal projective identification ♂♀ is being hindered. We could imagine that some elements internal to the patient inhibit this trajectory. We could also think that, in the analyst, when she is with this particular patient, ♂♀ cannot function in a commensal mode, and that neutrality is not sufficient to favour receptivity. Penetrability of ♂ is reduced, compromising the remodelling potentialities of ♀.

The container (box = ♀) in which the patient wants to drop a content (♂) is a "male box". Can "male box" be depicted by ♂♀ or ♂ ↔ ♀? At another level of psychical functioning, does "male box" represent a bisexual fantasy, or a primal scene in which psychical positions can shift around? It would seem, from the original point of view, that "male box" is a paradoxical container. It looks like a container that cannot take anything in because it carries a ♂ that prevents access. My association is to an antibody in immunology. It may somehow relate to the fantasy of a mother with a penis. The desire that mother be endowed with a penis would run contrary to the need to deposit some content in her psyche.

Sexual fantasy representations would be the touchstones of primary psychical movements in which the maternal ♂♀ apparatus could not put up with being penetrated by the infant's drive activity.

Winnicott's term for this is "impingement".

This brings us to the countertransference aspect of "mailbox". I shall explore only one aspect and one manifestation of this: "I understood that in 'mailbox' there is 'male' and I immediately said so to my patient." Then, "I understood, but my patient could not do anything with my understanding because I failed to make any links." Here, we reach the theme of the potential relationships between interpretation, insight, and working through.

"Male" seems to have become something like an exciting object in the analyst's mind, diminishing the potentialities of mutual transformation between container and contained. In this context, the thought "You see, I understood, here is what it means" may amount to some kind of evacuation.

It was, perhaps, experienced by the patient as a confirmation of the fact that she could not put ♂ in ♀ because of ♂.

Winnicott's term for this is "retaliation".

This is how Bion tries to shed light on the use of ♀:

It may make my meaning clearer if I say that I am in a state of receptive observation as opposed to a state in which I pass judgment on
what I observe. I can further describe it approximately by saying I
become absorbed in my task of observation or that I am absorbed in
the facts. (1962, p. 95)

Bion goes on to say that the use of ♀ "indicates that the reader's comprehension of my meaning", and this would be true also of the
analyst's comprehension, which "should contain an element that will
remain unsatisfied until he meets the appropriate realization" (p. 96).

This can be linked, in Freudian terms, to the necessary and specific
factors of analytical listening, that is, neutrality and free-floating attention, as well as to the dynamic relationship existing between the two
minds in the course of the psychoanalytical process.

Neutrality implies that one element (♂) should not be preferred
over the other (♀), and that it is best to let them lead their lives one
with the other (the ♂♀ apparatus). The reference here to the primal
scene is obvious, a primal scene understood as a primary representation of the encounter between infant and object, between psyche and
soma, giving birth to the life of the mind.

Free-floating attention implies that the analyst's psychical space
can let itself be penetrated by an infinite number of elements (♂)
which follow their unlimited trajectories and can, within that space,
remain dispersed and scattered. This aspect of free-floating attention
corresponds to the Freudian representation of "the dream's navel, the
spot where it reaches down into the unknown" (Freud, 1900a, p. 525).

The fluctuations of attention while it is free-floating give a containing function to the space where the unlimited phenomena are taking
place. The dynamic interaction between the fluctuations and the
unlimited trajectories allows for the possibility of bringing together
scattered and dispersed elements and favours the emergence of those
psychical events that we call interpretations. It is the containing function of free-floating attention.

The third element—"a check"—opens on to the potentialities of
polysemy in the analyst's listening, and their correlation with free-
floating attention, neutrality, and free association. The capacity to let
oneself be carried away by polysemy and to let it operate in our minds
with the help of free-floating attention goes hand in hand with
changes in vertex, with the mobility of identificatory positions in the
primal scene fantasy and with the infinite possibilities of combination

in bisexual fantasies along a spectrum going from masculinity to femininity. A "check" is a piece of paper with a name and an address on it; it has to do with some form of identity being deposited. It also, obviously, is related to money and its retention. Heard as a verb, to "check" means to control, to verify. It is very probably the case that the patient wanted to place a bridgehead and a homing head into the analyst in order to explore her interior and to control it. Exploration is also an attempt at checking and immobilising. If it is experienced by the analyst as an intrusion, the analyst can be tempted to safeguard the entrance by a "check"-point: ♂.

If we consider this from the perspective of the evolution of ideas concerning technique, we can identify some historical landmarks that have to do with the relationship between theory and the subjective implication of the analyst in the analytical process. Here are three aspects of the same question as expressed by Freud:

1. Theory: libido is masculine in essence.
2. Countertransference: it is difficult for me to be the mother in the transference, I feel so masculine.
3. Clinical illustration (a heavyweight in psychoanalytical legacy): the analytical relationship between Freud and Ferenczi. A letter that Ferenczi wrote to Groddeck[29] shows that the negative aspects of his transference with respect to Freud corresponded to character traits of Ferenczi's mother and confirm that, under cover of the *Vater* complex in the transference, Freud was unable to address and confront the negative maternal transference.

Four years after Ferenczi's death, Freud wrote "Analysis terminable and interminable" (1937c), a theoretical meditation arising from Ferenczi's reprimand, according to which Freud had not analysed his negative transference. It is no wonder that the idea of a so-called biological bedrock of bisexuality comes in the course of this meditation and is related to the negative therapeutic reaction.

How can a bedrock be transformed, other than by the use of dynamite?

One patient for many years dreamt about rocky mineral landscapes that could only be shaken up by his explosions of rage. In his dreams and associations, his mother was as hard as a rock—a marble statue or a barren stone vault. He had been brutally chased from paradise early in his life by the birth of his siblings, and also by certain traumatic events that had plunged his mother into an unreachable recess of depression. After many transference storms in the analysis, as he was slowly reconnecting with a desirable maternal object, symptoms of sexual impotency (premature ejaculation) began to appear. This gave rise to many sarcastic comments addressed to psychoanalysis and voiced by an internal father who was the principal saboteur of the patient's inner world. Reconnecting with a loving, loveable, and desired mother implied a cataclysmic change in his defences, triggering the worst aspects of his hostile superego, or, we could perhaps say, all the bad men in the chorus of his internal group.

Towards the end of his analysis, in a session when he felt that he did not have much to say, he reported "a little unimportant dream": he was eating an artichoke, but actually the artichoke was entirely made up of scallop meat (*coquille Saint-Jacques*, in French). He was eating it with a little spoon. It was extremely tender and smooth, and this surprised him because an artichoke is usually defended, as it were, by leaves that end like spikes; inside, before reaching the soft core, things that resemble brushes, like hay, have to be taken out—these are softer than the leaves, but still prickly. The patient started to go round and round in associative paths that knew no limit. If the artichoke was a peculiar kind of breast, the dream and the dream-work in the session, including my own free associations, became a very good breast indeed, yielding food for analysis: ♂♀ and ♂↔♀. I cannot indicate here all the associative paths, but the *coquille Saint-Jacques* was soon associated to Venus and the opening of the artichoke to cunnilingus, joining in a very elaborate and over-determined representation the nipple, the oral orifice, the tongue, the penis, and the vagina, the nipple as ♂ being transformed into ♀. A convex shape becoming concave, a saliency being transformed into a pregnancy. In the dream, as he was relishing the tender meat, he realised that there were one or two fish-bones—*arête* in French, which has the same sonority as *arrête*, the imperative form of the verb meaning "to stop". At one point, he said that he was thinking of the incredible intensity of excitation while performing cunnilingus, something that he had not experienced for a long time. I said, "It seems there is a little voice in this artichoke saying to you: *arrête*, stop." He laughed.

It is now time for me to stop writing and allow the mating of pictograms to go on.

CHAPTER EIGHT

Psychical metabolisations of the body in Piera Aulagnier's theory

With all the passion that she put into trying to imagine and think about the origins of mental life, Piera Aulagnier put forward a theory that she continued to develop over time; we can, therefore, try to grasp it from a historical point of view. At the same time, as they developed, her ideas gave more and more place and importance to the notions of history and historicising and to what she called the "effects of history"; it is the task of the "I" to put these in place of the effects of drive-related impulses. It was an extraordinarily moving moment when, in a paper that she read to a symposium in Bordeaux (this was to be her last one, because just two months later she died), Piera Aulagnier admitted to the audience, "Sometimes I wonder if my thinking has ever really succeeded in giving up the illusion that it will discover its own origins; perhaps that is what I am forever trying to do."

When her first book, *The Violence of Interpretation*, was published in 1975, the outcome of many years of thinking and writing, Piera Aulagnier was already well known, renowned, and held in high esteem. That book represents a turning point in the assertion of her ideas which, while acknowledging the various sources that had a significant influence on her, broke free of these and affirmed her independence, originality, and personal style.

What the analyst feels

At the origin of the important effort that she put into her theorisation and reformulation of metapsychology, Piera Aulagnier saw two factors drawn from her experience as a psychoanalyst, in particular with psychotic patients. Those two factors were based upon observations of splitting and dissociation. It should be emphasised that, in order to make those observations, Piera Aulagnier took as her starting-point her subjective experience in the analytical session, that is, what she "felt"—that, indeed, is how she puts it herself: applying the Freudian model of understanding to the response awakened in her by the experience of the encounter with a psychotic patient left out of the picture part of what she really felt within herself. Based on that acknowledgement of the dissociation between what the analyst experiences and psychoanalytical theory, she put forward the hypothesis of a split: analysts assume that their knowledge of mental life should make it possible to act on the phenomenon. However, "there exists a knowledge of the psychotic phenomenon which proves ineffective when confronted with the field of clinical experience" (Aulagnier, 1975, p. xxvii, retranslated for this edition).

It was because she gave priority to what she felt, arguing that "we must learn to depend on what our thinking experiences" (1975, p. xxvii), that Piera Aulagnier undertook her attempt at theorisation, the aim of which was "to give back access to part of what remained outside" (1975, p. xxvii). It was on that search for a relationship of coherence between thinking and feeling that she based her intellectual approach. That relationship of coherence was also a major issue in her theorisation of the development of the mind.

Giving back access to what had remained outside, that was her theoretical and clinical project. In my view, that way of putting it— "giving back access"—echoes other concerns that are less explicit in what she wrote in that book. *The Violence of Interpretation* puts the body once more at the very core of psychoanalytical thinking—indeed, as I shall try to show in my exploration of the idea of metabolisation, the body in all of its states and all of its dimensions, from the most somatic to the most erotogenic. In that sense, Aulagnier's book bears witness to a magnificent intellectual journey calling many things into question, thanks to which she was able, in the main, to break free of the influence of Lacan's theory and to discover or rediscover the access to the sources of her own personal epistemophilia.

As they developed more and more, Lacan's theorisations and thinking went further and further in the direction of putting to one side the body and the affects, in both the theory and practice of psychoanalytical treatment. By giving back access to thinking about the body in a way that was actually based on the body, Aulagnier called into question the complex issues raised by Freud but pushed aside by Lacan—who, in so doing, gave rise to a kind of prohibition against thinking among psychoanalysts in France, one that extended far beyond the Lacanian school of thought itself.

In that first book, Aulagnier mentions only two other authors—Freud and Lacan—and she enters into a discussion exclusively with them. With Freud, she affirms her affiliation with respect to him, placing herself in the continuity and ongoing development of his theorisation of the drives; with Lacan, she acknowledges what she owes to him, but criticises him and makes clear her differences with respect to his ideas.

To have some notion of the road that she travelled, it is necessary to read some of her earliest papers, written in the 1960s, when the French Psychoanalytical Society, where she had had her training, was coming to an end and the Ecole Freudienne de Paris (founded by Jacques Lacan in 1964) was being set up, together with the journal *La Psychanalyse* and, later, *L'Inconscient*—that is, before the Quatrième Groupe (Fourth Group) (founded by Piera Aulagnier, Jean-Paul Valabrega, and François Perrier in 1969) and *Topique* appeared on the scene. Independent thinking, theoretical interests, some formulations, temperament, style, all of these were already in place, although still in reference to—and with reverence for—a way of thinking that she was trying hard to stay with even though her own ideas were obviously in contradiction with it.

One example is the paper "Anxiety and identification" that she read to Lacan's seminar in May 1962. Over and beyond the compulsory reference to certain theoretical concepts (desire and demand, the phallus as signifier, ecstatic pleasure (*jouissance*), the signifier of desire, the Other), her way of treating clinical phenomena and of focusing her thinking on certain specific points is already highly personal and very different from the prevailing right-minded approach; her tendency to invent new terms is already present, too. Thus, a kind of "telescoping between fantasy and reality" is linked to the outbreak of anxiety, as well as the loss of identificatory markers; a still rudimentary outline of the idea of the "complementary object-zone" can be seen in her analysis of the mouth–breast part-object relationship, the activity of absorbing as a source of pleasure, the differentiation between "absorption–food" and, depending on the quality of the mother's response—the way in which she gives something—the introjection of a fantasy relationship. Even more surprising is the fact that she is already describing, in psychotic functioning, what she calls amputation and auto-mutilation, based on the idea clearly asserted, with no beating about the bush, that

> for the psychotic, the other person is introjected at the level of his/her own body. . . . However, insofar as the other person is introjected at the level of his/her own body and that introjection is the only thing that enables the psychotic to go on living, any disappearance of that other person would be the equivalent of an auto-mutilation that would bring the psychotic once again face to face with his/her fundamental drama. (Aulagnier, 1962, p. 144, translated for this edition)

That graphic résumé is all the more striking when we are familiar with the theoretical developments it would undergo some ten years later, when it became possible to think about the idea of pictographic activity. To illustrate her idea—so highly condensed at that point in time—with its connotations of theoretical reverie or floating theorisation (*théorisation flottante*), Aulagnier suggested an image, taking into consideration what she would later call spoken representation (*representation parlée*): "For the psychotic, the only possibility of identifying with a unified imaginary body would be that of identifying with the shadow that the body which is not his/her own might project in front of him/her" (1962, p. 144, translated for this edition).

In concluding that paper, she gives an example taken from her work with a schizophrenic patient. Over and beyond the power and the clinical beauty of that extract from a session, it is as if she were offering us a metaphor of what was lacking in psychoanalytical theory in order to give substance to how psychoanalysts listen to psychosis, as well as a foreshadowing of the blanks in theory that she herself would attempt to fill in, in a way that could be put into words and thought about. That patient, "whose speech, in its delusional form, was always mathematically exact" became all mixed up and at a loss for words immediately after mentioning some worrying thought that had come into his mind: he had been told that, when people have amputations, they can still feel things in the limbs that they no longer have. The patient said, "A ghost, then, is someone without any limbs, with no body, who, thanks only to his intelligence can perceive mistaken sensations in a body that he does not possess . . . That really scares me!"

The theoretical explanation with which Aulagnier ended her paper was, at that time in her thinking, well below the enigmatic force of what that patient said. But it was the impact of that enigma that led her to write in her preface to *The Violence of Interpretation*: "Confronted by this discourse, I have often felt that I was receiving it as *the wild interpretation made to the analyst of the non-evidence of the evident*" (2001, p. xxv). That was the starting point for, and the motive force behind, her research.

The life of the organism

Before exploring the various effects of the idea of metabolisation and their use in the body of her writing, I want first of all to underline the fact that Aulagnier saw her conception of mental life as being part of an overall theory of living beings and as one aspect of the phenomena involving the organism as a whole—a specific one, but not separable from the rest. We could even ask ourselves just how disembodied a certain kind of theorisation had become for her to feel on so many occasions the need to argue that the life of the body is fundamental to that of the mind:

> [W]hat do we mean by psychical life? If we mean any form of psychical activity, it requires only two conditions: the survival of the body and, to this end, the persistence of a libidinal cathexis resistant to a final victory of the death drive. (Aulagnier, 2001, p. 12)

Aulagnier emphasises the fact that mental life can take shape only once that activity has reached a certain threshold, the activation of which depends on a situation of encounter that never ends. I shall later clarify and illustrate the ideas of situation of encounter and borrowing from the model of the body; they lead to the concept of metabolisation and cannot be understood outside of that concept.

In her initial outline of the elementary forms of mental life, Aulagnier bases her thinking on a general aspect, the common denominator of the many phenomena that exist in the life of the organism:

> I set out from the hypothesis that the life of the organism is based upon a continuous oscillation between two elementary forms of activity that I call:
>
> • 'the taking-into-self',
> • 'the rejecting-outside-self'.
>
> These two activities are accompanied by a work of metabolization of the 'taken in', which transforms it into a raw material of one's own body, the residues of this operation being expelled from the body. Breathing and eating are a simple, clear example. (Aulagnier, 2001, pp. 22–23)

Similarly, the state of encounter that constitutes the essential condition for the earliest forms of mental life to be set up is initially defined from the most general point of view of living beings: "The peculiarity of the living being is its situation of continuous encounter with the physico-psychical milieu" (p. xxx).

In that definition, there is a very important element in the encounter—the fact that it is continuous, permanent, and lasts all through life. That brings to mind one of the fundamental aspects that Freud ascribed to the drives: their thrust, an aspect that confers on them a constant and permanent dimension that the organism—and, *a fortiori*, the mind—cannot avoid, hence the constant need for psychical working through. In Aulagnier's theory, that continuous aspect of the encounter blends with what, in the end, is her somewhat tragic conception of Eros, condensed in terms that we often come across in her writing: "condemned to cathect", "condemned to desire", "condemned to represent".

The need for defining tends to rigidify phenomena and to confer on them a static representation. Yet, in my view, one fundamental aspect of the encounter and of the productions of the "primal" (*l'originaire*)—the pictogram—is that they are in movement, always in the course of being produced. It is the "representative background", which is also a flux from which every human being is constructed and takes nourishment.

> My hypothesis concerning the primal, as creation repeating itself indefinitely throughout existence, implies an enigmatic interaction between what I call the 'representative background' against which every subject functions and an organic activity . . . (2001, p. 23)

The activity of metabolisation to some extent enables that enigmatic interaction to be represented.

The concept of metabolisation—which lends figurative and representative support to the primal activity of the mind and its productions, which are processed in a dimension in which physical and psychical are inseparable—comes from biology. It may well be worth pointing out that, before she came to psychoanalysis, Aulagnier intended to devote herself to fundamental research in biology; this, to some extent, throws light on the representative background from which she drew her theorising modelisations and metaphorisations. The concept of metabolisation draws our attention to the fact that the psyche is anchored and rooted in the soma, but it did not lead Aulagnier to adopt a biologistic (in the reductionist sense of the term) point of view; she was much closer to the frontiers between metabiology and metapsychology. The various aspects of metabolisation—transformation, change, assimilation, excretion, energy expenditure, absorption, integration—come into play, in both modelisation and metaphorisation. In this approach, it is necessary always to remain at the frontier between the two.

> Otherwise there is a risk of sliding either to the side of a biologization of psychical development, or, on the other hand, of opting for a theory of the signifying chain that ignores the role of the body and of the somatic models that it provides. (2001, p. 14)

Embodying the activity of representation

The idea of "borrowing" must be added to that of metabolisation in order to have a clearer understanding of how these somatic models can best be used in creating the forms of mental life.

In itself, metabolisation is not a concept that Aulagnier designated to describe one key aspect of her theorisation (which is the case with the idea of borrowing, as I shall explain later). Nevertheless, the term does occur remarkably often whenever the idea of representing a process of transformation and of psychical production arises—not only in the primal dimension, where, of course, the pictogram is the *par excellence* activity of representation, but also in the primary and secondary dimensions. Each of these processes is described as being one of metabolisation. Let us first of all try to delineate the different aspects of the process of metabolisation.

It is at work in every activity of representation and it gives rise to a twofold shaping:

> Every representation confronts a double shaping: the shaping of the relation imposed on the elements that make up the object repre-sented—here again the metaphor of the cellular work of metaboliza-tion describes my conception perfectly—and the shaping of the relation between the representative and the represented. (2001, p. 5)

What activates the process of metabolisation is simultaneously an encounter and a disruption: the encounter between psychical space and a space that is outside of the psyche, and the disruption in the equilibrium of energy that the body maintains via self-regulation. That disruption gives rise to a feeling indicative of what will later be called a state of suffering or distress in the body. The essential aim of triggering an activity of representation, the process of pictographic metabolisation, is to ignore the need, the body, in order to be once more, thanks to representation, in the earlier quiescent state. Accord-ing to that way of thinking, Thanatos is the prime mover in psychical activity, just as, for Freud, hate is the determining factor in the construction of the object. What is original in Aulagnier's thinking is the fact that, in her view, *the primary object is the body* and that primary hate is directed at the person's own body and its functioning.

Aulagnier takes up Freud's definition of the drives as "a measure of the demand made upon the mind for work in consequence of its connection with the body" (Freud, 1915c, p. 122), saying that it applies in every respect to what she is suggesting regarding pictographic activity. The primal process that leads to pictographic productions is, therefore, both an extension and a development of the concept of the drives as an activity of representation that lies at the frontier between somatic and psychical.

In order to understand the extent to which the activity of rep-resentation is "corporealised" in Aulagnier's theory, we have to take into consideration the concept of *borrowing*, borrowing from the somatic model and, in particular, the sensory one; the work of metabolisation is dependent upon the requirement of representability, which itself is determined by issues such as survival and self-preservation.

The material that is exclusive to the pictogram is the image of the bodily object; the body and the sense organisation are the somatic models that the primal process replicates in its representations. The sensory functions in general play a major role in somatic survival and in the possibility of libidinal cathexis. The psyche borrows from the body a model of activity—sensoriality—that is specific to it. It is this somatic model that is subjected to metabolisation into a substance appropriate to the requirement of representability. According to Aulagnier, the activity of representation is "the psychical equivalent of the work of metabolisation proper to organic activity" (2001, p. 3). Contrary to what occurs in the cellular structure but following the same model, "the element absorbed and metabolized is not a physical body but an element of information" (2001, p. 3).

Depending on whether it is a source of excitation and of pleasure or unpleasure, the element of information that comes from the sensory systems will be dealt with by the elementary forms of "taking-into-self" or "rejecting-outside-self". The element of information has to do with perception, and the process of metabolisation transforms it into a psychical element; the factor that determines that transformation is the feeling of pleasure or unpleasure which accompanies the perception. Pleasure facilitates the form and process of "taking-into" and reinforces the pictographic representation of auto-engendering; unpleasure, on the other hand, leads to "rejecting-outside" and to the auto-mutilation of the organ and the zone that lie at the source and centre of the excitation.

In that theorisation, the elementary forms of mental life could be described as "ex-corporised" out of the forms of somatic life. These "formal constraints", which we could describe as being microscopic or molecular, are more fundamental to the manner in which the earliest forms of mental life are shaped than those that we could call macroscopic—the bodily tendencies in the erotogenic zones, above all the oral one. The model of swallowing and that of vomiting reinforce and secondarily confirm these early stages of forms drawn from the manner in which the major functions of the organism are deployed—and not only sensoriality, perhaps, because, although it is highly important, sensoriality is not cut off—indeed, it cannot be entirely cut off—from the other systems.

Borrowing/anaclisis ("leaning on")

It is important to point out that "borrowing" is not the same thing as Freud's concept of anaclisis. Aulagnier was well aware of that, and she emphasised the difference within that enigmatic interaction between an organic activity and the "representative background".

> The heterogeneity between need and drive, posited at the outset by Freud, is a nodal concept of psychoanalytic theory; this heterogeneity, however, does not mean that one cannot find between these two entities a relation that is no longer one of support, but one of an effective and persistent dependence in the register of the represented. We shall find traces of this persistence in the scenic representations created by the primary, in which the preponderant place given to the image of the body will become apparent. (Aulagnier, 2001, p. 23)

If we follow that reasoning, we may well be surprised by the very decisive point of view that Aulagnier takes as regards the homogeneity and heterogeneity of substances between the various representing agencies. When she argues that the somatic model adopted by the psyche is metabolised into a completely heterogeneous material, we might well wonder why we have to look upon that heterogeneity as being complete, since, according to the model itself, every transformation via metabolisation still retains traces, in the new system and the new product, of the earlier state. If heterogeneity was as drastic as stated, how can she speak, for example, of the "particular texture of the pictogram" resulting from borrowing from the sensory model, or affirm in a very fundamental way that the pictogram is both a representation of affect and the affect of representation? In order to sustain the idea of complete heterogeneity, the metabolising agency would have to be wholly external to the process of metabolisation. But it is precisely the process of metabolisation that constitutes the metabolising agency itself—and this is what allows her to claim that the activity of representation represents the representing agency itself. It is that very complexity that enables us to break free of the traditional representation of an origin as being a point in space. What

Aulagnier is attempting to describe is not an origin as such, but a primal process.

This complex exploration, in its attempt to model the primal process behind the construction of mental life starting with organic activity, and the difficulties encountered in finding spoken representations sufficiently coherent with their object always, in my opinion, have to do with the limitations imposed on what can be theorised and thought about. Freud himself emphasised these, and Aulagnier often mentions them: the idea that consciousness is a sense-organ and ". . . that everything new that we have inferred must nevertheless be translated back into the language of our perceptions, from which it is simply impossible for us to free ourselves" (Freud, 1940a, p. 196).

In order to pursue the attempt to draw a distinction between borrowing and anaclisis (leaning on), I think that it would be interesting to reflect upon some comments that Aulagnier made concerning the idea of *the expectation of satisfaction in the sense organisation*. Those comments often follow on from some incidental remark she makes about the importance of

> . . . recent experiments of sensory disafferentiation [which] seem to prove that, during the waking period, parallel with such objects of need as food, air, an adequate intake of calories, a continuous supply of sensory information is also necessary: without it the psyche seems to have difficulty functioning without having to hallucinate the information that is lacking. (Aulagnier, 2001, p. 22)

Another enigma emphasised by Aulagnier enables her to introduce the idea of expectancy for the object that has a power of excitability; the response to that expectancy is just as vital, for the organism and for mental life, as is the satisfying of alimentary need. "[The] satisfaction of an expectation coming from the sense organization, enigmatic as the presence of this elementary need for information by the senses and this pleasure resulting from their activation still are for me" (p. 25, translation revised for this edition).

For Aulagnier, it is important to differentiate between the satisfaction of alimentary needs and the activation, for example, of the gustatory sense that corresponds temporally to them.

> I believe that what results from this initial encounter does not depend on the fortuitous juxtaposition of the pleasure of taste and the

satisfaction of alimentary need, but that there exists in the register of the sensibility an 'expectation' of the object that possesses an ability to excite and a 'need' of information that explains that the activation of the various sense zones has the property of being accompanied by what I call erogenous pleasure. . . . This cathexis of sensory activity is the very condition of existence of a psychical life, since it is *the condition for the cathexis of the activity of representation*. (p. 35)

It is through the link between this idea of expectation in the sense organisation and the object's response, the adaptation of which will depend on the object's own metabolisations, that Aulagnier describes a representation of the primary object that has its source in the emergence of the primal representative capacities: "Something felt in our body lies in the place that will later be occupied by the mother: to the anticipated I there corresponds an 'anticipated mother' through a bodily feeling" (Aulagnier, 1985, translated for this edition).

The metapsychological and clinical consequences of this differentiation between borrowing and anaclisis—which, as we can see, are, in principle, complementary—would be well worth exploring in some depth, but this would take me far beyond what I am attempting to describe in this chapter. I would simply, for the moment, say that the idea of the expectation of some specific response characteristic of the sense organisation links up with that of deprivation, which is very different from the non-satisfaction of needs in the oral sphere. Deprivation is part of the specific qualities of the object's response, qualities that are assumed to be necessary for the potentialities for somato–psychical development to take root and begin to connect up. Here again, it is a question of the threshold of excitability below which no activation can be triggered. Where there is no response sufficient enough to produce the expected activations, I think that, in some cases, the organism attempts to find within itself an ersatz of that quality through auto-excitation, giving rise to internal discharges that function as a kind of "as-if" equivalent. The hypothesis of the existence of an auto-excitation process is completely different from that of the illusion of auto-engendering; the latter opens on to a more and more advanced form of mentalization. Auto-excitation gives rise to a somatic feeling that remains somatic because it is not "qualified" by the sharing of an affect of pleasure or unpleasure. Clinically speaking, it belongs to the category of those pathologies that have been described, in various terms, as neo-realities. The auto-excitation circuit, which is dependent on the triggering of somatic manifestations in the search for the equivalents of psychical feelings necessary for development, cannot participate in the interplay of successive equivalences and substitutions that symbolisation makes for. It is no longer a matter of metabolisation, but of secretion. From that perspective, I think that, for example, given the lack of any necessary "qualifying" response in the early psychical environment, the organism may set up "anti-depressive techniques" that do not travel along the circuit of psychical representations, but directly through that of endogenous somatic excitations. In my view, what Aulagnier wrote is indicative of a similar way of thinking:

> In the absence of any circulation via the body of a shared experience of pleasure, the infant's psyche will not be given the 'aliment' of pleasure that it *needs* in a manner appropriate to assimilation or metabolization. There will be pleasure—it is a kind of vital energy, without which the psychical apparatus could not function—but its quality and properties will give rise to anomalies and above all to the resistance that that form of energy sets up against contributing to the relationship functions of the apparatus. (Aulagnier, 1985, p. 134, translated for this edition)

Before concluding this chapter, I would simply like to illustrate how Aulagnier also renewed our approach to speech and language in psychoanalysis. She did this by bringing together the points that I have raised and issues relating to access to language—again in the continuation of the questions raised by Freud—while, at the same time, distancing herself from a conception of speech and language as something purely external, as is the case in Lacan's theorisation of the Other, the treasure trove of signifiers and the defiles of signifiers. For Freud, the word, the word-presentation, provides a perceptual basis for bringing into consciousness unconscious representations. That conception is completely coherent with the idea that consciousness is a sense organ. Piera Aulagnier puts it thus:

> Thing-presentation is the prerequisite for word-presentation to be added to it: *the scenic primary follows the pictographic and prepares the way for the sayable*[30] that will . . . be separated from it by repressing that first material that was an essential part of its own flesh. (2001, pp. 52–53)

For Piera Aulagnier, psychical inscription of word-presentations is not limited to secondary processes, in her view, language is structured in terms of a system of meanings based on the nucleus of primary signs—there is a trajectory that goes from the perception of sound to the appropriation of a semantic field. In her approach to the issue of access to language, she insists on the idea of borrowing from sense organisation and the initial form of what is heard in the primal register itself:

> If, as I have proposed, there is a need for sensory information whose psychical counterpart is the wish to rediscover the pleasure associated with the excitation of the corresponding zones, we must accept the presence of a pleasure of hearing that at this stage has no connection with the meaningfulness of the noises emitted by the milieu and is connected only to the sensory quality of the audible. This hypothesis ought to have led me to examine the experiences of sensory discon-nection in hearing. (2001, p. 55)

In later developments of her thinking, Aulagnier laid more and more emphasis on the mother's emotions in her encounter with her infant and on the highly important role played by that emotion in somato–psychical integration, bearing witness to the somatic anchor-ing of the love that a mother has for the body of her particular child:

> This somatic component of the mother's emotion is transmitted from body to body, the contact with a body moved by emotion touches yours, a hand that touches you without any pleasure does not give rise to the same feeling as one that feels pleasure in touching you. (1985, p. 127, translated for this edition)

That paper was written in 1985, ten years after *The Violence of Interpretation* was published. In the meantime, Aulagnier's thinking had gone on developing, her style was no longer quite the same, and, above all, her conception of the role and interpreting function of the mother's mind changed significantly. In 1975, the idea of the "word-bearer" still owed much to Lacan's theory of the signifier, although she was already distancing herself from it and beginning to criticise it. In order to define the object that can be metabolised by the infant's psyche, Aulagnier calls upon the mother's discourse that makes it meaningful and upon the naming of it that bears witness to this. She would, therefore, appear to be close to Lacan's idea of the primacy of the signifier. However, her definition of the mother's discourse is entirely new and highly specific, because it considers the idea of discourse and that of the reality principle to be equivalent. The object of metabolisation is not the Real (in Lacan's meaning of the term), but a psychical object that has already been metabolised by the mother's psychical activity; therefore, it carries the stamp of the reality principle and is in keeping with the fate of the repressed. In that perspective, even if the primal dimension, by definition, knows nothing of the reality principle, that principle is, none the less, active, in that particular manner, from a very early stage in the primary dimension. In addition, Aulagnier argues that "the primal knows nothing of the signifier, even though the latter remains the attribute thanks to which the object lends itself to the kind of radical metabolization to which this process subjects it" (1985, p. 132, translated for this edition).

The anticipated mother

In her 1985 paper "Naissance d'un corps, origine d'une histoire" ("Birth of a body, origin of a history"), the concept of the word-bearer gives way to that of the "anticipated mother". In her definition of the "anticipated mother", Aulagnier makes no reference to a signifier, but to emotion, which, as she emphasises, has no particular place in psychoanalytical terminology (I myself would add here, "particularly in France"). Emotion is defined as the visible part of an affect, having a special relationship with the sensory aspect, as well as—in my understanding, at least—a signifying function of the body-ego:

> Emotion modifies the somatic state. . . . The person's body responds to that of the other, but since emotion involves the 'I' we could also say that the latter is moved by what its body gives it to know about and share in the experience of the other's body. (1985, p. 118, translated for this edition)

Even more than in *The Violence of Interpretation*, Aulagnier emphasises the vital importance of sensoriality in what she calls "giving life to the psychical apparatus". While the concept of the word-bearer required a definition of the object able to be psychically metabolised in terms of the effect of the signifier, here the same question is treated very differently:

> If we stay simply with this representative process [i.e., the primal], we come to realise that the object exists psychically only thanks to its unique power to modify the sensory (and therefore somatic) response and, in so doing, to act upon what is being felt mentally. (p. 118, translated for this edition)

It is with that somatic component of emotion as a starting point that we become able to think in terms of a history of somatic life and of a movement from the sensory body to one that is relation-based, that is, in terms of

> what will come into play for the body in its encounter with the *emotion* to which its manifestations give rise in the mother, an emotion the perception of which by the infant inaugurates the link between his/her psyche and this discourse and history that were there 'waiting'. (p. 125, translated for this edition)

I think it interesting to point out that it is precisely at this juncture in her theorisation—whether concerning the "word-bearer" in 1975, or the "anticipated mother" in 1985—that Aulagnier quotes extracts from Bion's writings and comments on them, each time making it perfectly clear where she does not agree with him. Although they share a common inspiration, more or less, in terms of pre-digestion and pre-metabolisation of the psychical object by the mother's mental activity, the concept of the container is not to be found in Aulagnier's texts. By emphasising the fact that, in order to give life to the psychical apparatus, the object must be endowed with a power of excitability, she invites us to think in paradoxical terms: it is this power of excitability which, by enabling the processual capacity of the psychical apparatus to be set in motion, acts as a protective shield against excitation.

This short foray into the substance of her wide-ranging and complex thinking puts us in touch with the importance that Aulagnier gives to the effects of the somatic dimension in the construction of what we call the mind, in a duality of language that we continue to maintain because we do not yet know how to think of the body differently, even though this approach tends to keep separate the different states of extremely complex phenomena that are, nevertheless, of the same kind. These thoughts on the effects of the auto-engendering of the mind based on its links with the somatic element enable us to think also about the somatic and psychical effects of psychoanalytical treatment, in other words, about how a word that is full of emotion can, in some circumstances, change the living matter.

CHAPTER NINE

Auto-engendering and auto-excitation: some hypotheses concerning the qualifying role of the object

T he Freudian approach has always taken as its starting point the outward signs—sometimes extremely severe ones—of mental pathology in human beings in order to raise fundamental questions about mental life in general, to set up models of its normal functioning, and to put forward hypotheses concerning how it comes about in living organisms. The paradoxes of masochism and the challenges that they represent for the pleasure principle, the guardian of our life, led Freud to envisage primary masochism as a process of metabolisation and of transformation that takes place in the encounter between a tendency towards inertia that rules over the organic world and a force of vital energy, the libido, which can survive only if it finds a way in which to oppose "the intended course of life" (Freud, 1924c, p. 160).

There are three terms in the very first paragraph of that paper that are well worth examining more closely: mysterious, economic, and drug.

It is indeed *mysterious* to have to think that, if the experience of pleasure lies at the heart of the earliest structures of mental life, it is the capacity to tolerate unpleasure that indicates to what extent it is possible to set up a psychical apparatus that is able to carry out the transformations, starting with somatic excitations, which are necessary for the development of mental life and the construction of psychical reality. The mystery is, therefore, that of the construction of the psyche, following the model of somatic functioning, and that of the kind of processes that enable the movement from quantitative to qualitative. Freud emphasised the fact that pleasure and unpleasure are not dependent on the quantitative factor (mental tension due to stimulus), but on some characteristic of it that he described as qualitative. It is the origin of that qualitative characteristic that remained a mystery to Freud. Although he suggested that there must be some relationship to the rhythm of internal modifications, he did not explore the part played in this "qualifying" by the primary object and the nature of its cathexis of the infant's physical and mental life. In this chapter, I shall, *inter alia*, attempt to show how we cannot think properly of this qualifying characteristic unless we take into consideration the essential role of the object and the primary environment—and, more specifically, the qualifying function of emotion. In so doing, I shall refer to certain aspects of the theorisation that we owe to Piera Aulagnier.

Economic

The issues raised by masochism have indeed to do with quantities of energy and thresholds of excitability upon which processes of transformation can—and must—come into play in order to ensure the survival of the organism via the setting up of an activity of representation. The function of that activity of representation is, in itself, ambiguous, because it is initially characterised by ignoring the body's vital needs and giving priority to hallucinatory fulfilment. That paradox led Aulagnier to argue that Thanatos is the primary agent of mental life, which is built up from hatred of the body and, at the same time, follows the model of somatic life.

A drug

This evokes a quite striking image: the pleasure principle would appear to be under the influence of a toxic substance that paralyses it through its action as a narcotic. Narcosis induces sleep, anaesthesia, and paralysis: wakefulness, sensoriality, sensitivity, and the motor functions are all affected. Later, we shall see other echoes of such representations in the idea of "expectation".

Borrowing from the somatic model

In one of her early articles, "Remarques sur le masochisme primaire" ("Some notes on primary masochism"), Aulagnier (1968) defines in the following terms Freud's way of thinking when he began to study masochism and the issues it raised:

> My aim is to analyse the implications that follow on from the trans-formation of energy, occurring, thanks to primary masochism, at the expense of an aim that originally was quite different: what is entailed by this activation, to the benefit of ego pleasure, of an energy, the aim of which was to oppose its existence. In other words, I shall try to define what comes into play when that energy, in its widest sense, becomes the psyche, when a purely economic principle must, in order to function properly, present itself as a wish and thus be able to call upon meaning, in the place of a principle of physics that to me is as impenetrable and foreign as the law of gravity and the principle of Archimedes. (Aulagnier, 1968, author's transcription for this edition)

Aulagnier goes on to say that if the death drive represents the most direct expression of an instinctual tendency to return to a previous state,

> primary masochism, in turn, represents the most direct expression of a drive seen as the necessary gateway between the organism's most prim-itive biological tendency and the representation that enables it to be expressed in the mental domain. (author's transcription for this edition)

Aulagnier is here emphasising, in my view, the extent to which the concept of primary masochism is directly related to that of the drive as defined by Freud, at the frontier between the somatic and psychi-cal dimensions, in terms of a process of metabolisation that produces the psychical representative of the drive. The concept of primary masochism is, thus, intrinsically linked to the body and to the effort that is put into thinking how a somatic element can be transformed into its psychical equivalent. Masochism, thus, belongs to the series of mentalization processes that enable the activity of representation to come into play, be sustained, and become more complex; these processes have their source in the capacity to bring about the hallucinatory fulfilment of a wish.

It is, therefore, not surprising that most of those who have taken an interest in illnesses with somatic manifestations have observed "deficiencies" or "failures" in the primary erotogenic masochism of these patients—in other words, a defect in the capacity to set up links between soma and psyche which could give rise to representative productions that obey the laws governing representability.

In my opinion, some aspects of Aulagnier's metapsychology lead to new avenues of research that might well prove profitable when we attempt to draw up hypotheses concerning the origin of those deficiencies and try to understand how, when the "royal road" of the activity of representation based on hallucinatory fulfilment seems to be partly blocked off, other avenues—substitutes, "palliatives", or "remedies"—can be set up; what are the mechanisms that govern these and what material do they make use of? In this way, we come close to the questions raised by Freud concerning the nature and topography of unconscious feelings and the concept of resistance coming from the id.

Aulagnier's thinking illustrates just how familiar she was with biology and physiology—the "representative background" from which she drew elements that helped her to work out her metapsychological conceptions. Her psychoanalytical ideas are, to a considerable extent, corporealised; they take support not only from the great "visible" bodily functions, with their anatomical localisation in the erotogenic zones, but also from the "infra-scopic" and silent functioning of the various systems—in particular sensitivity and sensoriality, and also cellular metabolism. These provided her with "somatic models", the use of which to describe mental functioning is not merely metaphorical.

The idea of "borrowing" is very much present in her theorisation. This indicates that her use of the somatic model is not simply a metaphorisation; in her view, the mind borrows from the somatic domain both material and modes of organisation that are subjected to a metabolisation (the primal pictographic activity) which transforms them in accordance with the requirements of figurability belonging to the primal dimension. According to Aulagnier, the activity of representation is "the psychical equivalent of the work of metabolisation proper to organic activity" (2001, p. 3). Every transformation via metabolisation preserves the trace of the preceding state. The essential material of the pictogram is the image of the corporeal thing, and the particular texture of the pictogram is the result of the borrowing made from the somatic sensory model. The element of information, which comes from the sensory systems and is the object of metabolisation, has to do with perception. It is the process of metabolisation that transforms it into a psychical element. The feeling of pleasure or unpleasure that accompanies the perception determines the form and quality of that transformation. Aulagnier often mentions the enigmatic interaction that exists between an organic activity and the representative background of mental life. That point of view introduces an important distinction between Freud's concept of anaclisis ("leaning on") and that of borrowing.

> The heterogeneity between need and drive, posited at the outset by Freud, is a nodal concept of psychoanalytic theory; this heterogeneity, however, does not mean that one cannot find between these two entities a relation that is no longer one of support, *but one of an effective and persistent dependence in the register of the represented*. (Aulagnier, 2001, p. 23, my italics)

In this theorisation, the activity of representation, whatever its specific domain (primal, primary, or secondary), can never be completely free of the formal and vital constraints belonging to the dimension of somatic functioning. As for these somatic models, Aulagnier gives pride of place to the sensory model and to the borrowing from it carried out by the psyche in order to represent itself; in this way, a very strong—and very Freudian—link is set up with perception. It is, however, entirely possible to consider that this borrowing from the somatic model can be extended to cover systems other than that of sensoriality; this is all the more so since no somatic system is ever completely shut off from all the others—and this is particularly true of the sensory system. The development of disciplines such as neuro-endocrinology and neuro-immunology has highlighted these avenues of communication. It is not inconceivable, even though the relationship is less immediately obvious, that the mind can also borrow, for the modelisation of its self-presentation, from somatic models that are much more "silent" in their functioning than the sensory one. The immune system may well be one example of this (cf. Chapter Thirteen, "A thirst from so long ago").

The notion of expectation

In *The Violence of Interpretation*, Aulagnier mentions on several occasions experiments in sensory disafferentiation, emphasising the fact that the results of these deserve to be thought about in much more detail. What interested her was the confirmation of her idea, which to my mind is an extension of that concerning borrowing from the somatic model, of an expectation of satisfaction on the part of the sensory model. According to Aulagnier,

> parallel with such objects of need as food, air, an adequate intake of calories, a continuous supply of sensory information is also necessary: without it the psyche seems to have difficulty functioning without having to hallucinate the information that is lacking. (2001, p. 22)

In the following pages, I shall argue that, to my way of thinking, hallucination is not the only form of substitution possible when that supply of specific sensory information is not available in cases in which we are dealing with pathologies that are not neurotic or psychotic in nature.

Aulagnier invites us to imagine, in addition to the fundamental and vital needs concerning basic metabolism, other needs—for "information" of a sensory kind—which are every bit as necessary for somato–psychical life and mental development, "enigmatic as the presence of this elementary need for information by the senses and this pleasure resulting from their activation still are for me" (2001, p. 25).

This is how she differentiates between the satisfaction of an alimentary need and the activation of the gustatory sense that corresponds temporally to it.

> I believe that what results from this initial encounter does not depend on the fortuitous juxtaposition of the pleasure of taste and the satisfaction of alimentary need, but that there exists in the register of the sensibility an 'expectation' of the object that possesses an ability to excite and a 'need' of information that explains that the activation of

> the various sense zones has the property of being accompanied by what I call erogenous pleasure. . . . This cathexis of sensory activity is the very condition of existence of a psychical life, since it is *the condition for the cathexis of the activity of representation*. (2001, p. 35)

The quality of the primary object's response to that expectation—the object that possesses an ability to excite—is decisive for the awakening of the potentialities for mental development that require the satisfaction of that need for sensory information and the pleasure to which it gives rise. It is the object that has a qualifying function via that feeling of pleasure that contributes to the quality of cathexis of mental life. I would add that the quality of that feeling of bodily pleasure also probably plays a part in somato–psychical integration—it does not involve merely mental cathexis. We could perhaps say that the psycho-corporeal quality (of the body-ego) of the object's response also has an impact on the development and maturation of the major physiological functions. In a later paper, "Naissance d'un corps, origine d'une histoire" ("Birth of a body, origin of a history") (Aulagnier, 1985), that bodily feeling becomes the first representative of the object. "Something felt in our body lies in the place that will later be occupied by the mother: to the 'anticipated I' there corresponds an 'anticipated mother' through a bodily feeling" (Aulagnier, 1985, p. 119, translated for this edition).

In that same paper, Aulagnier clearly places emotion at the very heart of her thinking; emotion bears witness to the somatic anchoring that the mother has for the body of her particular child. That conception seems to me to be fairly close to some aspects of Winnicott's theorisation of holding.

The quality of the object's power of excitability helps to go beyond certain thresholds of "activation". That idea brings us close to the difficulties raised by inertia (the Nirvana principle), and to what, towards the end of his life, Freud referred to as resistance from the id. The following extract from Aulagnier's paper seems to me to be particularly helpful in that respect:

> In the absence of any circulation via the body of a shared experience of pleasure, the infant's psyche will not be given the 'aliment' of pleasure that it *needs* in a manner appropriate to assimilation or metabolisation. There will be pleasure—it is a kind of vital energy, without which the psychical apparatus could not function—but its quality and

properties will give rise to anomalies and above all to the resistance that that form of energy sets up against contributing to the relationship functions of the apparatus. (Aulagnier, 1985, p. 134, translated for this edition)

The aliment of pleasure is, in itself, insufficient. Only the quality of certain specific responses from the object will be able, via the satisfaction of the expectation for sensory information, to activate the potential for psychical development. We can, perhaps, imagine that the quality of that response to the expectation will "nourish" the quality of the borrowing by the psyche from the sensory model, and, thereby, contribute to the processing functions of the activity of representation. To that expectation in the sense organisation for specific qualities of the response, there must correspond, in the maternal emotion that carries it along, a specific "knowing" that does not belong to the category of secondary processing. The exact nature of that "knowing" is still, to a great extent, enigmatic. Winnicott's hypothesis of the "normal madness" of the primary maternal preoccupation appears to me to lay the foundations for one way of thinking about this.

> This organized state (that would be an illness were it not for the fact of the pregnancy) could be compared with a withdrawn state, or a dissociated state, or a fugue, or even with a disturbance at a deeper level such as a schizoid episode in which some aspect of the personality takes over temporarily. . . . I do not believe that it is possible to understand the functioning of the mother at the very beginning of the infant's life without seeing that she must be able to reach this state of heightened sensitivity, almost an illness, and to recover from it. (Winnicott, 1975, p. 302)

Deprivation/frustration

It is important also to realise that the effect of a non-response to an expectation in the sense dimension is not a matter of frustration, but of deprivation.

This has two possible outcomes. In the first of these, we could say that the specific qualities of the object's response have corresponded to what the sense organisation was expecting and enabled the necessary threshold of activation to be overcome. Borrowing from the sensory model, given the experience of shared pleasure that accompanies the "qualifying" brought about by the mother's emotion, will contribute, thanks to the activity of primal metabolisation, to providing a modelisation and representative material that will compose the pictogram. The illusion of auto-engendering will still be in place and the somatic element will be able to take part in the more and more differentiated transformations and substitute operations that will go to make up psychical reality. That avenue, which is that of mentalization, implies a capacity for hallucinating any satisfaction that happens to be missing. The ability to hallucinate implies that an initial experience of satisfaction has indeed occurred.

In the other outcome, the specific qualities of the expected response are lacking, so that no activation that would have allowed the deployment of a developmental potential has occurred. Deprivation implies that something that was expected has not appeared, and that the non-response to that expectation cannot be compensated for through hallucinatory fulfilment. The idea of expecting leads to that of the organism "knowing" something about the conditions that have to be fulfilled in the encounter with the object endowed with a power of excitability so as to be "qualifying". With his idea of pre-conception, Bion was undoubtedly attempting to provide the wherewithal thanks to which hypothetical phenomena located in neighbouring zones could be thought about and put into words. Aulagnier's theory has less to do with an *a priori* form; it is more related to bodily feelings, although there is all the same the assumption of a "pre-knowing" or "pre-representation" of what is both necessary and expected.[31]

Given the absence of a qualifying response coming from the object and the inability to hallucinate the specific elements of the awaited response, we could perhaps argue that the organism which needs that response will try to procure it for/by itself, by attempting to trigger, somatically, an equivalent of the bodily feeling arising from the encounter between the expectation and the response. This would imply that, instead of following a path which, via the primal activity of metabolisation, leads from the somatic dimension to the activity of representation, the organism will try to find within itself an ersatz of the qualifying response by means of auto-excitation, so as to provoke internal discharges that will function as substitutes for the bodily feeling that Aulagnier called the "anticipated mother". That palliative procedure opens up a kind of diversion that, free of the illusion of auto-engendering, gives the illusion of a somatic self-sufficiency that negates the role of the object. The process of auto-excitation gives rise to a somatic feeling that remains somatic because it is not "qualified" by the sharing of an affect of pleasure or unpleasure. In so far as it is dependent on the triggering of somatic discharges of excitation in order to reach the threshold of excitability in its search for the equivalents of psychical feelings necessary for development, auto-excitation cannot participate in the interplay of successive equivalences and substitutions that symbolisation allows for. It necessarily remains under the aegis of the automatism of repetition. It is no longer a matter of metabolisation, but of secretion.

With the idea of libidinal sympathetic excitation, Freud put forward the hypothesis of the existence of a physiological mechanism at the beginning of life which would later disappear; this would provide the somatic model for what later, once brought back into and metabolised by the psychical agencies, would appear as erotogenic masochism. This infantile physiological mechanism shows that, given that an internal process—and pain in particular—constitutes a phenomenon of excitation, that excitation may itself contribute to reinforcing the sexual excitation that is a marginal effect of it.

The fact that this mechanism goes on operating over and beyond the activation of the primal activity of representation, now that a psychical apparatus is beginning to exist, indicates that the psychical apparatus does not succeed in metabolising some kinds of excitation; more specifically, sexual excitation, instead of being aroused via the mental circuit of the activity of representation, is triggered by "techniques" of internal excitation on a physiological level.

As to masochism, in which the source of excitation is pain as a kind of pseudo-drive, Freud pointed out that in the three kinds of masochism that he described—primary erotogenic masochism, feminine masochism, and moral masochism—physical pain is a very minor phenomenon; sexual excitation derives from an activity of processed fantasy representation that is sufficient for maintaining erotic tension and leading to orgasmic resolution. In addition, some sadomasochistic activities that involve physical cruelty and lead to somatic pain (they might even go as far as actual mutilation and the endangering of certain vital functions) are, in fact, illustrative of failures in erotogenic masochism. That masochism, which could perhaps better be described as auto-sadism, bears witness to the reckless and desperate search, in somatic terms, for physiological excitation as a substitute for libidinal excitation, for a psychical apparatus threatened with aphanisis, that is, extinction. The somatic feeling of pain, as a substitute for a mentalized bodily feeling, probably represents in such cases a means—perhaps the only one that they have at their disposal—of hanging on to the feeling of being alive (Miller, 1999). The "pain-aliment" might be the last barrier against "the intended course of life".

I suggested earlier in this chapter that the palliative road that might be set up, given the object's inability to facilitate, via its power of excitability, a response to the expectation of the sense organisation, could be an attempt at obtaining a response by means of auto-excitation. We could imagine internal discharge being brought about via shouts and motor movements, but there could also be a "perverted" use of the activity of representation, leading to its being disqualified. In that case, a psychical representative, which at this stage can be no more than a mixture of representation and affect, as in Aulagnier's description of the pictogram, may be employed as a means of triggering an internal discharge generating excitation instead of lending support to the psychical metabolisation of the somatic excitation. Part of the activity of representation is, thus, directed away from mental processing—which in principle leads to making sense of and giving meaning to what is felt at the somato–psychical level—in order to be used to trigger and activate a somatic process. Somatophilic attraction, with the aim of searching for quantities of excitation, would, thus, seem to be a consequence of a defect in the quality of the object's response and of an insufficiency in its power of excitability. That point of view opens up a paradox: the setting up of what Freud called the protective shield against stimuli is related to the object's power of excitability, the necessary requirement for the shift from quantity to quality to take place.

CHAPTER TEN

The potential impact of psychical processing on the restructuring of neural matter

I s there a difference in kind between what we call the body and what we refer to as the mind, or simply a different way of looking at these elements? Could we say that, once a certain level of complexity of mentalization is reached, the mind is to some extent autonomous with respect to its underlying neural—and, more generally, bodily—substrate? If there is no solution of continuity between the somatic and psychical structures, how can we imagine what takes place when something somatic is transformed into its psychical counterpart? What difference is there between psychical and subjective? What kinds of relationship are there between the soma, the psyche, and the affects? Between the soma, the psyche, and thinking? Between the soma, the psyche, and speech?

These questions are not the only ones that arise when we examine the role of the body in psychoanalysis; they simply open up a certain number of perspectives. They take on their own particular significance only because they are permanently linked to the overall question of a theory of representation—and, perhaps, even more generally, of that of symbolisation. Where lie the boundaries of the capacity to represent and of figurability? How far can we go into the depths of the soma in order to bring out the potentiality for meaning and signification?

If it is possible to see organic life as being "intelligent", is that intelligence reflected in the forms that mental life takes on? Do the modalities in which the life of the soma is structured, in their most biological and "silent" form as regards mental life, provide, nevertheless, some kinds of "model" for the structuring of the mind? Are these examples of what Kant called the "a priori principles of understanding" and of which Freud, in his own form of neo-Kantianism, often made use (primal fantasies)? This brings to mind one of the last things that Freud wrote:

> *August 22.* – Space may be the projection of the extension of the psychical apparatus. No other derivation is probable. Instead of Kant's *a priori* determinants of our psychical apparatus. Psyche is extended; knows nothing about it. (Freud, 1941f, p. 300)

In addition to the concept of representation, André Green introduced that of representance (Green, 1973); the term indicates a degree and a modality of representation based on a less clear-cut differentiation between representative and represented, between signifier and signified. The representance of an affect, therefore, indicates, in addition to the idea of discharge (which is, to all intents and purposes, simply quantitative), a valency of figuration in the actual perception of the discharge of the affect, one that leaves a memorised trace of a kind of differentiation between various body-states; this is in relation to an environment which is not necessarily, at that stage, perceived as being other. It is related also to what Freud called the pleasure/unpleasure principle and homoeostasis, that is, the maintaining of equilibrium between the major physiological functions that ensure survival.

These modalities of differentiation, by means of contrasting perceptions of different body-states, make up an initial value system, thereby setting up one of the earliest markers of the construction of meaning and of a "grammar", or "syntax", of bodily—and not simply somatic—signifiers.

The archaic magic of language

Let us take a look at two papers that Freud wrote, with a gap of almost fifty years between them: "Psychical (or mental) treatment" (1890a) and "Some elementary lessons in psycho-analysis" (1940b), which he wrote in the second half of 1938 while he was living in London, a paper that he thought of as an introduction to a new version of *An Outline of Psycho-Analysis* (1940a).

In his 1890 paper, Freud discusses hypnosis—this is the Freud that we are accustomed to calling "pre-psychoanalytical", but his psycho-analytical thinking is already at work: even although the vocabulary is not yet present, the questions that arise are already there. Freud writes of the power of words and of their magic:

> The words which we use in our everyday speech are nothing other than watered-down magic. But we shall have to follow a roundabout path in order to explain how science sets about restoring to words a part at least of their former magical power. (Freud 1890a, p. 283)

The power of language that can be expressed when certain conditions are met "produce such mental states and conditions in the patient as will be the most propitious for his recovery" (p. 292); these conditions modify states of consciousness and "[do] away with the autocratic power of the patient's mind which, as we have seen, interferes so capriciously with the influence of the mind over the body" (p. 298). He describes that autocratic power as "interfering" (p. 299).

That mental state, which resembles sleep to a considerable extent, "finds a parallel in the way in which some people sleep—for instance, a mother who is nursing her baby" (p. 295) (cf. Winnicott's "primary maternal preoccupation"). It expresses "the unsuspected power of the mind over the body" (p. 297); "in the hypnotized subject the influence of the mind over the body is extraordinarily increased" (p. 295). "This implies . . . an increase in the physical influence of an idea. Words have once more regained their magic" (p. 296). Freud argues that hypnosis "is in no sense a sleep like our nocturnal sleep or like the sleep produced by drugs. Changes occur in it and mental functions are retained during it which are absent in normal sleep" (p. 295). It would be difficult to give a better description of what we now refer to as the state that obtains during a psychoanalytical session, in which both analyst and analysand have a capacity for topographical and formal regression. Freud insists on the fact that psychical treatment is carried out via the psyche, the mind, and applies not only to disorders of a mental nature, but also to illnesses that have an "organic" basis to them.

Following on from Freud's conceptions of psychical treatment, this is how Edelman, in his book *Wider Than the Sky: The Phenomenal Gift of Consciousness*, describes certain phenomena that contribute to remodelling the brain.

> In both normal and abnormal states, [Edelman makes an explicit reference to "induced states such as those of a hypnotic trance"], the brain of an experienced individual attends continually to signals from the body and the environment, *but even more to signals from itself*. Whether in the dreams of REM sleep, or in imagery, or even in perceptual categorisation, a variety of sensory, motor, and higher-order conceptual processes are constantly in play. Given the mechanisms underlying memory and consciousness, both sensory and motor elements are always engaged. For example, in perception, there are contributions of motor elements—not acted out—that result from the premotor contributions of global mappings. And in visual imagery, the same reentrant circuits used in direct perception are reengaged, but without the more precise constraints of signals from without. In REM sleep, the brain truly speaks to itself in a special conscious state—one constrained neither by outside sensory input, nor by the tasks of motor output. (Edelman, 2004, pp. 143–144, my italics)

I find that idea of the brain speaking to itself during sleep very important, because it brings to mind the auto- or endo-psychical phenomena that are crucial to much of Freud's thinking. In my view, they are extremely important for our thinking not only about the earliest forms of mental life, including the elementary level of what Freud called the psychical representative of a drive, but also with regard to more developed levels which, in themselves, imply *a minima* the idea of personality—what nowadays we would refer to as a process of subjectivation or integration. I would say that what we call mental life—including its most elementary forms—always incorporates some phenomena that have to do with reflexivity and mirroring. I would now like to outline some ideas concerning what neurobiologists refer to as mirror neurons, suggesting some thoughts *a propos* of the initial elements of an intelligence of the soma that might provide models for the psyche.

Changeux introduced that concept, discovered by the neurophysiologist Giacomo Rizzolati, in his discussion of verbal and nonverbal communication between human beings, in particular the communication of thoughts. For Changeux, the model based on information technology and artificial intelligence is not pertinent here: "The brain is not an ordinary computer, fed with digital messages . . . The communication and comprehension of thoughts by means of language cannot be reduced to the decoding of a linguistic signal" (2009, p. 125). He goes on to quote something that Vygotsky (1962, p. 7) wrote: "The rational, intentional conveyance of experience and thought to others requires a mediating system", and in particular a spread of affects.

Mirror neurons "were discovered in the ventral premotor cortex, an area of the prefrontal cortex involved in the preparation of a movement" (Changeux, 2002, p. 196). By recording individually the neurons of that area in an alert monkey, Rizzolati and his colleagues observed that discharges occurred during voluntary movements of the hand and of the mouth—for example, when the monkey reaches for a peanut and brings it to its mouth. "Moreover, these firings are correlated with the global gesture rather than with its component movements. The researchers identified a 'neuronal vocabulary' of six basic motor acts" (Changeux, 2002, p. 197) (cf. the idea of "neurosemantics" and my attempt to discover a hypothetical somatic semantics; this may well mean that, as in linguistics, there exists a division into units): the neurons "grasping with the arm and mouth, grasping with the hand, holding, snatching, reaching, and carrying to the mouth and body" (Changeux, 2009).

> In the course of their experiments they made an unexpected discovery. Some of the neurons that fired when the monkey grasped or manipulated objects were also activated when the monkey *observed* the experimenter making the same gesture—as if they were both motor neurons and sensory neurons. The correlation of the activity of these mirror neurons, not only with the production of motor actions but also with their sensory representation suggested to Rizzolati and his team that these neurons were involved both in imitating movements and in understanding them . . .

> Both imaging studies and transcranial magnetic stimulation confirmed the presence of a system of mirror neurons in Broca's area. Broca's area is thus not exclusively devoted to language. It also is involved in the recognition of actions and contains representations of the hand as well as of the muscles involved in movements of the hand and the pronunciation of words. The discovery of motor neurons in this area led Rizzolati to suggest that mirror neurons play a role in speech

recognition. It may therefore be plausibly supposed, then, that the activation of Broca's area during the observation of a gesture is connected with the recognition not only of sounds produced by persons engaged in verbal communication but also of phonetic movements of the mouth and face. (Changeux, 2009, pp. 128–129)

Another of Freud's later aphorisms had to do with endoperception and the reflexive depth to which it gives rise: "Mysticism is the obscure self-perception of the realm outside of the ego, of the id" (Freud, 1941f, p. 300). With respect to self-perception, what Freud wrote there raises the hypothesis that the mind takes information from the reservoir of the drives that constitutes the id, the part of the mental apparatus that is rooted in the soma. In my view, it would be very interesting to think along these lines about the specific nature of mathematical thinking, that is, a representation not expressed in speech of the perception of models of mental functioning in the manner of self-perception, a sort of "thought process" of the body thinking itself through (see Introduction). One of the most difficult and yet fascinating aspects of that question is the relationship of pertinence between mathematical formulae and the state of the world.

That idea of a well-developed psychical construction that takes both its shape and its content from an intuition of the modalities in which the soma functions, providing a substrate for forms of thinking, can be found in other papers of Freud—this time in terms of a projection into the external world of an endoperception that has also a mirroring role:

In point of fact I believe that a large part of the mythological view of the world, which extends a long way into the most modern religions, *is nothing but psychology projected into the external world*. The obscure recognition (the endopsychic perception, as it were) of psychical factors and relations in the unconscious is mirrored – it is difficult to express it in other terms, and here the analogy with paranoia must come to our aid – in the construction of a *supernatural reality*, which is destined to be changed back once more by science into the *psychology of the unconscious*. One could venture . . . in this way . . . to transform *metaphysics* into *metapsychology*. (Freud, 1901b, pp. 258–259)

I began with Freud's 1890 paper on "psychical treatment", comparing it with his notes written in 1938 ("Some elementary lessons in psycho-analysis"). When, fifty years on, he went back to the idea of the essence of the mind, arguing that to identify it with being conscious would only lead to a dead end, Freud added that the drawback of such a definition is that it has the result of "divorcing psychical processes from the general context of events in the universe and of setting them in complete contrast to all others" (1940b, p. 283). In short, that way of looking at the situation would imply creating a split between the study of mental processes and the natural sciences. He goes on,

> But this would not do, since the fact could not long be overlooked that psychical phenomena are to a high degree dependent upon somatic influences and on their side have the most powerful effects upon somatic processes. . . . The psychical, whatever its nature may be, is in itself unconscious and probably similar in kind to all the other natural processes of which we have obtained knowledge. (1940b, p. 283)

Describing mental processes as unconscious implies that we see them as belonging not only to the overall category of natural phenomena, but also to the sphere of influence of the body. That influence is, in fact, bidirectional, because they are determined by the body and, at the same time, have an impact on it. The mind is unconscious not because it is opposed to consciousness, but because there is a somato–psychical continuity that does away with any parallelism between mind and body, and with any interaction between body and mind. What Freud is saying here is that the phenomena of consciousness are the product of the mind in its unconscious dimension. It is to that extent that we could argue that a metapsychology is also a kind of metabiology.

A psychical way of restoring neural matter

Some scientific articles can enhance my ideas concerning certain theoretical and technical issues that came to mind in the course of my clinical work and with respect to questions that Freud left unanswered. This is the case, for example, of an article published in *Le Monde*, dated 7 January 2004: "A mere visual illusion can bring relief to a phantom pain". Many amputees often still feel sensations linked to the limb that they have lost: this is particularly the case with pain, which may well be intense, hence the term "phantom pain". The physiological mechanism underlying this phenomenon has not yet been fully eluci-dated. However, recently developed techniques of brain imaging show that amputation leads to a restructuring of the motor area of the cortex corresponding to the nerve endings of the amputated limb. In the hours that follow, there occurs a restriction of the hand area to the advantage particularly of that of the face.[32] This phenomenon tends to support the idea of the plasticity of the brain, which has the ability to remodel and restructure; that idea has been significantly developed in modern neurobiology, in sharp contrast to that of a fairly great fixed-ness of brain organisation which prevailed when the model adopted to describe brain structuring was that of a cybernetic machine.

That limitation of the hand area is less pronounced in patients who have a myoelectric prosthesis that enables them to do certain things with their hand, in particular "grasping" movements, than in those who have simply an "aesthetic" prosthesis, that is, one that is inert. In a patient who had a double hand transplant, a displacement of the activation of the face area was found to have occurred: it returned to its usual place, thus freeing the area of the motor cortex correspond-ing to the hands.

It was by observing such phenomena that Pascal Giraux, of the rehabilitation unit in the Saint-Etienne faculty of medicine, and Angela Sirigu, of the Institute of Cognitive Science in Lyon, had the following idea: they would film the good arm in movement, then reverse the video image and project it on to where that of the handi-capped arm would normally be. During eight weeks, with three weekly sessions lasting one hour, the amputees visualised approxi-mately a hundred movements; in two of the three patients, whose injuries were more recent, the phantom pain diminished consider-ably—they were even able to stop taking the morphine-based pain-killers that had been prescribed to them. Six months after that phase of treatment, its effects were still operative. Brain imaging carried out before and after the eight weeks of remedial education showed that the motor cortex area corresponding to the forearm, atrophied as a result of the accident, had recovered its original dimension. In their preliminary hypotheses, the researchers who carried out this experi-ment emphasise the fact that vision might lead to a restructuring of brain activity. In addition, they draw attention to more general phenomena that bring into play the representation that the patient has of his/her body: "Our hypothesis is that the fact of seeing one's hand in movement reintroduces a consistency in the brain with the representation that the patient has of his/her body".

What, therefore, would appear to underlie phantom pain is the discrepancy between the image of the self—the internal model permanently generated by the brain in order to guide one's actions—and the injured body. Seeing the limb functioning once again appears to diminish that mismatch, even though the patient is conscious of the fact that there is some trickery involved.

Rather than contenting ourselves with the somewhat mechanistic explanations that give a pre-eminent role to visual perception in these restructurings, we ought perhaps to see such phenomena as more complex. This might help us to draw up some hypothetical models concerning the manner in which psychical forms of treatment may operate and encourage us, in our thinking about these, to examine different aspects of that technique which might facilitate some kinds of restructuring rather than others.

In my view, one important aspect of that experiment is that it demonstrates that a significant change in a subjective state is accompanied by some restructuring of neural matter. It shows also that that restructuring is the product of what we call psychical work, a work of integration that brings together and reunites.

What is brought into play in that experiment is an illusion, in the context of a subjective experience of physical and mental distress that sets up a great deal of expectancy—what we could call the desire to recover.[33] The perception of virtual movements is accompanied by what is referred to as an illusion; we could quite legitimately see that combination between perception and illusion as being similar to a hallucinatory phenomenon, or, at least, as the perceptual underpinning allied to a hallucinated valency concerning "hallucinated" motor movements. To return to Edelman's notion of re-entrant phenomena that I mentioned above: "[In] visual imagery, the same reentrant circuits used in direct perception are reengaged, *but without the more precise constraints of signals from without*" (my italics).[34] This implies that the form of perceptual phenomena is again made use of, outside of the purely perceptual phenomena themselves, and re-entered into phenomena of a quite different order, deflected away from their perceptual function so as to enter into a system that is, henceforth, one of re-presentation, one which is part of how I would define psychical processes.

One other aspect that is important to emphasise: the patient sees in the image of the arm and hand that are carrying out certain movements the image of his/her own arm and hand. In this way, specular recognition is brought into play as well as phenomena relating to the representation of a rediscovered self, and this together with a whole series of affect-related phenomena (modifications in the perception of the individual's internal state) that at the same time make use of the complex circuitry of the "emotional brain" and the corresponding neuro-mediatory discharge. To this, we must add a further level of complexity: not only do these individuals see an image of themselves which re-establishes a unified sense of self, they have also an experience in thought and in words of something that they could put to themselves thus: "What I am seeing there is *my* hand and *my* arm moving". One final level of complexity: the setting for that experiment had been imagined by some other person, someone who had a theory about suffering and about what can be done to diminish it, and who thereupon suggested a treatment procedure to someone else, someone who wanted to be relieved of his/her pain. That final level of complexity is that of the phenomena surrounding intersubjectivity which influence the effectiveness of what is taking place: among these, of course, are transference phenomena, although, in this particular instance, they are not employed explicitly as instruments of the treatment.

That description of the various levels of complexity which can contribute to our understanding of that experience may bring to mind certain issues involved in the work of psychoanalytical treatment: working on unconscious representations that border on what is perceived and what is hallucinated in the dynamics of an intersubjective relationship laden with affects, mobilising integration phenomena relating to identity and identification, the drives and language, leading to a series of re-entrant phenomena (repetition, remembering, and working through) that overcome the effects of resistance due not only to the need to open up other pathways, but also to the latency period required in order to structure or restructure new associative "networks".

Let us now try to explore these points more fully, this time focusing more on the metapsychological and clinical aspects. For Freud, pain was a kind of pseudo-drive, linked to the idea of libidinal sympathetic excitation.

> In the case of a great number of internal processes sexual excitation arises as a concomitant effect, as soon as the intensity of those processes passes beyond certain quantitative limits. . . . In accordance with this, the excitation of pain and unpleasure would be bound to have the same result, too. The occurrence of such a libidinal sympathetic excitation when there is tension due to pain and unpleasure would be an infantile physiological mechanism which ceases to operate later on. It . . . would provide the physiological foundation on which the psychical structure of erotogenic masochism would afterwards be erected. (1924c, p. 163)

I have suggested that the system of representance may be set up in response to certain failures in hallucinatory wish-fulfilment, which is, in principle, the starting point of the "royal road" that leads to psychical representations that are more and more elaborate, linked to language and participating in an infinite series of substitutions. (Compare Chapters Nine, on auto-engendering, and Eight, on the processes of bodily metabolisation.) That parallel road of representance develops through substituting bodily sensations for psychical representations, seeking excitation rather than following the path to satisfaction via the psychical representative. The discriminant of the value system in this circuit is the contrast between feeling oneself to be alive and feeling oneself to be dead (i.e., beyond the pleasure–unpleasure principle). Sensations are sought through triggering an internal discharge, thereby deflecting the "silent" physiological functioning to the advantage of a system of minimal representance: being alive/being dead. The somatic functioning employed for that purpose does not belong to a symbolic system or to a symbol-generating function linked to the structure of language. It is dominated by a quantitative factor; hardly economical and subject to repetition, it functions in terms of exhaustion. Although not semantic, it does signify something. This type of functioning is encountered in patients with addictive pathologies and in those described as somatic.

In her exploration of psychosis, Aulagnier has described defence mechanisms, set up very early, that are extremely costly: in these, the individual is amputated of the complementary object zone. This entails a quite remarkable self-mutilation of part of the individual's capacity for psychical metabolisation of what he/she experiences.

> The wish to destroy the object will always be accompanied, in the primal, by the wish to annihilate an erogenous, sensory zone, as well

as the activity of which that zone is the seat: at this stage, the object seen may be rejected only by abandoning the visual zone and the activity proper to it. In this mutilation of a zone-function as source of pleasure, we find the archaic prototype of the castration that the primary will have to reshape. In the primal, any organ of pleasure may become what is cut off in order to undo the unpleasure for which it suddenly seems to be responsible. (Aulagnier, 2001, pp. 28–29)

The amputation referred to here is that of a psychical function which, at that stage, can hardly be distinguished from a bodily function. My hypothesis is that these primitive defence mechanisms described by Aulagnier in the primal and in pictographic functioning bring about losses of substance that create an amputation in neural matter, as well as bringing to an abrupt end the development of neuronal associative networks that constitute the infant's emotional and cognitive brain.

To return to the model of the phantom limb, I would suggest that there might exist phantom pains that correspond to the very early amputation of that function zone. Everyone who has worked with schizophrenic patients will have come up against that clinical element: the patients speak of pains that may well be very severe, pains which they feel physically, yet which do not correspond to any detectable lesion. In her writings, Aulagnier often expresses her regret at not having explored more fully the issues raised by experiences of sensory disafferentiation. As for technique, particularly in the case of psychotic patients, she made use of the following metaphor: from time to time we have to *paint with words*. In my view, that metaphorical representation of what we have to introduce into certain kinds of treatment is, as yet, a very embryonic expression of the representation that we can have of various forms of material and of how we can make use of them in a given clinical situation. Painting with words describes an extreme and paradoxical situation in which we have to make use of words so that they play the part of a sensory function in order to *let the patient see* a modality of psychical processes that are deeply embodied, inaccessible to representations by means of language, a modality that enables the patient to recover the mirroring function of the pictographic activity that he/she destroyed early in life in an attempt to survive. Simply saying that we are painting with words means that we do not enter into the extraordinary complexity of the intersubjective events that are brought into play, in which the very forms of the analyst's psychical functioning are involved in the attempt to give the patient the equivalent—without the help of machines that project images—of that ingenious device invented for amputees. We could imagine that, in this case, it is the analyst's psychical functioning that is projected on to the locus where the amputation took place, giving an image of what had begun to exist and could have gone on developing. (Compare, in the Introduction, the example of an analyst's visual hallucination during a session with a schizophrenic patient.) It is with respect to these phenomena, which we call intersubjective, that we must develop our thinking in order to be able to conceive of the materiality of their existence. The neurosciences, as such, do not deal with this topic, but perhaps with an interdisciplinary approach—which, after all, is a highly developed form of intersubjectivity—this might well be possible.

A patient with autistic barriers

Now, a few words about a clinical situation. The patient, a dancer and choreographer of contemporary dance, was nearing the end of a lengthy period of psychoanalysis. I had spoken about that patient in the course of a symposium on autism in order to illustrate the concept of autistic enclaves and autistic barriers as they are sometimes found in the treatment of adult patients.

"Constant" discovered with me something that he knew about concerning his early childhood, although he had never fully realised the impact of it: there were absolutely no photographs of him as a baby until his first birthday, and his parents had never spoken to him about that early period in his life; he realised that it was not so much that he himself had never dared to ask them about it, the idea simply never came into his head. Complete silence with regard to the first year of his life. All he knew was that he had been looked after by a nanny and that he had been abruptly separated from her when his parents took him back. When he rediscovered that absence of words and images referring to his early childhood, he said, "It's strange; when I go to visit my parents now, I feel something that is difficult to describe, something to do with death, it's in the atmosphere, the sounds, the noises, the smells, the whole atmosphere around them, it's probably what I can recapture of what I must have felt as a child."

Another striking event in his childhood: when he was ten days old, he almost died of dehydration. It was a very hot day and his mother seems to have left him in his pram, wrapped up in blankets. He became dehydrated. When his mother realised this, his face was completely blue and he looked as though he was dead. He was saved, in extremis, and put in the care of a nanny . . .

He told me that he often had a feeling of emptiness, of being suspended above an immense void—on one side, he could see his birth, on the other, his death. Something had to be constructed, but he always had the impression that some initial element was missing, thereby preventing him from building anything at all. When I drew a parallel between what he had just said and the void of any representations concerning his early life, he told me for the first time of an experience that he had been having ever since he was a child, one that still existed from time to time: he could feel himself turning into a stone. When he was in that feeling of being a stone—"the stone-me", as he put it—it made him very anxious. In addition to those phases of autistic immobilisation and encapsulation in a shell carapace, he told me of experiences in which he felt that his perception of his body in space was being modified in a manner that has been described as feelings of depersonalisation; to make a clearer distinction between these, Aulagnier refers to experiences of decorporisation.

Three years ago, he had a very pleasant encounter with a young man who, a few days later, told Constant that he was HIV-positive. All that Constant said was, "At that point, everything came to a halt." He was paralysed by the terrifying fear that he felt at the idea of death present in his friend, and that he might be contaminated by it, and, at the same time, what came into his mind was that, by penetrating the young man, he was putting part of himself that was alive into his partner, thereby keeping him alive. In order to protect himself from the mortal danger represented by the proximity of that loving/loved body, a source of pleasure for him, and with the dreadful fear that he might once again have to put some distance between himself and that source of happiness, Constant again had recourse to his autistic defences. One evening, his partner, after they had had sex, switched on the television and watched it without saying anything. Then he fell asleep. Constant stayed by his side all night, without sleeping, but feeling himself to be turning into a stone. At dawn, through the open window, he heard birds singing outside. It was unbearable. He began to cry. I asked him if the distress that he had felt was linked to the contrast he may have experienced between his feeling of turning into stone and the birds singing and flying freely around outside. "Yes, that's exactly what it was. My crying woke him up. I tried to explain it to him. He said that there was nothing he could do for me, but that I could perhaps close the window. Then he fell asleep again. Time passed. I went to the window to close it, and I almost jumped out."

After a long period of processing that lasted several years, Constant began one session by telling me that, when he woke up, he remembered what he had been dreaming about, with a feeling of well-being that surprised him. In the dream, he was arriving at his parents' house—but a completely new one, very big and modern. He met his parents inside the house. His contact with them was easy and direct. It was all very pleasant. He felt that he was being made welcome.

We went on to explore the feeling of wellbeing that he had when he thought about that dream. We related it to the possibility of accepting and taking on board the feeling of having changed. The new house that he went into was Constant himself and his way of inhabiting everything that was new inside himself. His internal parents had changed and he was able to set up a peaceful relationship with them.

During the whole of that session, he spoke of the times when, in fact, he found it difficult to recognise himself. He was experiencing new ways of being and a new sense of self, but to describe them he still did not have representations or words that were sufficiently clear, identifiable and stabilised. Therefore, he tended to fall back on what was already familiar to him, already recorded, so as to express what he was experiencing—even though all those previous elements had become obsolete.

Henceforth, he was spending every night at his new partner's. He went on, "But . . . for the past five nights, we haven't had sex together . . ." He was getting ready to follow a path (and to draw me along it with him) with which he was perfectly familiar: the feeling of being completely rejected, banished from the world of human beings, giving rise to the feeling that he was turning into a stone. I thought of the compulsive "willing slave" aspect of his sexuality when he first asked for an appointment with me. I said that perhaps we could think of things differently: being in a tender and loving relationship with his partner without feeling obliged to have sex in order to preserve the sensation of a living contact with him—perhaps that was something new for him, but something with which he was comfortable. It would not stop him feeling that he was still loved and still the object of desire. I was, therefore, deliberately entering into a spoken description of what could be called a prospective construction of his psychical functioning, in the remembered present thanks to an anticipated future.

He went on to tell me about one evening when he came home late. His partner had cooked dinner and had already eaten. He served up the meal that he had prepared, spoke with Constant a little, then went over to sit in an armchair in order to go on reading a newspaper. Constant said, "It was horrible", and I thought that what was about to fall on him at that point was the well-known paradigmatic scenario in which he would feel himself turning into a stone beside his sleeping lover, then head for the window in order to jump out in an enacted representation in which the wish to be born became mixed up with the collapse into death. I invited him to continue. He made an effort to stand back a little from the distress that threatened to overcome him. Later, his partner asked him why he was sad. He tried to explain, but became confused because he could not find the right words, and fell asleep.

Several times during the session the patient remarked that, in different contexts, he no longer felt that he had to cling to something, to hang on. He went on, "In fact, something inside me has loosened up. You know the pain that I used to feel almost permanently [he pointed to his stomach, solar plexus, and sternum], well, it's completely gone."

At that point he was going through a very difficult time in his work as a choreographer and dancer: from time to time he would even think of stopping completely, because he felt that he no longer knew why or how he was dancing. He took on a little job as a salesman in a shop that sold children's clothing. He spoke of the regular hours, the simplicity of the work, the friendly environment. "It's hard for me to think this—and hard to admit it in your presence—but I really like it. I like that kind of life." He put on an expression of disbelief.

"I think that what you like is the idea of having what is usually called a 'normal' life, like everybody else. I think you're telling me about how comfortable you feel, and that's tied up with the way you're living in your new house." I went on to tell him that what was coming into my mind at that point was our very first meeting, when he could not manage to sit comfortably in the armchair—he kept on slipping, to such an extent that I held out a cushion for him. He then felt the need to tell me gently, "You know, it wasn't the armchair, it really was me." "Yes, the picture I had was that you had no proper foundation in life, and that that was both highly uncomfortable and distressing. But today you have shown me that you no longer need to cling on to something in order not to feel abandoned, you no longer need to remain uncomfortable in order to give rise to those feelings of pain that give you the impression that you exist."

Towards the end of the session, we spoke about the difficulty that he was having concerning the idea of going on with his dancing as being inextricably linked to all those elements which were changing and which were still hard to identify and put into words. He could no longer dance "as before" because that corresponded to a relationship to his body, to sensations and to a perception of himself that were out of date. I went on to suggest that something was developing deep inside him that would result in a new way of dancing.

CHAPTER ELEVEN

Homeostasis in the process of psychoanalytical treatment

T he work of psychoanalysis implies processes that are both intrapsychic and intersubjective. Although metapsychology provides us with theoretical hypotheses concerning what is taking place in the intrapsychic sphere, this is much less the case when it comes to the topographical, economic, and dynamic aspects of intersubjectivity.

The emergence of the transference, its setting-up, its modulations, its dynamics and its identification are the necessary, but not sufficient, conditions for the analytical process to come to fruition in the course of treatment.

What makes possible the emergence of the transference? Why is its recognition as such useful? What enables us to make use of the transference as a lever for overcoming resistance, facilitating the movement away from enacted repetition towards the construction of psychical scenarios that can be thought about, encouraging the working through of retrospective elements of the transference by means of speculative reconstructions, and providing the opportunity, in the transference, for prospective elements to appear, thereby shaping a new kind of self-perception in the relationship to the other person?

Working on a patient's transference is an agent of transformation.

The mainspring of this work of transformation is the work done via the drives as it is deployed *within* the transference relationship. It is the analyst's position as a third-party figure with respect to the process (the internal setting) that enables this drive-related work to be constantly directed towards an attempt at mentalization rather than being discharged through actual *in situ* satisfaction.

If we describe what takes place in an analytical session simply in terms of working through and transference–countertransference phenomena, we might as well have said nothing. When we try to think about all the phenomena that might arise during a session, the extreme complexity and multi-dimensionality of everything that can happen simultaneously soon gives us a feeling of vertigo.

Homeostasis

Somewhat more modestly, I would like to start with the idea of homeostasis in my inventory of a certain number of phenomena and mechanisms which, during any given session, contribute to creating disturbances or, on the contrary, to getting things back on their feet. I shall draw a somewhat artificial distinction between phenomena and mechanisms.

First, though, a brief reminder. The concept of homeostasis was introduced by the physiologist W. B. Cannon in his book *Wisdom of the Body*, published in 1932. The concept refers to the physiological processes thanks to which the body tends to keep the composition of the bloodstream constant. Thus, it refers also to the notion of "internal milieu" proposed by Claude Bernard. "Thus the idea of homeostasis clearly implies a dynamic equilibrium characteristic of the human body, and in no way a reduction of tension to a minimum level" (Laplanche & Pontalis, 1973, p. 346). There is obviously here a reference to Freud's Nirvana principle, the principle of pleasure–unpleasure and the principle of constancy; Freud himself sometimes found it difficult to distinguish between them in his writings.

If the concept of homeostasis is imported into descriptions of psychical phenomena during psychoanalytical treatment, this is because different spheres (or milieux) are in relationship with one another and in each of them there is a certain equilibrium in the energy deployed in the system. Three such elements can be highlighted:

- the circulation of energy within the psychical apparatus, with modulation of, and adjustments to, its variations;
- a relationship between the psychical apparatus and the organism;
- a relationship between the organism and the external environment.

In the analytical situation, each individual is the locus of relationships between these different milieux. There are, therefore, variations in, and adjustments to, the internal homoeostasis in its relationship to the other milieux. There is also the creation of a system made up of the pairing between the two psychical apparatuses at work; it seems perfectly possible that this, too, sets up its own homoeostasis.

Let us now take a look at some of the phenomena that might emerge during a psychoanalytical session.

First, the drive-related activity of both protagonists is constantly being stimulated, although direct satisfaction is, to some extent, prevented. (I say "to some extent" because much component-drive satisfaction remains possible: visual, auditory, the voice is an important drive-related object, olfactory—taken together, these could create what one might describe, following Anzieu, as a sensory envelope, which itself may function like a skin.) There is also, therefore, via the synergy between zones and the exchanges between formal and bodily signifiers, the creation of a psychical skin as the sensory organ of what we refer to as a psychical container.

Beginning with the elementary kinds of drive activity (the psychical representative of the drive), there unfolds a path that leads from the drive representative to more elaborate psychical formations—in particular, fantasy, but also reverie, day-dreaming, dreams, hallucinations, and sometimes transitory delusional elements.

Mood is stimulated, with all sorts of manifestations of the emotions and discharge of the affects of pleasure or unpleasure: with the affects, mechanisms to repress the affects; with manifestations of anxiety, defence mechanisms to counter anxiety.

There are more or less important variations in homoeostasis, as well as struggles to preserve homoeostasis whenever its equilibrium is seriously threatened by turbulence in the emotions. Every threat of breakdown in homoeostatic equilibrium triggers the earliest of mechanisms linked to states of primary distress in order to re-establish that equilibrium. Modifications in one's internal states lead to the actual re-experiencing of infantile helplessness rather than to memories or reminiscences of it. They constitute an implicit appeal addressed to a "helpful person", that is, to the primary container dimension of the analytical situation. If it is not possible to establish some kind of contact with the analyst as representing that container, the analysand will have to call upon "self-based" processes in order to compensate for failures in holding. These self-based mechanisms have recourse to the prematurity of the ego and always bring about some degree of splitting between intellectual processes and the psyche–soma. Ferenczi's term comes to mind here: the analysand turns into a "wise baby".

Every disturbance in homeostasis that occurs during a session is linked to the perception of modifications in one's bodily state; this might lead to having recourse to corresponding body-based defences which, more specifically, call upon the neurovegetative system: sympathetic or parasympathetic reactions (the most common of which is either vasodilatation accompanied by feelings of heat or vasoconstriction accompanied by paleness and feelings of inner cold), variations in metabolism that modify endoperceptions, hyperventilation that modifies the state of wakefulness, vertigo, all kinds of algia, paraesthesia, tensing of the muscles, and spasms.

Unbinding (between affect and representation) produced by the rule of free association leads to disturbances in psychical economy that create a level of instability in the system, one that may be conducive to qualitative restructurings and semantic redistributions. Nevertheless, when the rule of free association is announced, thereby emphasising thinking and word associations, this may facilitate some degree of putting aside the perception of internal states. Sometimes, all one has to do with an analysand who reports a dream is to ask him/her "What do you feel in that dream?" in order to enable the emergence of associations related to endocorporeal perceptions that have acquired a signifying function with regard to primary symbolisation and identificatory tendencies.

The earliest forms of the ego

Variations in homeostasis during a session, in the presence of the transference object, put the functions of the primitive ego (which Freud called the body-ego) to the test in its primary capacity of discriminating between actual and hallucinatory wish-fulfilment.

Freud saw in the earliest forms of the ego a function that, by opposing the principle of inertia of the complete draining-away of quantities of energy, finds itself in the sphere of the principle of constancy and takes on the role of guardian of psychical and biological life. It is, therefore, linked to self-preservation, and, from a phylogenetic perspective, it is linked also to the choice of mechanisms that, via evolution, are conducive to the survival of the species through the preservation of the individuals who make up that species.

That function is simultaneously:

- the outcome of the biological necessities for survival;
- the earliest form of structuring of a mental apparatus that brings together, in the beginnings of a functional unity, those separate manifestations of elementary kinds of mental life that we refer to as representatives of the drives; these are the endoperceptions of the signifying character of movements of the body searching for satisfaction and experiencing both satisfaction and frustration.

The function of discrimination, which constitutes the primary ego, is an initial structuring of what—after a lengthy series of successive non-linear integrations governed by their deferred and retroactive impact (*après-coup*)—will end up being a psychical personality.

The function of discrimination between internal and external reality sets up the primary ego as the initial representation of a differentiation between inside and outside. The earliest forms of the ego are, therefore, both a function and a representation of the object of that function. The form of the ego is co-dependent on the reality that it structures.

That very particular way of describing the beginnings of the ego, not as an entity (i.e., as something whole or positive) but as a function of discrimination (i.e., in relation to something else and negative), has some parallels with Freud's description of thoughts: they are not made up of memory traces, but of something that exists between memory traces.

Simultaneously with the phenomena that I have just described, there exists a certain number of mechanisms which enable

- the integration and transformation of these phenomena intra-psychically;
- the communication and spreading of these phenomena from one psyche to another (this is what we refer to as intersubjectivity).

Descriptions of these phenomena have changed and become more complex as psychoanalytical theory has evolved over the years. They still have to do with what we refer to as the sense of identity and identification, the foundations for what will become the psychical personality. They attempt to account for the construction of a human being possessing speech, based on a certain number of elementary phenomena that guarantee the existence of biological life but cannot account for the construction of the individual-as-subject.

It is this biological and neurophysiological prematurity that makes primary dependence the necessary condition first for the emergence of mental life and then for the structuring of a psychical individual as a person. The work of mentalization (or de-somatising), beginning with elementary biological phenomena, participates in the maturation of the central nervous system and of the organism as a whole; it has also an impact on the maturation of the neurophysiological apparatus.

There are many differences in the theories drawn up to explain the beginnings of mental life and of individuation. Nevertheless, over and beyond their differences, all of these hypotheses take as their starting point the fact that, in the human infant, there is no *ab initio* structured entity that perceives and thinks of him/herself as an individual subject distinct from all others and from external reality. In its earliest form, psychical substance makes no distinction between what it feels and produces, the psychical reality of those in its environment, and the reality of the world. That primary state of relative non-differentiation is the raw material upon which differentiations will later be built. That original commonality, however, will continue to leave its mark on the relationships of separation that will be set up between the now differentiated parts. That experience of continuity between somato–psychical substances of individuals who are "in reality" distinct from one another is what lays the foundation not only for separation–individuation, but also for the subsequent capacity to scale down, under certain conditions, the frontiers that define separate psychical spaces. It lies at the heart of intersubjectivity. It is worth pointing out that many specialists, following Winnicott, have emphasised the fact that it is the experience of the illusion of space–time continuity that lies at the very heart of the capacity for individuation. *A contrario*, people who have not been able to experience fully (i.e., to a sufficiently repeated and prolonged degree) that illusion are the ones who encounter the most difficulties in separation–individuation.

The experience of the feeling of going on being (which is an illusion maintained thanks to the quality of holding and set up against the vicissitudes of the chaotic turbulence of the life of the drives) thus becomes a requisite for the birth of an individual-as-subject who can begin to have feelings of hate and love. The various somato–psychical experiences that come into play here are the states of unintegration, integration, and disintegration, as described by Winnicott.

Here is another model of the birth of the psychical individual through the dynamic and transformative interplay between disparate elements that are brought together to form a whole: Melanie Klein's description of the movement away from the paranoid–schizoid position to the depressive position. Bion introduced a significant transformation of that pattern in order to make use of it as one of the dynamic foundations of normal mental life all the way through to adulthood: he drew an arrow heading in both directions between Ps and D (Ps ↔ D). Mental life is, thus, a constant dialectic interplay between breaking apart and coming together. In both models (Klein's and Bion's), transformations occur under the influence of drive energy and emotional turbulence, thereby giving rise to somato–psychical transformations and structural reorganisations.

It would be impossible to understand these major developments that structure psychical individuation without taking into consideration the fundamental mechanisms described by Freud, Ferenczi, and Klein: incorporation, introjection, identification, projection, and projective identification.

These various mechanisms take their shape and content from those bodily activities that predominate in experiences of satisfaction and in the relationship between the internal and external worlds. If the ego is first and foremost a body-ego, this is also because the early kinds of psychical propensity that set up intrapersonal and interpersonal relationships have as their basis a grammar and a syntax that are directly borrowed from movements of the body. According to Freud, bodily movements cathected by the libido in the erotogenic zones (one of the important features of which is that they constitute pathways between internal and external) shape the architecture of the personality and the forms that intersubjective exchanges will take on.

The object, too, is, first and foremost, a body-object.

CHAPTER TWELVE

Psychoanalysis and neurobiology: an imagined dialogue

Some parallels can be drawn in our thinking with the issues raised in contemporary neurobiology relating to fundamental questions to which we have no definite answer. In my opinion, however, if any kind of productive dialogue is to be set up, it must be based on material drawn from clinical experience. I would add that the clinical experience of which I am talking must necessarily include the workings of the analyst's mind.

The emotional mind and minded emotion

Here is a brief clinical extract, the sole aim of which is to try to highlight one particular way in which change can be seen to be brought about in the course of the work of an analysis.

The patient is a woman of a certain age—she is, shall we say, of an age to be a grandmother with adolescent grandchildren. She describes herself as being somewhat strait-laced; her background is that of the Protestant bourgeoisie, with enough clergymen and Swiss-German nannies to buttress her moral standards. She reports a dream that left her completely stunned: in the dream, she was a man and she was

169

looking at a handsome young man, naked, with his back to her; she felt desire for him. "I even felt that I was having an erection." "Just a few years ago, I would never have been able to tell you about that dream." She thinks for a moment, then says, "No, in fact, just a few years ago I would quite simply not have been able to have that dream. To have a dream like that, you have to have enough confidence to think that you might be understood." What had changed was her ability to dream. That new acquisition depends on the development of the quality of intersubjective communication.

Joseph Ledoux has written a remarkable book: *The Emotional Brain* (Ledoux, 1998). I admire the freedom of thought that he expresses in it, the sheer depth of his knowledge and the subtlety of his analyses. In Chapter Eight, he attempts to define from a neurobiological stand-point—and in a somewhat abrupt manner—the processes at work in psychotherapy: "Psychotherapy: quite simply another way to rewire the brain". Somewhat blunt, but, when all is said and done, just as acceptable as the more global definition, according to which psychical treatment brings about a neuronal restructuring: the idea is to create a synaptic potentialising in the brain circuits that control the amygdala, helping the cortex to control the amygdala. Why not? But when he makes a brief comparison between the different modes of action in behaviour therapy and psychoanalysis, I am really quite surprised to read what he says, because my own representations of the complex mechanisms that are brought into play in the work of analysis are quite different:

> Psychoanalysis, with its emphasis on conscious insight and conscious appraisals, may involve the control of the amygdala by explicit knowl-edge through the temporal lobe memory system and other cortical areas involved in conscious awareness. (Ledoux, 1998, p. 265)

Since I do appreciate Ledoux's subtlety when he talks of neuro-biology, I think to myself that I really would like to be able to talk to him about the clinical work of psychoanalysis. For example, the changes brought about in my state of consciousness when I listen to my Protestant patient, changes which, through time, perhaps help her to put her cortex to sleep a little and let her amygdala say what it wants to say, if I can put it like that. I always give pride of place to dreams in the work of analysis, not only as the royal road leading towards the unconscious representations of a wish by means of free associations, but also as bearing witness to the work of processing that takes place in the treatment. Not all analysts would share that point of view; indeed, some leave very little room for dream-work and its interpretation in the course of an analysis. One of the interesting aspects of a debate that could be set up between analysts, or between analysts and neurobiologists, has to do with the distinction that Freud made between the manifest content and the latent content of a dream. Do we still pay attention only to free associations arising from the latent content in order to reveal the unconscious desire behind a dream, or do we treat the manifest content also as being important—and, if we do, what do we do with it, how do we think about it?

Another patient, while she was thinking about how her two daughters had developed so differently, spoke of the difficult circumstances in which the younger of the two was born. For the first time, she realised that she had been so unhappy about that second birth that, during the baby's first few months, she had looked after her more or less automatically, without really feeling anything. In speaking of the impact of that primary environment on her baby's development, she put it very simply: "All that time, my heart wasn't in it." I would like to put, in words just as simple, the question that runs through the whole of this chapter—to both analysts and neurobiologists: is there any significant difference in the mutative potentiality of what the analyst says depending on whether his/her heart is in it or not? In other words, depending on the circuitry involved for processing that intervention over time.

The "body loop" and the "as if loop" (Damasio)

In his book *Descartes' Error*, Damasio (1994) introduces a concept that seems to me to be relevant to that question: the concept of the "body loop" and that of the "as if loop", described in the chapter entitled "The body as theatre of the emotions". An emotion is perceived via a loop that starts in the brain, goes towards the body, then comes back to the brain again. That is the body loop. However, there exists an "as if" mechanism that enables the emotion to be simulated exclusively in the brain by short-circuiting the body. That is the "as if" loop. According to Damasio, the perception of emotions by means of the "as if" mechanism, which is more "economical", is of a very different quality from a perception of emotions that has travelled through the body. This is how he explains his point of view:

> [An] emotion is not induced by neural routes alone. There is also the chemical route. What is played out in the body is constructed anew, moment by moment, and is not an exact replica of anything that happened before. I suspect that the body states are not algorithmically-predictable[sic] by the brain, but rather that the brain waits for the body to report what actually has transpired. . . . If all our feelings were of the "as if" type, we would have no notion of the ever-changing modulation of affect that is such a salient trait of our mind. (2005[1994], pp. 157–158)

This, of course, brings to mind Winnicott's theoretical developments concerning the false self, Phyllis Greenacre's concept of "as if" personalities, and John Klauber's idea of the analytical false self. Drawing such a parallel is, of course, something of a "leap" that will be met with disapproval on the part of epistemologists, but, all the same, it would be fascinating to be able to discuss this with Damasio, taking clinical work as our starting point.

This leads me to the issue that Damasio expressed thus: "I have not explained *how* we feel a feeling". When I read "How do we feel a feeling?", my impression is that the author of that sentence is attempting to explore, from his own point of view as a neurobiologist, an issue that concerns theory, clinical work, and the way in which a psychoanalyst listens attentively to the patient. This brings immediately to mind what Freud said about the sense organ being "the system of consciousness" (1950, p. 252); he argued that unconscious sensations are the only elements that go directly from the Unconscious to consciousness without going through the Preconscious system where the connections with word-presentations take place. This makes me think of those patients who cannot "feel" their emotions, those who enact them rather than feel them, or in order not to feel them, and those who constantly need to stimulate themselves in order to feel that they are alive. Then I think of the importance that Winnicott attached, for the construction of the human mind, to what he called the feeling of going on being and the interruptions in that feeling of continuity that give rise to primitive agony, which may jeopardise, sometimes irreparably, the development of somato–psychical potentialities. Damasio himself writes of "ongoing body-states"—perhaps body-states that are constantly dynamic? Indeed, he emphasises the state of permanent change that applies to them, and their reconstruction—body-states that are constantly evolving. When Damasio differentiates between "background feelings", "secondary feelings", and their relationship to the concept of the "neural self", this gives rise to a great number of ideas and questions in my mind.

For example, trying to understand how his description can enhance the theoretical representations of certain basic conditions for the development of a mind, that is, what in our vocabulary we call primary repression and primary identification. I would like, for example, to discuss with him the phases of great turbulence experienced by patients who, in the course of their analysis, are undergoing significant changes: the feelings of internal catastrophe that they experience at that point, sometimes accompanied by physical sensations of pain, of being torn apart. These "catastrophic" occurrences are crucial in enabling new kinds of integration; our representations of identification and dis-identification are not, in themselves, sufficient for helping us to think about the issues involved: these developments take on an integrative function only if they are mentally "contained", as though by a skin. Is it possible to think in neurobiological terms about what we are trying to describe via such terms as the container, the mother's capacity for reverie, the psychical skin (terms borrowed from Bion and from Anzieu)? I think that the beginnings of a dialogue are well and truly present when I read the following extract:

> If feeling happy or sad corresponds in good part to a change in the neural representation of ongoing body states, then the explanation requires that the chemicals act on the sources of those neural representations, that is, the body proper itself, and the many levels of neural circuitry whose activity patterns represent the body. (Damasio, 2005[1994], p. 161)

That makes me think of Piera Aulagnier, of her conception of primal psychical activity in terms of a pictographic activity that is the representation of affect and the affect of representation, both inextricably linked, and, more specifically, of the idea of borrowing from the sensory and bodily model in order to have the required material for the primal construction of the activity of representation. How far does that borrowing go, what does it imprint on the psyche of its reminiscences concerning somatic functioning, what somatic sources are required for such borrowing? Those questions give rise to a certain number of speculations when I read the following extract from Wolf Fridman's book, *Le cerveau mobile. De l'immunité au système immunitaire* (The Mobile Brain: from Immunity to the Immune System):

> The molecules that constitute the immune system, and in particular the antibodies, possess within themselves images of the universe. . . . Where is this immunological brain? Everywhere and everywhere at the same time. . . . The cells that go to make it up are constantly circulating through the organism, picking up information, digesting it, communicating it to other cells, multiplying and taking decisions on how to proceed. A mobile brain, constantly enriched by new cells, constantly on the alert, is present in every single part of our body. (Fridman, 1991, translated for this edition)

To avoid any misunderstanding, I must emphasise that I am not attempting to set up a simplistic analogy here. I know that the representations in molecules as described by Fridman belong to a different state of matter from mental representations in the psyche, and I do not believe that there exists any kind of linear causality going directly from one to the other. I am simply making use of the idea of something being borrowed from the somatic sphere in order to construct models of the mind. To this, I would add the question: to what extent, in the infinitely small dimension of the mechanisms of somatic functioning, can we have a representation of something being borrowed in order to construct some forms of mentalization?

In principle, a psychoanalyst listens, hears, understands, and interprets. An interpretation will overcome repression and, thereby, enable the lifting of infantile amnesia. However, what might appear to be a series of cognitive operations is accompanied by some mobilisation of passion in the form of the most primitive and powerful emotions linked to infantile sexuality and to life-involving issues that correspond to primary dependence and the infant's prematurity. From the very beginning of his work and right up to the end, Freud emphasised the threefold dimension of what is at stake in psychoanalytical treatment: dynamic, topographical, and economic—that is, the energy dimension of the forces at work between different psychical *loci*.

Epigenesis and plasticity

Freud's initial representations of the mechanisms at work in psycho-analytical treatment became more complex as he had to deal with difficulties in, and failures of, the treatments that he conducted; these forced him to revise his original theoretical models. He introduced some degree of embodying/corporisation of psychical reality, with the emphasis being laid more and more on substance, its consistency, and its resistance. In those developments, *The Ego and the Id* (1923b) represents a significant stage. In that book, Freud states that "the conscious ego . . . is first and foremost a body-ego" (p. 27). He added to that definition in 1927, when he wrote in a footnote:

> The ego is ultimately derived from bodily sensations, chiefly from those springing from the surface of the body. It may thus be regarded as a mental projection of the surface of the body, besides, as we have seen above, representing the superficies of the mental apparatus. (1923b, p. 26)

In his theorisations, Freud reflects on the body in terms of somato–psychical continuity and reversibility; his thinking is fundamentally monistic in that it is a constant effort to think simultaneously in terms of the body and the mind, seen as different states of a single substance. From his perspective as a neurobiologist, Damasio puts it thus: "The mind is embodied, not just embrained".

From a scientific point of view, the variations in the analytical setting should be explored in terms of the appropriateness of the therapeutic instruments in different clinical situations. In some cases, the contrast between conscious and unconscious or the mechanism of repression might not be a sufficiently operational model to account for a series of clinical facts. Another model has to be called upon: part of the ego is unconscious, and the contrast is between a coherent ego and one that is repressed and split-off from it, with the operative mechanism being that of splitting. Indeed, Freud saw splitting as a rift in the fabric of the ego—"a rift in the ego" (1940e, p. 276). In his view, going from one model to another implied modifying some part of psychoanalytical practice.

Although Freud said that something had to be modified, he did not say exactly what. The easy way out would be to invent a new technique, something external to a transformation in the subjective experience of the analyst involved in the process with his/her patient. However, the only modification that may in the end enable access to the patient's psychical reality in order to change it is a modification of the analyst's subjective state, one which, in my view, has to do with the analyst's body-ego and the psychical stirrings that he/she allows to take place internally. Winnicott made use of Freud's idea of the body-ego to illustrate the inner modification that is required if the work of transformation is to take place (it could be described as a work of metabolisation between affects, emotions, representations, words, language, and sensoriality): "I personally do my work very much from the body-ego, so to speak" (Winnicott, 1965, p. 161). He did not, however, go in to any more detail on that particular point.

In reading the various articles written by, for example, Changeux, Damasio, and Edelman, we can see that there are a certain number of major topics that they all deal with, although each has his own way of thinking about them. One such topic is the hyper-complexity and the non-linearity of the causality that comes into play in the development and functioning of the nervous system and, more specifically, of the brain. Another fundamental theme: the plasticity of neuronal structures and the possibility of their being remodelled according to the different experiences encountered in the outside world; such encounters are necessary in order to activate developmental potentialities, because spontaneous brain activity is not, in itself, sufficient for promoting development.

The epigenetic model contrasts with the representation of brain structuring based on a predetermined genetic programme. The shaping of the adult brain lies, to some extent, outside the absolute control of the genes. "It is properly regarded as an epigenetic evolutionary process characterized by variation and selection that begins during embryonic development and continues after birth" (Changeux, 2009, p. 184).

If we look at the classic question of innate *vs.* acquired from this perspective, not in terms of a contrast but as interlinked elements, we could say that genes are the means by which the environment enables the individual to shape him/herself via a process of self-structuring and self-excitation.

That epigenetic plasticity of neuronal structures evokes a progressive form of structuring in which each new experience leaves its mark; in turn, this will remodel retroactively the markers that structured earlier experiences. These retroactive effects in the construction of "thinking matter" (Changeux) enable the progressive integration of what experience teaches us in its relationship to survival. Others, such as Edelman, have spoken of re-entrant circuits, feedback loops, and re-entrant maps. These descriptions of the complex and non-linear modalities of the processes by which neural matter is structured echo, to some extent, the manner in which Freud tried to describe the structuring of psychical reality in terms of a complex temporality brought about by the deferred retroactive and restructuring impact of *Nachträglichkeit*. Indeed, it is precisely that representation of a temporality governed by deferred retroactive impacts that enables us to conceive of the possibility of psychical change taking place in the course of a psychoanalysis. It goes hand-in-hand with the model of regression in psychoanalytical treatment, a bidirectional movement between regression and progression in all three of its aspects: temporal, topographical, and formal.

Another topic that often crops up: the fundamental part played by emotions and affects in the development of cognitive functions in all of their profusion. This is a major topic in Damasio's and Ledoux's articles and also, although to a slightly lesser extent, in those of Edelman.

The epigenetic model and the concept of plasticity mean that there is some connection between the development of the brain and the environment in general (external and internal stimuli). What, in this vast domain, relates more specifically to psychoanalysis has to do with the influence of the quality of the subjective states of the human environment on the development and structuring not only of the thinking matter of the brain, but also of the major systems that go to make up the body; the thinking matter is dependent on these, and vice versa: a relationship of co-dependence. To what extent does the quality of the intersubjective link determine the activation of the potentiality for development and, therefore, the quality of the shaping and structuring of the organism in its entirety? That fascinating question does not simply express a kind of general interest for the development of human beings; it has direct repercussions on the representations that we may have of what is at stake as regards the therapeutic effectiveness of our psychical instruments in the course of psychoanalytical treatment.

In order to explore properly the idea of the body in psychoanalysis, we have to go back to the concept of the drives.

When we look in some detail at the way in which Freud defined the drives, it is obvious that the idea of work is central to those definitions; it is via the idea of work—the work of the mind—that we can best approach what, in modern psychoanalytical parlance, we refer to as "subjective appropriation". That is one way of designating the phenomena that help us to conceive of the movement from a somatic dimension, seen as a purely organic functioning without any space for the reflexivity that constitutes the individual-as-subject, to a bodily dimension that is brought into the mind, libidinalised, and participates in the signifying relationships that constitute intersubjectivity.

Take, for example, Freud's paper on "Instincts and their vicissitudes" (1915c), which is part of his writings on metapsychology.

In that paper, Freud begins by focusing on the difference between physiological stimulation and the drives. A strong light that falls on the eye is a physiological stimulus that may have some impact on the psyche, but its source lies in the external world. An instinctual (or drive-related) stimulus has to do with a need; it comes from within the organism and does not operate as a force giving a momentary impact that can be disposed of by a single action—its impact is always a constant one. A dryness of the mucous membrane of the pharynx and the irritation of the mucous membrane of the stomach are internal processes and, as such, are the organic foundations from which needs such as thirst and hunger arise; they are drive-related stimulations.

The only means of doing away with the constant thrust of a need coming from inside the body is to bring about an internal modification that amounts to "an appropriate ("adequate") alteration of the internal source of stimulation" (Freud, 1915c, p. 119). This is what we call "satisfaction".

The introduction of the concept of the drives makes more complex the simple physiological pattern of reflex.

According to Freud, the complexity of drive-related phenomena is what underlies the development of the nervous system. Drives

make far higher demands[35] [than physiological stimuli] on the nervous system and cause it to undertake involved and interconnected activities by which the external world is so changed as to afford satisfaction to the internal source of stimulation. (p. 120)

Freud went on to say that the drives "are the true motive forces behind the advances that have led the nervous system, with its unlimited capacities [cf. what we now refer to as plasticity], to its present high level of development" (p. 120).

Darwin was often on the horizon of Freud's thinking as it developed. This probably led him to add an evolutionist hypothesis to his theorising of the development of the nervous system influenced by drive-related stimulation:

> There is naturally nothing to prevent our supposing that the instincts themselves are, at least in part, precipitates of the effects of external stimulation, which in the course of phylogenesis have brought about modifications in the living substance. (Freud, 1915c, p. 120)

We can see here, as is often the case, that this evolutionist idea has a Lamarckian note to it—Freud's hypothesis here, as in the case of trauma, is that of transmission via sedimentation from generation to generation.

Let us go back to the subject of differentiation with respect to drive-related stimulation. In the two examples that Freud mentioned, the mucous membrane of the pharynx and that of the stomach, the differential criterion does not involve simply the idea of internal as opposed to external. The other aspect—one which Freud does not seem concerned to highlight, which is perhaps why his theory of the drives has often been accused of being solipsistic—is that the need to which the drive-related stimulation bears witness cannot be satisfied, given the prematurity of the infant, other than through the intervention of some *external* object. The concept of the drives, and of the work of processing involving the drives, is, therefore, from the outset, linked to that of primary dependence in order to survive—in other words, intersubjectivity. It was only in Winnicott's time that the concept of the subjective object could be theorised: not only is the external object that provides satisfaction through actually modifying external reality not perceived as being external, it is necessary, for the individual's somato–psychical development, that he/she maintains the illusion for a sufficiently long period of time that those modifications were brought about by the individual him/herself (omnipotence) and that the external reality of the object, as such, should not be acknowledged too soon. That idea of illusion, which in Winnicott's theory lies at the very heart of the earliest capacities for development of the self and the ego, can be seen as complementary to Freud's concept of hallucinatory satisfaction, but it does not constitute a substitute for this.

No description of the drives could suffice to account for the workings of the mind in their globality—and even less for the setting-up of what Freud called the mental apparatus or that of a psychical personality. In his paper "On narcissism: an introduction" (1914c), Freud emphasises the fact that "we are bound to suppose that a unity comparable to the ego cannot exist in the individual from the start; the ego has to be developed" (p. 77). He then goes on, "The auto-erotic instincts, however, are there from the very first; so there must be something added to auto-erotism – a new psychical action – in order to bring about narcissism" (p. 77).

It is that "new action", one that is certainly not limited to a single phenomenon, which leads to the construction of the earliest forms of what we call the ego and the personality of an individual. There are prolegomena of that capacity in Freud's description of the elements that go to make up the earliest forms of representative activity based on the somatic excitability that we refer to as the drives. I shall, therefore, quote the very first definition of the drives that Freud suggested in his paper "Instincts and their vicissitudes" (1915c), and then break it up into its component parts.

> If now we apply ourselves to considering mental life from a *biological* point of view, an 'instinct' appears to us as a concept on the frontier between the mental and the somatic, as the psychical representative of the stimuli originating from within the organism and reaching the mind, as a measure of the demand made upon the mind for work in consequence of its connection with the body. (1915c, pp. 121–122)

Almost every word in that definition deserves to be studied in detail and commented upon. Mental life is thought of and observed "from a biological point of view"—this lends support to the idea that metapsychology is also a form of metabiology and that mental life is included in it as emanating from its biological substrate. It implies also that it was thanks to his familiarity with, and knowledge of, the innermost workings of physiology, and in particular of neurophysiology, that Freud was able to theorise the birth of mental life and the construction both of the mental apparatus and of the personality. The most important question would seem not to be so much that of "the discovery of the unconscious" as that of a form of mental life distinct from discursive conscious awareness, distinct from, but not divorced from, the life of the organism.

The difficulty lies in drawing up the frontiers of, and the pathways between, somatic and mental life. In my opinion, that concern and this area of research are also part of contemporary neurosciences via the complex studies that they have initiated in an attempt to define and highlight the neurobiological mechanisms that govern the emergence of consciousness. I think that the term "consciousness", applied to what neurobiologists are attempting to explore, also includes what psychoanalysts call mental life, that is, a set of phenomena, the substrate of which is organic, which give rise to a representation of the self and of the world, and of oneself as a representing agent.

The emergence of subjective experience

A drive can be defined by three terms. It is a frontier concept, a representative, and a measure.

A drive is a concept; in other contexts, Freud spoke of myths or mythology. It is an attempt to have some representation of a phenomenon that exists—as he put it in another context—in a way that is unknown to us; it is a concept in the sense of a modelisation that attempts to describe a movement, a transition, a transformation. It is a frontier concept because it attempts to describe the movement from one reality state to another. A drive is simultaneously the sensitive substance of stimulation, the path followed by that stimulation and the effects that it has on an "agency" that is, as yet, not clearly defined because "at the very beginning" there is no organised ego that can take on board the impact or the information coming from drive-related stimulation. A drive, therefore, "represents" the internal state of the organism, but for an entity that does not, or does not yet, exist. In addition, my hypothesis is that it is the repeated experiencing of that drive-related trajectory that will participate in the construction of an entity that is capable of perceiving it. Therein lies the essential difficulty of that description: when Freud says that the instincts (i.e., the drives) are a representative of the internal stimulation reaching the mind, thereby offering it an image of the state that the body is in, he is postulating the existence of something "already there" in the mind, something that is able to analyse information coming from the body; yet, it is precisely that information which, since it is "psychical", will go to make up the psyche. This, therefore, evokes a system of self-regulation and self-structuring that is built up via reciprocal interactions, the frontiers of which are the constraints of their expression arising from the constitution and the unknown aspects of the experience.

Edelman and Tononi try to deal with very similar issues in their attempt to construct a theory of the phenomena of consciousness and of the conditions under which they may emerge.

> Something is definitely missing in attempts to identify the neural basis of consciousness with this or that set of neurons. Again, we confront the world knot. By what mysterious transformation would the firing of neurons located in a particular place in the brain or endowed with a particular biochemical property become subjective experience, while the firing of other neurons would not? . . . We take the position that consciousness is not an object but a process. (Edelman & Tononi, 2000, pp. 8–9)

What I said earlier about the function of representance of a drive for a mind that is not there for taking it in but to the construction of which it makes a contribution, raises the issue of the integrating function of a system in the absence of an agency that can actually accomplish that integration.

This is how Edelman and Tononi deal with the problem of the coherence of a perceptual scenario in spite of the wide variety of sensory stimuli.

> Our ability to act coherently in the presence of diverse, often conflicting, sensory stimuli requires a process of neural interaction across many levels of organisation without any superordinate map to guide the process. This is the so-called binding problem: How can a set of diverse and functionally segregated maps cohere without a higher-order controller? . . . Since there is no superordinate map that coordinates the binding of the participating maps, the question arises: How does binding actually take place? (Edelman & Tononi, 2000, pp. 106–107)

The answer to that question has to do with the idea of re-entry, which is part of an evolutionist conception of brain development that

Edelman calls the "theory of neuronal group selection". Without going into too much detail, I would, none the less, draw the reader's attention to the fact that the concept of re-entry is not completely foreign to Freud's idea of *Nachträglichkeit* (deferred retroactive impact/*après-coup*). Re-entry is a process that facilitates the integration of the dispersed neuronal states that accompany consciousness; their variability and differentiation are considerable.

The question of binding, of integrating, in the absence of any "superordinate map", looked at from a neurobiological point of view may rejoin that of subjectivation and subjectivity considered from a psychoanalytical point of view.

This might be where the intrapsychic point of view is limiting in both neurobiological and psychoanalytical perspectives. It might be necessary at this point to add an even higher level of complexity to the neurobiological approach.

Within the epigenetic factors contributing to brain development, does the intersubjective factor have a specific role to play in the binding and integrating function? Binding very probably varies according to the quality of the "tuning" of the intersubjective dimension. Would neurobiologists ever be interested in trying to explore the phenomena Winnicott described as the normal madness of the primary maternal preoccupation, including phenomena which seem to imply a topographical continuity between the infant's psyche and the maternal psyche?

What is the "good-enough" subjective, emotional input expected by the organism from the primary care-givers for the brain to develop to the best of its potentialities? What is the impact of micro-traumatic or traumatic discontinuities in holding and/or of impingements on brain development? How does the organism manage to compensate for these sudden disturbances in intersubjective homeostasis through the phenomena of self-regulation providing a kind of self-cure? How can we relate these compensation phenomena of self-cure to later phenomena of mental disorders? Many more questions than answers . . .

CHAPTER THIRTEEN

A thirst from so long ago: soma, body, and early traumas

Expectation and the environment

T he concepts of crisis and of the repetition of crises would seem to imply a movement of disorganising mobilisation in the face of a repeated impossibility to resolve a problem; that movement bears witness also to the search for some reorganisation via the integration of a new element enabling a different pattern of the relationships between the various elements of the conflict to be set up. A crisis follows on from a conflict situation and represents an attempt at overcoming that conflict. When crises occur repeatedly, this is an indication that something expected has not, in fact, been found, that some encounter or other did not take place, that the crisis is not, in itself, resolvable. In the context of psychoanalytical treatment, we could say that the working-through process has not been carried out. The repetition of crises could then be seen from two points of view: that of the compulsion to repeat, which lies short of the pleasure principle, and that of the persistent expectation for a response, more or less adequate, from the primary object; the absence of that response produces not a fixation, but an inhibition in development and a failure of integration. These two perspectives are not necessarily contradictory.

The notion of expectation implies that of an encounter (an encounter equivalent to a meaningful interpretation), and that of organisers of the psyche which are "waiting" to be awakened and put into action so that the individual's mental development may be as good as possible—thus, it implies also notions such as growth, virtuality, and potentiality, and its epistemological domain extends from phylogenesis to ontogenesis, from the idea of instinct to that of symbolic.

All through his work, Freud gave pride of place to symbols and the symbolic dimension—in particular from *The Interpretation of Dreams* on. The latest definition that he gave of those elements appears in *Moses and Monotheism: Three Essays*.

> In this we have in mind the example of what is certainly the 'innate' symbolism which derives from the period of the development of speech, which is familiar to all children without their being instructed, and which is the same among all peoples despite their different languages. (1939a, p. 132)

That phylogenetic conception of symbolism is linked to the concept of "the psychical precipitates of the primaeval period" (1939a, p. 132), which constitute a genetic inheritance, following an idea that Freud never really gave up in spite of the scientific refutation[36] of Lamarck's theories: that of the heredity of acquired characteristics preserved by a kind of sedimentation and handed down "directly" to future generations, that is, not via a psychical reacquisition through an interchange between individuals. What I am attempting to emphasise here is how the notion of expectation, as I am trying to outline it, is present in Freud's thinking: "[something] which, in each fresh generation, called not for acquisition but only for awakening" (Freud, 1939a, p. 132).

Another very important idea, since it provides the instruments for trying to think about the "uncoupling" from psyche to soma (a hypothesis that may well apply to certain somatic illnesses), is, in some situations, the recourse and return to instinct: "We find that in a number of important relations our children react, not in a manner corresponding to their own experience, but instinctively, like the animals, in a manner that is only explicable as phylogenetic acquisition" (Freud, 1939a, pp. 132–133).

The human organism is, therefore, waiting for some response, for some nourishment coming from the primaeval psychical environment which will trigger and activate the processes of growth and development, enhancing them or paralysing them, and, thereby, enabling, preventing, or distorting the various possible integrations. In his conceptualisation of holding and the environment, Winnicott focused particularly on those aspects that involve the maternal side of the primary mental environment and of the "expectation" of the *infans*—although he did let it be understood that the idea of the environment went further than that of the primary object. For any scientific study of adaptation and the environment, which Winnicott sincerely hoped for, there would have to be some extension of the idea of holding to include the paternal aspect. I shall try to show how the fundamental benchmarks of that issue are already present in what Freud said, sometimes in a highly speculative manner.

In his exploration of the question of expectation, Freud goes a long way into the destiny of humankind. He describes the restoration, after a long moment of somewhat obscure developments, of the sovereignty of the father of the primal horde, a restoration that enables their "feelings towards him" (1912–1913, p. 160) to be repeated. The way in which Freud expresses that idea is also pervaded by intense feelings:

> The first effect of meeting the being who had so long been missed and longed for was overwhelming and was like the traditional description of the law-giving from Mount Sinai. . . . A child's emotional impulses are intensely and inexhaustibly deep to a degree quite other than those of an adult; only religious ecstasy can bring them back. A rapture of devotion to God was thus the first reaction to the return of the great father. (1939a, pp. 133–134)

It should be pointed out that the other aspect, the libidinal one, of the issues surrounding expectation—more familiar, perhaps, because it follows on from the hallucinatory fulfilment of wishes—is that of the impossibility, by its very nature, of ever obtaining absolute satisfaction. Freud always insisted on the fact that, at the very heart of satisfaction itself, there always remains some non-satisfaction. Absolute satisfaction is not compatible with the preservation of mental life, or probably with that of biological life. It is that aspect of the issues involving expectation that Freud expresses in the following extract, written just a few days before his death:

> The ultimate ground of all intellectual inhibitions and all inhibitions of work seems to be the inhibition of masturbation in childhood. But

perhaps it goes deeper; perhaps it is not its inhibition by external influences but its unsatisfying nature in itself. There is always something lacking for complete discharge and satisfaction—en attendant toujours quelque chose qui ne venait point [Always waiting for something which never came]. (1941f, p. 300)

In *Moses and Monotheism*, expectation involved someone who did not appear on the scene—"the great father"—whereas here there is a waiting for "something" which, by its very nature, cannot provide the expected satisfaction. This implies that there exists *a representation of satisfaction that is independent of the actual experience of satisfaction*. Paradoxically, we have to go back to Freud's *Project for a Scientific Psychology* before we can see the situation in all of its complexity, through the introduction of something extraneous and of the quality of the object's response:

At first, the human organism is incapable of bringing about the specific action [i.e., getting rid, for the time being, of the release of $Q\dot\eta$ in the interior of the body]. It takes place by *extraneous help*, when the attention of an experienced person is drawn to the child's state. . . . In this way this path of discharge acquires a secondary function of the highest importance, that of *communication*. (Freud, 1950a, p. 318)

The hypothesis of somato–psychical integration, thanks to the quality of response from the human psychical environment in those early days, is already present in what Freud says in that extract, and it is linked to the idea of prematuration. In those early phases, we could think of the human organism as being "on hold", "expecting" a certain number of sufficiently specific responses; the quality of soma–psyche growth, still relatively undifferentiated, will depend on this, not only for the future development of mental life but also for the maturative integration of the major biological functions. Probably no experimental protocol will ever be able to prove, to a sufficiently detailed and dependable degree, the validity of these hypotheses. None the less, recent advances in immunobiology tend to lend support to that way of thinking, although we may have to be as cautious as Gabriel Gachelin with respect to hasty analogies and the uncalled-for use of metaphors. The idea of somato–psychical integration seems to me to be coherent with the definition of drives as "a measure of the demand made upon the mind for work in consequence of its

connection with the body" (Freud, 1915c, p. 122). Advances in immunology lead to a smaller and smaller gap between the central
nervous system and the immune system, to such an extent that we
could now speak in terms of an "immunological brain"[37] and, therefore, approach the question of memory from a different perspective,
the immunological one. That would undoubtedly have fascinated
Freud, offering him a different model of memory traces. It is the
immunologists who speak about the capacity for integration.

> It is clear that the cells of the immune system have on their surface
> very many receptors, including those involved in receiving messages
> originating in the nervous system. Those cells are capable of integra-
> tion, that is, of the quantitative modulation of their function as deter-
> mined by their state of differentiation. Modulations by various
> neuropeptides of the normal physiological activity of lymphocytes
> have been observed *in vitro*, in sufficiently physiological doses for us
> to imagine that these same phenomena exist *in vivo*. (Gachelin, 1995,
> p. 12, translated for this edition)

The bodily memory of early trauma

I shall, for the moment, leave aside these theoretical speculations and
focus on clinical matters, taking as an example the two analyses that
Juliet had. When she first asked me for an appointment, she was
worried because a somatic disorder was endangering the sporting
career that she had so brilliantly started upon. The problems manifested themselves in recurrent bouts, which were of two kinds: very
painful stomach pains and searing attacks of conjunctivitis that made
her eyes puff up to such an extent that she could not open them.
During the three years that her analytical psychotherapy lasted, in a
face-to-face situation, interpretations were basically made along two
axes: on the one hand, unconscious guilt feelings and aggressiveness
towards her mother, reinforced in particular by the fact that her
mother fell seriously ill while Juliet was going through puberty, and,
on the other, bisexuality as expressed in Juliet's dreams and fantasies.
All the signs pointed to a hysterical neurosis, with her somatisations
as conversion-related elements. With regard to her conjunctivitis, this
was interpreted in relation to many fantasies involving the primal
scene. Her stomach pains were linked to fantasies about the maternal

penis and her firm belief that she had a penis in her stomach that was about to grow and become manifest—the pain she felt was a confirmation of this. These representations were replaced by others, more in line with the genital destiny of women, the child of the father taking over from the maternal penis.

The somatic symptoms disappeared completely. After three years, we ended the treatment: Juliet's career was no longer put at risk by her somatisations and she was thinking about having children. Several years went by before I heard anything further from her. Then, one day, she asked for another appointment. She did not look much older, but she had certainly matured. She had continued her sporting career at a very high level and was now a mother. During the three years of her psychotherapy, we had remained in the domain of the "hallucinosis of corporeity" that is the hallmark of conversion hysteria (David, Fain, Marty, & de M'Uzan, 1968). When she came to see me ten years later, the somatic manifestation of her problems was quite different; it had nothing to do with the metaphorical logics of conversion and reconversion based on symbolic transformation. After a training session in preparation for an important competition, done in very difficult conditions of bitter cold with a particularly sadistic coach, Juliet suffered for the first time in her life from rheumatism in her upper and lower limbs, and this very soon became incapacitating. She consulted several rheumatologists, all of whom diagnosed a "system disorder", with a very high sedimentation coefficient and the presence of antigens specific to progressive rheumatic illnesses; the last rheumatologist whom she consulted said that that pathology belonged to the category of autoimmune diseases. As we know, in such diseases, the body, through its immunological defences, does not recognise itself any more and proceeds to attack and to reject itself as if it were a foreign body. Further developments in immunological research have shown that, in fact, a phenomenon known as the suppressor must remain active so as to prevent the immune system from attacking itself as if it were not-itself. "From that perspective, there is therefore no exception to the capacity for recognition of the individual's immune system: the preservation of the integrity of the immunological self is the result of an active process of suppression" (Gachelin, 1985, pp. 73–74, translated for this edition).

It follows that, in autoimmune diseases, the organism's attack on itself might be the result of the lifting of the active process of

suppression. We could perhaps suggest that the absence of a sufficiently adapted psychical response by the infant's early environment
might bring about some weakness in the setting up of these suppres-
sive functions, and that a later traumatic reactivation might inhibit
them and facilitate the development of an autoimmune disease—or
perhaps encourage the "expression" of an antigen that until then had
remained silent. We can see here how, in the course of this brief
description, the question of meaning arises—not in the sense of some
kind of psychologising, but quite clearly in that of the boundaries
within which meaning and "intelligence" can cover a wider area, not
yet psychical, but not without meaning and potential impact on the
psyche. As Gachelin puts it, rather splendidly,

> If we stand back for just a few seconds from the mechanising approach
> inherent in the biologist's research work, that hypothesis (i.e., the
> capacity for integration of different messages by a cell, the modulation
> by various neuropeptides of the normal physiological activity of
> lymphocytes) leads to the need for biologists to make use of a concept
> similar to that of representation or even to that of meaning. (Gachelin,
> 1985, p. 18, translated for this edition)

In principle, the organic phenomenon of the autoimmune process
takes place outside of the psychical apparatus, but that, in itself, does
not imply that it is meaningless or that it does not represent anything.
Yet, that meaning and that representation are not of the same order as
mental representations and meanings. Does that lead to the conclusion that there is no link, no relationship between those phenomena
and mental life? And if some connection does exist, how can we envisage a possible causal relationship between these two sets of phenomena? To summarise the question in probably far too concise a manner:
is there any connection between self-hatred and autoimmune
processes? If there does exist a connection, it is presumably not a
direct link; maintaining the classic distinction between psychical and
somatic makes it difficult to think about that connection other than in
terms of a directly causal relationship. We could indeed turn around
Gachelin's suggestion—"The stakes are high if, as I think, it is a matter
of transposing from the sphere of mental life to that of somatic components" (1995, p. 12, translated for this edition)—and argue that it
might be a question of transposing something from the sphere of
somatics to that of components of mental life. Furthermore, if we get

rid of the question by arguing that there is no connection between them at all and that the psychical and somatic dimensions are domains that not only follow different causalities, but also are completely separate from each other, would we not once again find ourselves in those pre-psychoanalytical days of separation between mind and body? We can try to set up some differences, the first of which would be between the dimension of conversion and that of somatic illness, although there exists a whole area of indetermination between the two, the most stimulating for our thinking. We could try to differentiate between secondary and primary causality. By the term secondary causality, I mean bringing the effects of the somatic illness back into the mind and interpreting them.

In Juliet's case, for example, her articular pain, the restrictions on her movements and her incapacitating symptoms were of course "interpreted" in different ways by her psyche. The intervention of unconscious guilt feelings, the reactivation of an early cruel superego, and the re-experiencing of sadistic maternal imagos full of hate meant that Juliet felt herself being cruelly punished for wanting to have freedom of movement, condemned because of her success, nailed to the ground for having too successfully defied the laws of gravity (of the maternal and paternal psyche), obliged henceforth to live like an elderly invalid, identified with her maternal grandmother who, at the end of her life, was very disabled, caught up once again in the tightly-woven mesh of a parental mental hold on her. This does not mean that we are entitled to take the easy way out and think that somatic illnesses can be explained via a direct cause-and-effect relationship—drawing the conclusion that they are the result or the outcome of unconscious guilt feelings, of maternal imagos, or that being in the grip of some problem situation is enough to explain the onset of a somatic illness. Here, it is not a matter of bodily symptoms that "illustrate" a mental conflict. There is a whole physiological system (in this case, the immune system) which is manifested via a dysfunction that arouses, activates, and triggers a certain number of potentially pathogenic elements (the presence of specific antigens)—but these might well have remained silent indefinitely (here, again, we come across the idea of potentiality, to which we refer also in the psychical domain). The classic idea of susceptibility to disease is important here. Inflammatory, one might say. But what sets on fire those particular conditions? In Juliet's case, it was the context of the traumatic experience of mental coldness and a physical cold spell that combined together. This brings us to the question of primary causality. Does the traumatic experience have a disorganising impact on the mind, and if so, why? As we saw, ten years before, Juliet had been able to metabolise the mental conflicts linked to the trauma, while preserving the fantasy links between her mind and the bodily expression of her psychological conflicts. In this more recent situation, I had the feeling, as I listened to Juliet, that "something had given way", "something had become unhinged"—a fairly global impression that is given concrete expression in those two verbal metaphors, but it may also be "contaminated" by theoretical representations. On the one hand, we have a type of mental functioning that enables integration between psyche and soma to be maintained, a psychical "meshing" that holds together representations and biological coherence; one of the theoretical representations of this "holding together" is, of course, Eros. On the other hand, we have a disunity, unbinding (here, it is the figure of Thanatos that comes to mind), although we could also think in terms of a kind of "de-qualification" of the drives that can no longer be defined as the outcome of the work imposed on the mind because of its link to the bodily element. Part of that corporeal dimension, thus, lies beyond psychical "jurisdiction" (psychical metabolism) and acts on its own behalf, outside of any zone of influence. There is in that the model of de-cathexis, of disunity, of separation with respect to what until then had managed to coexist. We could say that this soma that unhinges *itself* had been in a kind of intimate relationship with the psyche. In an attempt to find some analogy, I would say that this soma "remembers" its union with the psyche and that the shadow of the psyche is still falling on it.

Beside this model of de-cathexis and disunity, we must make room for the hypothesis of another kind of phenomenon that might come more from the model of non-cathexis and non-integration rather than disintegration. In my view, this second hypothesis is impossible to understand unless we refer to Winnicott's idea of early failures in the environment, failures which are more or less important, and which entail more or less widespread defects in psyche–soma integration. Thus, some somatic "zones" evade any psychical cathexis or mentalizing. These somatic enclaves remain alien to psychical life. They are somatic elements that, outside of any psychical link, may function as primitive elements of communication with the primary bodily environment. They are not representational, but they can be triggered into a somatic discharge that produces a meaningful bodily sensation. They are "expecting" a psychical response that might enable integration. This implies that "something" in the human organism is waiting for a psychical response of a particular kind, one that will help the organism's somato–psychical potentialities to develop fully.

Primitive agony and defects in psyche–soma integration

Juliet resumed her analysis, and fairly quickly we moved towards three sessions per week with her lying on the couch. She continued to have regular consultations on the somatic level with the same doctor; there was no change in her medication other than a gradual reduction in the prescribed doses. She had biological tests on a regular basis, every three months, more or less. When she told me about these, I was, therefore, able to draw a comparison between the fluctuations in her mental productions, the quality of my listening to her, and the biological data. One striking element was that every improvement— sometimes spectacular and "incomprehensible", according to her doctor—corresponded to phases in her psychoanalytical treatment in which I noticed a degree of processing that made use of various highly productive psychical elements: dreams, reverie, fantasies, the intensification of the positive transference making it possible to formulate transference interpretations and share the affects aroused; what was most difficult—and relatively rare in her analysis—was bringing the negative transference into play. On the other hand, the phases devoid of any affects, with nightmares, de-cathexis by both of us of the analytical process, loss of quality in her free associations, and the aridity of my attempts at listening to her always corresponded to an aggravation in the results of her biological tests. What a pity that the conditions in which psychoanalysis is carried out do not make for a more objective and more refined assessment when we compare these different parameters. What a pity for psychoanalytical research, and also for our scientific dialogue with biologists.

Here is one of Juliet's dreams, which may give a clearer picture of the process of somato–psychical reintegration as it can occur thanks to the dream-work processing that is part of the psychoanalytical process.

From a window in the building opposite, she sees a little girl fall—she had slipped while she was on the sloping roof of the pantry.[38] Then a cat falls down. Then another little girl. Juliet begins to feel anxious; she calls the emergency ambulance service and the fire brigade. The first little girl is not to be found anywhere.

Her free associations draw the following picture: anxiety about falling, fear of sliding, desperate attempt to hold on. That makes her think of two conflicting tendencies: hold on/let go; this, in turn, leads her to think about the intense fear of losing herself and about a reaction consisting in holding on, in containing herself. Then she thinks about what she feels in her joints when she is having attacks of rheumatism: it is like an infinity of little links, little ropes, which, by tightening up and retracting around her joints, grab hold of them and immobilise them.

She associates the pantry to a stomach sticking out. She thinks of a pregnant woman, then what comes into her mind are images of a catastrophic birth: nobody is there to catch or to carry the baby, who falls down.

In that dream, there is a representation of a catastrophe in which the main character is in an endless fall (what Winnicott called "primitive agony"), with the risk of losing his/her entire being. That fall into a void, which is associated with a birth in which nobody is there to welcome the baby, is prevented thanks to a movement of the whole person and the whole body in an attempt to hold back. In the hypothesis of a primitive bodily ego, this would amount to a primary defence via a physical response in an attempt to deal with the absence of any holding. It could also be the case that, secondarily, that primary defence is "enhanced" by representations specific to the anal phase, particularly in a family in which control and anality dominate their psychical exchanges.

We could perhaps now proceed to the following aetiological representation: the traumatic moment (cold, sadism) has awakened the bodily memory of an early catastrophe experienced at that time in terms of primitive agony. Through regression, the primitive defence is again called upon, over-determined by anality in its relation to the muscle structure. Tenseness and contraction lead to immobilisation, which prevents the person from falling endlessly. The inflammatory reaction could, therefore, be seen as a consequence, localised and mechanical, of that contraction.

It is obvious that that explanation, even though it correctly describes some aspects of the phenomenon, leaves aside the most difficult
part: the inflammation is not localised—if that were the case, there
would be no increase in the sedimentation coefficient or a significantly
higher level of a specific antigen. Here, we are dealing with the
reaction of a system in its entirety. Could we then say, with the already
tested Freudian model in mind, that the morbid attack is paradoxically an attempt at recovery?

In order to clarify that hypothesis, it was necessary to wait until
some new elements made their way into the analysis. In one particularly dramatic phase, when her closest friend was dying of a rare
autoimmune disease and needed continuous artificial respiration,
Juliet had a very harrowing dream, as she had done before: she found
herself trapped between planks of wood that hemmed her in and
immobilised her; she had a terrible feeling of coldness. In attempting
to associate to this dream, she remembered something that had happened when she was very young, something that her parents had told
her about: when she was just six months old, she was rushed to hospital and placed in a sterile atmosphere. Her parents were not allowed
to touch her—all they could do, during their visits, was to look at her
from behind a glass wall. That early traumatic situation lasted for one
month. A situation of terrible infantile distress, through the sudden
loss of everything to do with her familiar human environment, accompanied by a sensorial loss—olfactive, tactile, visual, and auditory—
with regard to the maternal presence and the stream of words that are
part of holding, thrust into a non-human environment, with sensory
deprivation (the coldness), in which she was no longer "held" but
manipulated and where there was no longer any feeling of continuity
of being. Just as in her dream, "the first little girl" was lost, nowhere
to be found.

Juliet did not appear to have recourse to autistic defences in order
to survive that trauma of the lengthy breakdown in her feeling of
continuity of being. She managed to structure things more in a
neurotic manner: there was no instrumental thinking or residues of
autistic withdrawal. The relationship between autistic defence and
immunological defence is, nevertheless, a question that arises from
both the clinical and the theoretical point of view. In child psychiatry,
we often observe that children with autism do not suffer from infec-
tious diseases, although they tend to lose part of that immunity as

they gradually emerge from autism and set up psychical defensive modalities that are less substantial. Somatisation may occur during their treatment in patients who present marked autistic features as they begin to abandon their autistic defences. For example, one patient, after several years of psychotherapy, felt that his relationships with other people, his sensitivity, his sensoriality, and his ability to experience emotions were coming to life, to the point where that sensitivity became a hyperaesthesia of contact accompanied by a pathological change in his perception of hot and cold; further tests revealed the initial signs of multiple sclerosis, the imaging of which was practically undetectable, which fortunately remained quiescent. We could, of course, argue that there is no relation at all between these two kinds of phenomenon, and, fortunately enough, revealing them experimentally is impossible. Nevertheless, repeated observations of such coincidences can only encourage us to bring together and compare seemingly similar data.

As everybody agrees, there is, between six and eight months, a very important phase of structuring for future mental life, the phase that Melanie Klein called depressive. That is the time when the infant, in the presence of an unknown face, turns his/her head and eyes away. We know also that children with autism turn away from their mother's face, and that they are remarkably well protected against all kinds of diseases and infections, an immunity that they tend to lose as they begin to emerge from their autistic state. The autistic defence would appear to lie on the frontier between a psychical defence and a somatic, immunological one. We can also—quite rightly, in my view—draw a parallel (without putting them in the same dimension of reality) between the paradoxical behaviour of the infant with autism who turns away from the mother's face as if it were that of a stranger, and the autoimmune reaction of the organism that treats its own body as if it were a foreign body. Perhaps, here, it would be apposite to mention the fact that, during her pregnancy, the mother and the foetus are, in principle, protected against any immunological response of rejection with regard to that foreign body, the foetus.

If an autoimmune response can be triggered as a result of trauma that repeats the threat of annihilation through primitive agony, and if that response is, paradoxically, an attempt at recovery, the reason might be that, in such a situation, the body has turned into a threatening stranger and then, through psyche–soma disintegration, has once again become an external space. The defence is no longer psychical but somatic, and aims at the rejection of all or part of the body by the organism itself. There is, perhaps, here a somatic version of the model of the pictogram of auto-engendering described by Piera Aulagnier as constitutive of the primal process of the psyche, with the autoimmune response becoming for the somatic dimension what the pictogram of rejection is for its psychical counterpart.[39]

However speculative these hypotheses, I think it important to emphasise the fact that the traumatic impact of these early situations—as was the case with Juliet—derives, to a great extent, from the sudden loss of a human psychical response. This loss reinforces in the *infans* the expectation of an awakening of the potentialities for mental organisation and the construction of a mental space. This does not exclude the idea of a deferred retroactive effect, the *après-coup*, because the disorganising impact of trauma depends on the quality of psychical construction both in the individual concerned and in the environment. The question arises, too, of the importance of any possible verbal processing: in Juliet's case, the traumatic event occurred before the acquisition of speech, and this determines the type of modalities of figuration to which the *infans* can have recourse in order to survive. If that mental nourishing of the ego, necessary for the development of the early primitive ego—the bodily ego, as Freud put it—is lacking, the fragile psyche of the early stages of life might turn towards the organism in order to obtain some "response", just as previously it could make use of the human psychical environment.

It might well be that the earliest modalities of mental life take support from certain forms of the silent "intelligence" of biological life. Not by simply copying them, but by taking support from them, using them as a model, in order to go beyond them—by bringing about a change in status, in a way unknown to us, by becoming mental, thereby implementing the idea of the anaclisis of the sexual drives with respect to those of self-preservation. In their comments on what Freud said of the bodily ego in *The Ego and the Id* (1923b), Laplanche and Pontalis write (1973, p. 147), "Such statements suggest that we search for the basis of the agency of the ego in an actual psychical operation consisting in the 'projection' of the organism into the psyche".

What happens if the psychical operation of differentiation of a psychical agency, consisting in the projection of the organism outside of itself, is not done properly?

When her friend died, that very night Juliet dreamt that she was lifting him up from behind by holding his arms and trying as hard as she could to pull him in the opposite direction from where he was being drawn.

The dream was so clear that it was easy to comment on it; I simply maintained an approving silence. One week later, Juliet was very much out of breath and anxious when she arrived for her session. In the space of a few days, she had had many fits of choking and breath-lessness—her general practitioner was already thinking in terms of asthma attacks. I did not for one moment believe in the asthma hypothesis; we were able to analyse how Juliet held on to her friend not simply with all her psychical strength but also with all the bodily strength she could muster, to the point of having spasms in her bronchioles functioning as sphincters. Thus, we went through, in the reverse direction, the limits of conversion somatisation by means of a psychical movement of secondary identification. Holding on to her friend, being like him, merging into him. She had first met him at an international sports event where comparisons had been drawn between them to the effect that, in their particular sport, they were the feminine and masculine versions of the same competitor. They were a pair of opposites brought together to such a degree of complementar-ity that they were united as if they made up a single body, like the bringing together of the two exiled parts of an androgyne, or the two separated halves of a *sumbolôn*. When death took from her a loved object, it tore from her at the same time a part of herself, that other half, of the opposite sex, which guaranteed her narcissistic complete-ness: bisexual wholeness, perhaps, given the lack of psychical inte-gration of bisexuality, but at least we were now in an environment in which separation and mourning again became thinkable and no longer forced her, when not representable, to separate from herself and from her own body.

A delusion of corporeity

I shall now discuss the case of a patient, "Damien", who also presented a major somatic pathology. I shall restrict myself to those aspects of his treatment that will enable me to evoke the very partic-ular states of mind which, from time to time, occur in the analyst and which can contribute to producing some degree of psychical effectiveness in the treatment. Damien brought me into some mental states that I would call "borderline"; they were, nevertheless, necessary if any processing of what was taking place was to be carried out. Some borderline psychotic patients never stop trying to infuriate the analyst by repeatedly attacking his/her life narcissism in such a way that the analyst may be brought to the point of enactments that amount to retaliation; Damien put me into a kind of trance, almost a state of lethargy, which, in my view, was very similar to hypnosis. What I find interesting also, in this case, is to explore how and why hypnosis may once again emerge in the analytical situation—what are we to think of that and what can we make of it? In my opinion, hypnosis, when it ventures back into the practice and the experience of psychoanalysis, does not have the same meaning or the same function as in Charcot's day or when Freud was beginning his work, a whole century ago. Now it is more a question of the hypnotic impact that the analytical situation and the rules that govern it might, at times, have, this time on the analyst. The perspective is, thus, reversed. It is now quite ordinary, following André Green, to think of dreams and dream-work as the model for the work of analysis; the hypnotic dimension reinforces, via *hupnos* (sleep), the bodily aspect of the process during the session. In such a context, we ought perhaps to turn Freud's statement round and say that sleep, in its bodily aspect, is the guardian of dreams—a reparatory sleep.

Damien was in his twenties when he asked me for an appointment. He had a degree in engineering, was in a situation of intense emotional isolation, and spoke in a monotonous voice, with no hint of emotion and poor in content. His voice was muffled because of congestion—permanent and, he said, allergic—in his ears, nose, and throat; ever since he was a child, he had suffered from eczema. He was prone to what he called "fits", which occurred quite frequently, particularly when he was on his own. These would start off with itching sensations that initially he would try to ignore, then he would let himself go and scratch as though in a frenzy. He would also smack himself in the face, great slaps with both hands until his face became puffed up. These fits, these attacks, were often accompanied by visions—which, at my request, but with a great deal of difficulty, he described—abstract shapes, with a kind of special luminosity, and white.

That multiform symptomatology took up most of what Damien had to say; the periodic return of those fits overwhelmed him. The overall picture was one of somatic acting combined with enactment. The plethora of symptoms constituted a heterogeneous intersection, at the frontiers of several morbid potentialities, the whole appearing as an invention playing the part, in his psychical economy, of an identificatory compromise functioning as a stabiliser and ultimate barrier. The psychical elements at work in all of this were often very difficult to grasp and to draw into the open.

Scratching was experienced as an orgiastic frenzy, which, at face value, could pass as an erotic equivalent. The compulsive aspect of the struggle against the temptation to scratch himself was indicative of a ferocious fight with a cruel superego; the moment when he let it all go and began to scratch himself was experienced as a transgressive release tinted with guilt feelings. The issue was that of resisting something that was irresistible, of playing with barely describable sensations, and of being continuously at the point where things would split apart; there was also an element of turning activity into passivity. The struggle against itching was the active phase; the letting-himself-go that followed was passive, although the fingers that were scratching were tremendously active. The interplay of excitation, satisfaction, and non-satisfaction was a subtle one. During the struggle phase, his hand would touch his skin lightly, in an attempt at relief but, at the same time, in order to provoke an increase in the almost painful internal tension that was felt as a sensation in the thickness of the dermis, a sensation that lay on the border between pleasant quivering and painful tension. While he was scratching himself, a kind of extremist madness seized hold of him: scratching gave him a great deal of pleasure, but that pleasure did not bring about any discharge—on the contrary, it only reinforced the itching and the wish to calm it down. Damien was drawn more and more into the fury of going further, further and further, in his mad desire to reach something that constantly kept out of reach, something that had to be looked for inside himself by getting through the barrier of the skin. He wanted to break through the surface in order to reach something inside. The sexual dimension was, of course, very much to the fore here—a masturbatory equivalent with no orgasmic outcome was what immediately came to mind, with an enacted representation of foreplay and coitus. Nevertheless, it is the dimension of attack that was foremost in the manifestation of drive-related activity, as if the psyche and body were deprived of any protective shield against excitation that could modulate the attack of the drives, manifested in a savage, uncontrolled, anarchic, and chaotic way.

The blows that Damien gave himself were a later addition to these fits; my impression was that they were a self-soothing technique,[40] an attempt to deal with the impossibility of calling upon the resources of masochism in order to bind together the aggressive and sexual components. Those slaps may have represented a punishment, but they had no effective processing attached to them, thus bearing witness to the failure of any attempt at setting up a fantasy scenario. I think that they were an attempt at constructing a kind of fixation point for the unbound and unbinding excitation involving pain, a rallying point towards which could be drawn a structuring narcissistic cathexis that could take it as its focal point.

Those fits occurred in an atmosphere that Damien described as bizarre; it made me think of the atmosphere of strangeness of the aura that precedes another kind of fit—an attack of epilepsy. The visions that he described were similar to hallucinations of elementary shapes, more organic-looking than geometrical; he twice gave me drawings of these so that I might have a better picture of them (see Figure 1). Those

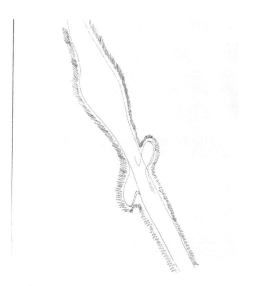

Figure 1.   Damien's drawing of the shape of his "visions".

shapes were surrounded by a halo, which, in the way it was drawn, reminded me of the cilia in some protozoans. Could these have been a hallucinatory equivalent of what Frances Tustin called autistic shapes?

It is not difficult to imagine how hard it was to tolerate a face-to-face setting three times per week with someone who was locked into that kind of self-persecutory system, concentrated in the sensations of the surface of his body which constituted, like the shirt of Nessus, a straitjacket of painful excitation. Neither is it hard to imagine the moments of despair and despondency that Damien experienced when faced with his inability to break free of that corporeal madness and with my inability to offer him any relief that would be other than short-lived. With respect to conversion hysteria, I spoke of the "hallucinosis of corporeity"; here we could perhaps think in terms of a "delusion of corporeity" in which a persecutory form of madness appears to have become encysted in bodily sensations. That corporeal madness seemed to protect Damien from a psychotic form of hypochondriasis and from the psychical structuring of a delusional and persecutory system. These ideas find an echo in the developments that Winnicott described in his book *Human Nature*, in which he says that it is quite usual to hear a discussion of

> the psychology of a psycho-somatic disorder with no mention of the positive value to the patient of the anchoring of some aspect of the psyche to some part of the body. There is psychotic anxiety underlying psychosomatic disorder even although in many cases at more superficial levels there can be clearly shown to be hypochondriacal or neurotic factors. (1988, p. 123)

As the analysis progressed, my impression was that those fits often occurred in situations that ought to have mobilised representations to do with separation and the mental pain resulting from the need to think about it (consciously or unconsciously). Instead of that, it was a fit of itching that arrived on the scene. Those situations could involve either an intolerable excess of presence or the sudden interruption of a pleasant relationship—for example, a long and pleasant phone conversation with an attractive woman. My representations of the phenomenon were, depending on the circumstances, either a kind of outburst of bodily anger, similar to the instinctive skin changes that occur in some animals when they want to keep an enemy at a distance, or images of coming unstuck and being torn from the surface of the skin, thereby re-creating, in the form of quasi-hallucinatory tactile sensations, the illusion or the ghost of a lost contact. Piera Aulagnier's clinical and theoretical remarks come to mind here; Frances Tustin, in fact, found them interesting, too, so there may well have been a certain coming-together of minds in exploring those phenomena.

> Faced with the sudden emergence of an affect, which steers clear of the conditions that would make it thinkable as well as of those that would allow it to be fantasized, and confronted with the absence of any connection to primary and secondary processes, the psyche can avoid its own total nothingness, i.e. the loss of any attribute of existence, only by hallucinating, not an object but a *sensory perception*; it will hallucinate the complementary object of an erotogenic zone—or, more precisely, a substitute-object that exists only through its power of excitability. (Aulagnier 1986, p. 399, translated for this edition)

I must make it clear that, in Damien's case—a psychosomatic illness, not a clear-cut psychosis—it was not a matter of a hallucinatory sensory perception, but of cutaneous sensations that did have some hallucinatory valency. They hemmed in the psychotic potentiality and absorbed it, thus preventing it from unfolding; also, by hemming it in like that, they contained it and kept it in reserve, ready, if need be, to let it open up if the defensive function, with its fixating and stabilising potential, of that alliance between hallucinatory feeling and pain were no longer enough.

At this point it would be a good idea to take another look at what Freud said about unconscious and conscious sensations in *The Ego and the Id* (1923b). Freud insists on the need to differentiate between unconscious representations and unconscious feelings, which are often wrongly mistaken for each other:

> We then come to speak, in a condensed and not entirely correct manner, of 'unconscious feelings', keeping up an analogy with unconscious ideas which is not altogether justifiable. Actually the difference is that, whereas with *Ucs. ideas* connecting links must be created before they can be brought into the Cs., with *feelings*, which are themselves transmitted directly, this does not occur. In other words: the distinction between Cs. and Pcs. has no meaning where feelings are

concerned; the *Pcs.* here drops out – and feelings are either conscious or unconscious. Even when they are attached to word-presentations, their becoming conscious is not due to that circumstance, but they become so directly. (Freud, 1923b, pp. 22–23)

With respect to the skin as the most appropriate interface for bodily figuration, we see it taking over from the protective shield against excitation and from the preconscious system in the topographical model, and from the bodily ego as the projection of a surface in the structural model.[41] With regard to the modalities of internal perception, it would be interesting to explore the differences—formal, in particular—between feeling, affect, and sentiment. Melanie Klein's followers developed the concept of memories in feeling, and what Bion tried to describe in terms of beta-elements and ideograms is in the same vein.

Regression, hypnoid states, reparatory sleep

I shall now report some sequences from Damien's sessions. On one particular day, as was his usual habit, he reeled off a monotonous list of cutaneous symptoms and the feeling of desperation that accompanied them. I found myself in a somewhat vague state, trying not to let myself be overcome by an impression of helplessness and discouragement that Damien was unconsciously trying to induce in me. I let things go. The image that then came into my mind was that of automatic piloting, yet I was not in the grip of thoughts that aimed to "pull me out" of the session. It was more a kind of numbness. All of a sudden, something like a breaking apart happened inside me, and I was startled. At the same time, I heard the words: "It'll end up being the death of me". I experienced a powerful affect that gave me a painful sense of a situation that had no clear representation, while at the same time there came into my mind the image of Damien's father collapsing slowly between two cars, an image that I identified as taken from a dream that Damien had reported some considerable time before—one of his very few dreams, if not the only one. Almost without taking the time to think, I said, "It's your father who is pronouncing those words, he's the one who's saying 'it'll end up being the death of me'. Why does he say that?" There followed a silence during which

I could see that Damien was in the grip of a very intense emotion. After a while, his eyes filled with tears, then he began to cry uncontrollably: "I've just remembered something, I was told about it, but I have a vague memory of it, too. When I was 2½ or three years old, I became dehydrated. My mother, who is always very much in control of herself, did not want to worry too much, and our family doctor thought that it wouldn't be necessary to have me taken to hospital. But my health suddenly deteriorated, and when they asked him to come back, I was, it seemed, in a very bad way indeed. They phoned the emergency medical service. My father was terribly upset because they said to my parents that I might not survive the journey to the hospital. He wanted to come in the ambulance with me, but they said no. He got into his car with the idea of following the ambulance, but he didn't manage to do that because it was being driven so fast that he lost sight of it." Damien again began to cry. "I've never given a thought to what my father might have felt."

"What your father felt and was thinking as he saw the ambulance going out of sight, without knowing if he'd ever see you alive again— 'it'll end up being the death of me'; but maybe it has also something to do with what *you* were feeling and going through at that time, and then later, when you were in intensive care." Much later, it became possible for Damien to have some representation of his mother's ambivalence and to wonder about the unconscious death wishes that his mother might have had: "In fact, by insisting on not wanting to worry too much, she nearly let me die."

After that session, Damien and his father had lunch together. That, in itself, was quite an event, because his father had always stayed in the background, overshadowed by Damien's mother, a woman stiffened by her narcissistic wounds who was determined to keep the whole family under her draconian control, using each of her children to make good the flaws in a very high ideal.[42] While they were having lunch, Damien was bold enough to mention to his father that dramatic event from early childhood; his father told him of the dreadful pain he had felt when he was not allowed to accompany his son in the ambulance, thinking that he was going to die. As they were talking about it, Damien's father began to cry. Damien was astonished by that storm of affects, accustomed as he was to knowing how to behave in their family, under the strict leadership of his mother, who kept under control not only her own feelings but also those of the people near and dear to her. In addition to the liberating effect of sharing those intense feelings, helping him to process them, Damien began to remember more details about certain bodily sensations that followed on from his dehydration and also those that resulted from the invasive procedures that were necessary for reanimating him. He had often told me about the strange feelings he had in his throat, pharynx, and nasal fossae; sometimes, he seemed to bring them about voluntarily and play around with them, just as the children with autism described by Frances Tustin played with autistic sensation-shapes. Those sensations were, for Damien, like shapes that filled up cavities, slipped along the mucous membranes, filled, blocked. All of this lay somewhere between unpleasant and pleasant, but it was a burden on him. All of these descriptions that I am giving in the space of a few lines were the fruit of a slow and patient attempt to put words to those feelings, which I strongly encouraged Damien to do, with the impression of having won a tiny little victory over organic opacity. Damien would play around in his imagination with the idea of being able physically to seize hold of one of those shapes, to start pulling on it, to feel that it was moving, to keep on pulling and pulling until it all came out, and then he would feel, in his imagination, the joy of deliverance, of relief, of freedom.

From that point on, in a later stage of his psychoanalytical therapy, Damien had, during his sessions, phases of what we could also call "fits"; these seemed, from a semiological point of view, to resemble states of depersonalisation. To the abstract shapes and sensations were added images and thoughts, in a dynamic movement that "ravished" him—in the literal as well as metaphorical sense of the word. These "fits" during the sessions usually began with a feeling that something was changing in his experience of his body, with the sensation that his legs were becoming lighter, soon followed by his whole body. Gradually, Damien felt himself to be getting lighter and lighter, he was floating, he had the impression that he was levitating. With a mixture of apprehension and delight, he played around with holding back and letting himself go, letting himself feel things instead of repressing and suppressing them. Once he had reached a certain state, he would no longer want to move or even to speak in case that might bring an end to that very moving and fascinating experience. He would remain silent, alone but in my presence, "savouring", visiting, and exploring everything that was taking place inside him; afterwards, he would tell me that it was so rich, intense, varied, and rapid that no words would ever be able to give an account of what was sweeping through him in images and in thoughts.

In my view, this kind of occurrence during a session is deeply conducive to some form of processing. This might not be the case were they to occur outside of the context and process of analytical treatment (which, in any case, facilitates their occurrence), without the presence of the analyst during the session and the analyst's mental work that accompanies them. In that context, I see such phenomena moving in the direction of the infant's capacity to be alone in the presence of his/her mother, rather than as some kind of psychotic withdrawal that urgently demands an interpretation in terms of the spoken representation of which Aulagnier writes with respect to schizophrenic patients (which, anyway, was not the case with Damien) in her paper "Withdrawal into hallucination":

> A complete silence falls, the look on his face changes, becomes fixed, and there is often the impression of a change in the rhythm of his breathing. . . . I cannot give a better description of that experience than this: a feeling of being struck by a verdict of non-existence. . . . To explain a little more what I mean by a verdict of non-existence, a word used by Orwell comes into my mind: we turn into an un-person, . . . we become an object that cannot be perceived. (Aulagnier, 1986, p. 396, translated for this edition)

Damien was not that kind of patient, but, all the same . . . it could be surmised that he had experienced, in that dramatic moment when he was torn away in a life-threatening situation and thrust into a foreign world, that of the hospital, something similar to what, in Aulagnier's view, happens to those schizophrenic patients during a session:

> The subject no longer exists, he cannot exist any longer, he has never existed other than as that perceiving function (auditory, olfactory, proprioceptive) inextricably linked to what is perceived: the subject is that noise, that smell, that feeling and he is at the same time that fragment and only that fragment of the sensory body mobilised and stimulated by what is perceived. (Aulagnier, 1986, p. 396, translated for this edition)

I think also that this sudden separation suddenly confronted him with the lack of any introjection of a warm and caring maternal presence that could take care of him in the absence of the real object. It seems that the mother figure had to be an addictive object, leaving very little space for symbolising her absence. In what occurred with Damien during his sessions, there was, to my mind, no mental immobilisation but quite the contrary—a relaunching of the psyche–soma, a terrific remobilisation through re-binding, which, however, only took effect and became meaningful within the containing envelope of the analyst's capacity for reverie, which manifested itself first and foremost through the presence of a reflective attitude, and also via an attentive silence or a dreamlike comment, depending on the precise moment. I often had the feeling, during those phases, that we were thrust into an atmosphere of hypnosis, or, at any rate, into what I would think of as the modifications in wakeful consciousness brought about by a hypnotic trance, something of which I have no direct experience. This was particularly the case in the course of one such phase when Damien felt that he was being drawn very far away and kept repeating, "I don't know what's happening to me, I'm frightened, I'm afraid to let myself go, where will it all end? I feel I'm getting close to something, it's unbelievable, it's there, just next to me, I can almost touch it, but I'm not going to do so, I'm too scared." Then, suddenly, he said that he felt something impossible to describe, something in his stomach; then he whispered, "I'm hungry, I'm thirsty, I'm so thirsty, I've been thirsty for so long, it's a thirst from so long ago . . .".

After that session, Damien began to fall asleep while travelling by train to his sessions. He said that that sleep—quite short and not particularly deep—made him feel very relaxed, with a feeling of having rested and recovered. He described something like "a round and soft shape touching [his] mouth and [his] face"; he then had the impression that he was drinking some nourishing liquid. It took him a long time before he was able to think that these dream-like sensations had perhaps something to do with the memory of a happy and enjoyable breast-feeding.

CHAPTER FOURTEEN

Pain: a therapeutics of survival?
Some elements for further thought

"The attributes of life were at some time evoked in inanimate matter by the action of a force of whose nature we can form no conception"

(Freud, 1920g, p. 28)

"[We] know nothing of the nature of the excitatory process that takes place in the elements of the psychical systems"

(Freud, 1920g, pp. 30–31)

Bob Flanagan's *Sick* is a film that is only just tolerable, because it lays bare in all of its rawness a man's mental and physical distress and the frontiers of experience to which his unremitting desire for survival leads him. In the darkness of the cinema, we hear first of all the noise made by someone who has difficulty breathing, then coughing fits. Then we see the tormented face of an adult male sucking on a baby's bottle. Next, that male is subjected to various attempts at force-feeding that suffocate him, a cream tart is thrown at his face, he is slapped several times, then subjected to several attempts to strangle him. These images follow one another very quickly, in a syncopated rhythm, which only adds to their traumatic character. Later, we learn that the baby's bottle was full of piss. That elderly baby with a face like a sad clown is Bob Flanagan. Since birth he has suffered from an incurable disorder: cystic fibrosis. The life expectancy of those who suffer from that illness is rarely more than twenty-five years; Flanagan, thanks to an unremitting struggle, managed to live until he was forty-three, by transforming his body into an object of physical ill-treatment and a work of art.

The transformational use of masochism

At the same time as he was undergoing medical treatment, he invented and inflicted upon himself a treatment by pain in order to try to keep himself alive. He succeeded also in finding a woman who agreed to subject him tirelessly to that pain in a display of hatred that controlled and kept a tight hold on any expression of love. What began as a chance encounter in which that masochistic man revealed the latent sadistic tendencies of a woman and used her as a means to an end, a torturer devoted to him and always available for him, developed into a strange story of love in which the avowal of the most naked kind of love and the disavowal of hate became the hallmark of the defeat of survival and the acceptance of death.

When he meets Sheree, Bob is twenty-eight years old. He has reached an age at which, according to medical science, he ought to be dead. His mother tells of how, as a little baby, the eldest of her five children, he showed signs of suffering that she could not understand. It was when he was eighteen months old that the paediatricians concluded that he was suffering from cystic fibrosis. After his early experiences of suffering—incomprehensible, unthinkable, unacceptable, and impossible to process—he had to put up with medical "ill-treatments", and many of them, repeated, interminable, and irrevocable. Bob went on growing, with intermittent stays in hospital and despite the deaths, in infancy, of two of his younger sisters, who also suffered from cystic fibrosis. He developed into a serious-minded little boy, shy, sensitive, and very intelligent. In 1962, he appeared on a television show (*The Steven Allen Show*), his hair neatly combed and wearing his Sunday best, where he tried to sell a work of art that he himself had produced. When the host asked him what he wanted to be when he grew up, he replied, "I'll be a doctor." His mother explained that he was a very well behaved boy, and his brother said that Bob was his "moral cop", always ready to criticise and sermonise him because of his masturbating.

Bob explains that behind that façade of the nice little boy who had no faults there lay a child, then an adolescent, who very early on indulged in strange erotic rituals with a hint of masochism about them. For example, he liked to spend whole nights lying naked on his bed, exposed to the freezing cold wind blowing through his bedroom window that he had opened wide. Not long after this, in addition to that exciting exposure to bad weather, he began to spread glue all over his body. When he speaks about that, he remembers the sweat test[43] in the course of which doctors enclosed him, naked, in a plastic bag. Then he discovered the delight of being tied up and, again during the night, he spent hours with his wrists tied together, very high up on the doorframe. He adds, with a laugh, that his parents were puzzled by the wearing away of the wood on that part of the doorframe. Then he began to flog himself with a nail-studded belt. Still laughing, he describes how his blood was scattered all over the bathroom walls and how he had to clean it all up in a hurry when his brother hammered impatiently on the door, wondering what on earth he was doing.

His mother blames herself for not having realised any of this: "Where was I all that time, where was I?" "We were a very closely-knit family," says Bob's father. His mother adds, "I think he began to hate that body of his, which was making him suffer so much." The correctness of that interpretation made by his mother finds a chilling echo in Sheree's comment, according to which a talented sadistic mistress must have motherly skills.

An image emerges from that series of video pictures showing scenes of sadomasochistic scenarios in which the body is being more and more seriously injured and tortured—that of the figure of a sadistic stand-in for maternal care. When we leave the close-up shots, in which we see tortured flesh, and get a more overall picture, in which the bodies of both protagonists can be seen in their entirety, we often have the illusion of a mother taking care of her baby or of a nurse treating a patient.

That other scene, in which maternal care is depicted in the form of hate and persecution, is an externalised and enacted representation of a persecutor–persecuted relationship between body (the illness) and mind. In that way of presenting it, the soma–psyche relationship, experienced early in life in the persecutory dimension of pain—a senseless form of pain, the intensity and potential eruption of which could not be controlled—is structured in terms of a persecutory relationship outside of the psyche and controlled by it. It is no longer the mind that is the *locus* of senseless pain or the object of persecutory hate—the body is the object of this.

One of the questions that we might ask ourselves concerning Bob Flanagan's mental development has to do with the early organisation of the superego and the maternal imago. A great deal of the suffering experienced by the early ego because of his illness was impossible to process by means of maternal reverie (cf. what Bob's mother said about her failure to understand what was causing him to suffer); to put it in Piera Aulagnier's terms, it lay beyond the scope of the word-bearer's interpreting and identifying function. The cause of all that suffering and of the lack of any adequate response to soothe it can be attributed by the suffering *infans*, in an attempt to find some meaningful causality, only to the primary object, the imago representation of which must, therefore, be built up as persecutory. In that semiology, in which the desperate search for an inflow of multiple excitations is uppermost, the accent is put on the dimension of psychical economy. As always, we must beware of any conception that might reify in terms of a "purely" quantitative dimension. As de M'Uzan puts it in "A case of masochistic perversion" (de M'Uzan, 1973, p. 465): "In other words, quantity is transmuted into quality, and the pure economics of instinctual energies move into the sphere of qualitative significance". Any excess of excitation is attributed and "bound" to the object; the increase in primary destructive aggressiveness towards the object, the increase in hate for the object and its repression can only lead to the construction of an early form of the superego that is particularly ferocious.

Faced with the turmoil of pain and hate impossible to process, the individual may find different structural ways out: the neurotic solution, with the reaction formations of an obsessional structure, or the psychotic solution either of a melancholic or of a delusional and persecutory type. It would seem that, very early on, Bob Flanagan "chose" the masochistic solution, a feminine erotogenic masochism that went all the way to the psychotic end of self-destruction through self-mutilation.

It could, perhaps, be said, all the same, that in this particular case, the masochistic solution, in its therapeutic dimension, remained incomplete; given the presence within him of a fatal illness, it remained the province of masturbatory fantasy activity accompanied from time to time by self-inflicted enactments. For that solution to fulfil its anti-lethal function, that is, of survival, Bob Flanagan had to meet, in reality, a female partner who would be equal to his fantasies and to the challenge he issued. The encounter between Bob and Sheree revealed and actualised two psychical potentialities, thereby sealing the fate of each of them.

Some remarkable images show Sheree's family together in the kitchen. In the middle, her mother; for long out of shot, her father, with her mother hurling insults at him; on the periphery, as if they were "just passing through" in order to make some ironic comments about their mother, her three brothers. Her mother is very much centre-stage, and those few minutes are enough to give us the image of a woman physically and mentally tough, inflexible, and extraordinarily violent; in a murderous rage, she lashes out at Sheree's father with a note of peremptory contempt in her voice, which is curt, shrill, cutting, and exhausting, pouring out verdicts and judgements against which no appeal is possible. We could imagine that, when she met Bob, something of Sheree's unconscious identification with her paranoiac mother was revealed to her, as well as her alienation with respect to her mother and her desire to be rid of her. Sadomasochistic acts and the enactment of scenarios in which she plays the part of the hating mother were probably, for her also, the opportunity of externalising and "dealing with" a psychical reality enclosed within her like a foreign body.

It was almost immediately after their first meeting that Bob decided to make a video recording of the times when they were together, of what they said to each other, and of their sadomasochistic scenarios. The idea was to make a copy of the inscription of painful traces on his body via filming the scene, a putting into pictures which undoubtedly had the aim of securing the memory of those traces and stabilising it, in the same way as his various masochistic acts were aimed at binding, re-binding, inscribing, tying, and attaching. Filming and recording reduplicated the externalisation of the scenario by placing it in a medium that would serve as memory. As Sheree puts it on several occasions, "A lot of memory is involved in SM." Work on the thresholds of intensity, memories of the sensations and sensorial-ity excluded from language and from the activity of representation. The sadomasochistic experience keeps alive the fiction of a memory based on the body from which the individual and his/her past history are excluded, but which enables them to exist elsewhere and in a different way, sheltered from the deadly grip of illness. That "else-where" and "in a different way" echo the question raised by Bob's mother: "But where was I all that time?" (i.e., while my little boy was in agony as an infant and while, as an adolescent, he was all alone, giving himself over to masochistic acts).

The body, the skin, the scenario are duplicates and mirrors, the function of which is to catch, secure, and keep hold of the forces of psychical and biological unbinding that were at work inside Bob's body. They have a secondary narcissistic and identificatory function: after a certain lapse of time, Bob transformed his videos into works of art that could be marketed; he appeared on stage and gave performances in art galleries: the body as an object of pain was trans-formed into a work of art that could be presented, thought about, and interpreted.[44]

That shift from the private scene to public exhibition is complex and includes many different aspects. The sublimatory component indicates an unshakeable intention to make himself heard and to bear witness to something by plunging the spectator into the throes of a theatre of cruelty difficult to tolerate, in which the affects that are mobilised go from castration anxiety to being shut inside a body and a destiny that are beyond recall: "Here is my body," he says. "I will never have another one."

Beyond traumatic fascination

Bob Flanagan had to win the bet: to do things in such a way that the biggest possible number of people could endure the spectacle of his suffering, while, at the same time, thinking about him and reflecting an image of him that could be cathected by human beings. Through his performances, his writings, his songs, his videos, and his exhibi-tions, we are brought face to face with a test that is barely thinkable, one in which we must try to overcome the traumatic fascination with the sensorial element—especially the visual one—and to break free of it while continuing to think about the meaning of the particular human experience that we are being asked to share, in an attempt to find, over and beyond anxiety and horror, a range of emotions that belong to another dimension.

When I saw the film *Sick*, I was so quickly overwhelmed by anxiety that at several points I thought that I would not agree to subjecting myself to any more of it—I did indeed almost leave the cinema. What helped me to stay with it was the realisation that came to me fairly quickly that, in spite of the traumatic impact of the images, I was beginning to be deeply interested in something completely different, something that helped me sense the intelligence, the sensitivity, and sometimes the humour behind it; thanks to that, I was able to open myself up to the incredibly tragic and human dimension of what that man was trying to make us understand. At no point is this a perverse film that transforms the spectator into a sadistic voyeur—and that, given the nature of the images, is, in itself, quite an exploit. Sheree herself remarks somewhat shrewdly that the increasing importance of Bob's artistic activity constituted a breach of their sadomasochistic contract: "I have lost that power over him now that he has become an artist."

In order to reach that point, it was necessary for Bob first of all to meet Sheree, for a woman to take on board what Bob was asking for, for that demand to awaken an echo in her, and for her to respond to it in a way that made it meaningful. Sheree agreed to play with him; she was not afraid of embodying the mother who hated in a deadly way—in fact, she took pleasure in so doing. The contract was to draw close to the corridors of death, up to the point of imitating death at times[45] by inflicting pain and destruction out of desire and pleasure. That challenge to death goes hand-in-hand with the denial of death, the importance of which becomes clear to us only at the end when Bob Flanagan, dying, says to Sheree: "Am I dying? I don't understand. It's all so stupid. I never believed this in my life, I don't understand it."

A year before he died, on his forty-second birthday, we have the impression that, for the first time, Bob is quite clearly depressed. The hyperactivity that kept him watchful at all times in order to provide the "counter-current" required to fight every inch of the way against the ineluctable advance of death was no longer possible; the formidable war machine of his "survival technique" could no longer function as it used to. Sheree tries to stimulate him into participating in a sado-masochistic game, but that does not work any more. Then we see him taking down one of his exhibitions: his sadness is palpable in the slowness of his movements and in the look on his face. There follows a sequence in which he violently reproaches Sheree for smoking hashish. She again tries to rekindle the flame of their sadomasochistic functioning: "If you loved me, you would submit yourself to me." To no avail. He looks at her and makes the following declaration, until then unthinkable in the context of his unremitting struggle but which now marks his acceptance of death: "I am not submissive to anybody. I just love you." He would, indeed, die not long after this, and in his last moments—filmed right up to the end, as he had wished—he kept on saying to her, "Baby, I love you so much. Am I dying? I don't understand." In the days leading up to this, Sheree said how difficult it was for her to imagine him dead, adding, "He's not a maso any more. Life has beaten him down." Yes, life, with its programmed death: ". . . the living organism struggles most energetically against events (dangers, in fact) which might help it to attain its life's aim [i.e., death]" (Freud, 1920g, p. 39).

That testimony by a man determined to live whatever the cost and—we could perhaps add—in defiance of the verdict of biology, raises so many questions in our mind that they cannot all be discussed here. In addition, the tragic dimension of that human experience, the courage and the intelligence shown by that man in his mad desire to live, demand of us some modesty in our theorisation—while, at the same time, awakening in us a powerful desire to understand and to bring on to the stage the "witch metapsychology", who had already been put to the test in *Beyond the Pleasure Principle* (Freud, 1920g), yet who is still attempting to continue her witches' Sabbath . . . in the beyond. Bob Flanagan goes to the very heart of the issues raised and left open by Freud concerning the nature of mental processes in their very corporeity, the nature of their relationship to the soma.

Flanagan seems to suggest a kind of theoretical hypothesis, the validity of which he never stopped proclaiming: I succeeded, thanks to a specific form of psychical action, in thwarting the biological verdict of programmed death. I compensated for a defect in somatic synthesis by initiating and permanently maintaining a particular process of an exciting nature that we usually call pain; the barrier that it set up with respect to the somatic processes of fatal unbinding was all the more effective in that it was inflicted on me by another human being who represented both my mother and my body.

Is it possible to subscribe to that theoretical hypothesis without reservation? Of course not, because it bears witness to a *chutzpah*[46] that is almost as important as are our metapsychological hypotheses. After all, that man, Bob Flanagan, demonstrates a degree of megalomania— excusable enough, of course, given the circumstances in which he found himself as an infant—that is worthy of Ferenczi's wise baby. Moreover, he has the cheek to know this and to proclaim it: "It makes me feel invincible. I'm nothing but a big baby."

It would seem indisputable that that megalomania was manifested, via the drive to control everything, through his acts of masochism, in a kind of omnipotent control over the object.

The body as primary persecutory object

It should be pointed out, all the same, that that object is not only another person representing the primary object responsible for the "specific action"; in Flanagan's case, the object is also—and above all—his own body, which has to be kept under his permanent control in order to "keep it all together". That little tear in the usually silent organic network, the tiny little deficit of protein that implies the unending repetition of that same defective coding, constitute an irreparable hole in the continuity of good biological and physiological functioning, which, in principle, usually tries to keep out of the lime- light. Dehydration thickens the mucus, which obstructs the bronchi, so that it has to be evacuated in order not to suffocate, then it all starts up again. How to get rid of this? There is no way. Perhaps by expelling the body as a whole? Maybe. How? A pictogram of rejection, in which a mouth in the act of vomiting ends up vomiting itself after having flung outside all the internal spaces and their contents, might perhaps be one way of trying to have some kind of representation of these primary experiences. We are far short of the psychical mechanism of projection; it is probable that the need to get rid of a part of bodily functioning by expelling it could perhaps compromise the setting up of projection, projective identification, and introjection.

What could be the impact of that little tear in the organic fabric on primary repression, that is, on the possibility of setting up mental processes and spaces? What could, as a result, be forever impossible in primary repression—a lack that one would have to try to compensate for via indefinite repetition? It could be said that this constitutes a situation of primary trauma that prevents, on the one hand, the setting up of the various stages leading to the kind of functioning that is dominated by the pleasure principle and governed by hallucinatory wish fulfilment, and, on the other, the construction of a defensive barrier maintained by anxiety.

We could go back to the question raised by Freud in *Beyond the Pleasure Principle* concerning traumatic dreams:

> We may assume, rather, that dreams are here helping to carry out another task [i.e., not that of allowing the dreamer a hallucinatory fulfilment of his wishes], which must be accomplished before the dominance of the pleasure principle can even begin. . . . If there is a 'beyond the pleasure principle', it is only consistent to grant that there was also a time before the purpose of dreams was the fulfilment of wishes. (Freud, 1920g, pp. 32–33)

When we watch *Sick* and listen to what Bob Flanagan says, we could think of the scenarios that he acts out on the stage of reality and that he is obliged to repeat over and over again (and, we could add, in higher and higher doses and more and more frequently, as if it were a matter of drug addiction) as being the equivalent, when awake, of traumatic dreams. But their aim is not—or not only—to give rise to anxiety that will enable an escape from the excitation that is part of the trauma, as is the case with traumatic dreams. What, paradoxically, is sought for is pain, that is, an increase in excitation that is a response to the primary excitation aroused by the congenital organic lesion. According to Freud, "The specific unpleasure of physical pain is probably the result of the protective shield having been broken through in a limited area" (1920g, p. 30) It could be argued that the pain that Bob Flanagan wanted to experience was on a more primitive level than the perverse masochistic mode—which, in his case, was only secondary.[47] That would take us in the direction of the tendency, described by Freud as primitive, to repeat, the function of which in this case is to make good a primary defect in the biological organic "fabric" that tends to disrupt the setting up of the pleasure principle and to prevent the mental processing function of the primary object's specific action. Part of the drive structure based on hallucinatory wish fulfilment cannot function as such; something takes over from it as a kind of neo-formation—in this case, pain, which functions entirely as a pseudo-instinct, as Freud defined it. This brings us back to Freud's theory of the counter-current, by means of which he attempted to account for a kind of functioning that lies beyond (in fact, far short of) the pleasure principle. An attempt has to be made to stop the unremitting emergence of excitations, brought about by the biological defect, through the counter-current of energy produced by the activity of physical pain in terms of a pseudo-drive. This is how Freud puts it:

> The higher the system's own quiescent cathexis, the greater seems to be its binding force; conversely, therefore, the lower its cathexis, the less capacity will it have for taking up inflowing energy and the more violent must be the consequences of such a breach in the protective shield against stimuli. (1920g, p. 30)

That enormous task—necessarily doomed *in fine* to failure—in some ways resembles setting up a kind of dam in an attempt to control the Pacific Ocean. Paradoxically, the aim of all this energetic turmoil is to succeed in preserving a zone relatively free of damage, sheltered from the forces of psychical and biological unbinding.

CHAPTER FIFTEEN

Brutality of fact: the power of painting according to Francis Bacon

Some years ago, the Metropolitan Museum in New York organised an exhibition entitled "Van Gogh in Saint-Remy and Auvers", which brought together almost all of the paintings that Van Gogh did in the last year of his life. What abundance, what profusion, what sumptuousness! How could it be imagined that such pictorial exultation would lead to suicide? As I left the museum, I thought to myself that Van Gogh did not die of some drying-up of his resources—quite the contrary: of an overflowing, an excess of what impelled him to paint, which in the end perhaps "splintered" the figurative capacities that he had developed. That idea of "splintering" is a familiar one for psychoanalysts because it brings to mind the traumatic dream of the Wolf-Man and Freud's comment on it: "[It] was not only a single sexual current that started from the primal scene but a whole set of them, that his sexual life was positively splintered up by it" (1918b, pp. 43–44).

Francis Bacon was a great admirer of Van Gogh. This is what he said about him:

> [A] great work of art . . . has its own power. Because it has re-invented its own realism. And Van Gogh is one of my great heroes because I

think that he was able to be almost literal and yet by the way he put on the paint give you a marvellous vision of the reality of things. . . . The living quality is what you have to get. (Sylvester, 1993, pp. 173–174)

In 1947, Antonin Artaud wrote *Van Gogh: the Man Suicided by Society*. Bacon was still at the very beginning of his artistic career; he himself said that it began around 1943–1944, even though he had begun to paint before then. This is how Artaud speaks of Bacon's "hero":

> It is what strikes me most in Van Gogh: the painter of painters, who, without going any further in what is called painting, and what *is* painting, neither setting aside the tube, nor the brush, nor the frame-work, nor the *motif,* nor the canvas, nor the intrinsic beauty of the subject or the object, managed to impassion nature. . . . That is why no one since Van Gogh has known how to shake the great cymbal, the superhuman gong, perpetually superhuman, following the frustrated order from which real-life objects ring out, when one has known how to open one's ears to understand the surging of their tidal flow. That is how the light of the candlestick rings forth, that the glow from the candlestick on the green straw-bottomed chair rings out like the breathing of a loving body near the body of a sleeping invalid. . . . No one has ever written or painted, sculpted, modelled, built, invented, except to get out of hell. And to get out of hell, I prefer the landscaped natures of this quiet convulsive man to the swarming compositions of Breughel the Elder or Hieronymus Bosch who, compared to him, are only artists while Van Gogh is only a poor ignoramus determined not to deceive himself. (1964, pp. 142–149)

Artaud, who had just spent several years in what has come to be known as convalescent homes, died soon afterwards. "I too am like poor Van Gogh, I no longer think, but every day I manage more and more finely terrific internal turmoils and I would like to see any doctor come and reproach me for tiring myself" (1964).

Artaud had never seen any of Bacon's paintings, and I think that if Bacon had read any of Artaud's writings, he would have said so at some point. To some extent, then, it is through Van Gogh that they meet each other and talk to each other. The questions about reality that they raise and that they ask of us are similar to one another; they are like those that Freud, in his own way, explored while listening to the Wolf-Man and in his reading of *Senatspräsident* Schreber's memoirs. Perhaps we could say that Van Gogh and Artaud "failed", whereas Bacon "succeeded", in the same way as Freud put it in a letter to Ferenczi (6 October 1910): "I have succeeded where the paranoiac fails" (Brabant, Falzeder, & Giampieri-Deutsch, 1993, p. 221). In any case, the analysis of the Wolf Man was a failure. What Freud, Bacon, Van Gogh, and Artaud produced in their work was, in many ways, a success. As for how they lived . . . as Artaud puts it: "You can say all you want about the mental health of Van Gogh who, during his life-time, cooked only one of his hands, and other than that did no more than cut off his left ear" (1964, p. 135).

It would be better to put on hold what we think we know when we talk about the schizophrenic's concrete thinking, and try to listen to what Artaud tells us about the body and what Bacon and Van Gogh try to bring into view. I have read several times *The Theatre and Its Double* (1958), substituting, in my thoughts, "psychoanalyst" and "psychoanalysis" for "actor" and "theatre". This has quite a startling result. In his definition of the work of the actor, Artaud speaks of "affective athleticism":

> The actor is like the physical athlete, but with this surprising differ-ence: his affective organism is analogous to the organism of the athlete, is parallel to it, as if it were its double, although not acting upon the same plane. The actor is an athlete of the heart. (1964, p. 133)

Bacon, Van Gogh, and Winnicott are now beginning to enter into a dialogue together, under the patronage of Freud, aided and assisted by Artaud, with *Senatspräsident* Schreber in the wings, in the shade of the tree carrying the wolves. Bacon for the flesh, Artaud for affective athleticism, and Winnicott for having written these somewhat out-of-the-ordinary lines for a psychoanalyst:

> I would rather be remembered as maintaining that in between the patient and the analyst is the analyst's professional attitude, his tech-nique, *the work that he does with his mind*. Now, I say this without fear, because I'm not an intellectual and in fact I personally do my work very much from the body-ego, so to speak. (Winnicott, 1965, p. 161)

It was that same Winnicott who wrote to Victor Smirnoff on 19 November 1958 in an attempt to finalise how a certain number of difficult expressions should be translated into French:

Here am I trying in my summary to relate experiencing to the transitional phenomena. I am implying that actual experiencing does not stem directly either from the individual's psychic reality nor from the individual's external relationships. This sounds rather startling but you can perhaps get my meaning if you think of a Van Gogh experiencing, that is to say, feeling real, when painting one of his pictures, but feeling unreal in his relationships with external reality and in his private withdrawn inner life. (Winnicott, 1998, p. 124)

At this point, we could perhaps set up a dialogue between Freud and Winnicott, through the intermediary of the Wolf-Man. Sergei Pankejeff felt that he was wrapped in a veil, which cut him off from reality:

The world, he said, was hidden from him by a veil; and our psychoanalytic training forbids our assuming that these words can have been without significance or have been chosen at haphazard. The veil was torn, strange to say, in one situation only; and that was at the moment when, as a result of an enema, he passed a motion through his anus. He then felt well again, and for a very short while he saw the world clearly. . . . Nor did he keep to the veil. It became still more elusive, as a feeling of twilight, '*ténèbres*', and of other impalpable things. (Freud, 1918b, p. 99)

It is precisely those impalpable things that painters attempt to bring out into the open by giving them some kind of representation that bestows on them a certain reality—and, in so doing, they might be attempting to make themselves feel more real.

When we enter into an unknown museum or art gallery, there are several ways in which we can try to make contact with the paintings on display. We might have prepared for the visit in every detail and, catalogue in hand, go methodically from one work of art to the next. That is the erudite's way of proceeding. Or we can enter on an impulse, not heeding any information given at the reception desk, cheerfully going through ticket control and strolling around just like that, our eyes wandering around somewhat vaguely until, intrigued by something barely glimpsed, at the frontier between consciousness and the visual field, some pressing internal need makes us slow down and come to a halt, even though we do not yet know why, in the grip of an emotion that reaches down to the very depths of our being.

Although those two ways of proceeding are not incompatible, and a vast number of intermediate levels is possible, my own preference has always been for the second of these, the first moment of an opening up to the power of the work of art and its role in opening us up to our own selves, to the object and to the world, all of this inextricably tied together. That is what really accounts for the compelling force of that pull towards reality that a work of art gives rise to within us, in much the same way as we talk of an indraught of air. The other way is that of the erudite; this one—always assuming that we have to give it a name—could be called that of the noble savage. Some points of convergence with the psychoanalytical method will have been noticed *en passant*, to do with free-floating attention and putting all judgement on hold.

The power that stems from a painting has as much—if not more—to do with its materiality, its texture, and the painter's gestures as he works on the canvas, as with the image that it is supposed to represent. It is what remains of those living inscriptions that manages to separate out from the surface of the canvas in order to make the person looking at it feel something of a reality that cannot be reduced to a description, even one full of imagery. Everything that makes a painting as untalkative as possible. Everything, too, that means that a painting is not restricted to the power of its image in terms of an enclosed and finite entity, but never stops evoking its very genesis, how it became possible to engender it, the always-open potentialities of its production. The most perfect of paintings is never finished: a work in progress. The power of a work of art is light years away from the fascination of the image that makes the eyes and thinking focus on it and see it as the fetishistic form of a fossil of reality. This is how Bacon saw the issue of the image as it appeared to him in his work as a painter:

> Certainly one is more relaxed when the image that one has within one's sensations – you see there is a kind of sensational image within the very, you could say, structure of your being, which is not to do with a mental image – when that image, through accident, begins to form. (Sylvester, 1993, p. 160)

That image lying at the very heart of sensation is, in fact, neither an image nor a representation, and even less a fantasy. It is closer to an affect in its dimension of representing (and perhaps also to what Winnicott referred to as experiencing in the extract I quoted above, or to what the Kleinians call memories in feeling). In *Le discours vivant*, André Green (1973) explores the place and the meaning of affect in Freud's theory of the drives, and writes: "Affect is looking at a body seized by emotion" (Green, 1973, translated for this edition).

Until the very end of his life, Freud tried to give an account of the first psychical expression of the drives "which originate from the somatic organization" (Freud, 1940a, p. 145). For Freud, that first psychical expression of the drives, where there is no clear separation between the representative element and the energy charge of the affect, occurs "in forms unknown to us" (1940a, p. 145). When Francis Bacon tried to figure out what was happening inside himself at the point where that image, at the heart of sensation, took shape, he emphasised the fact that it "seems to have been organically, by chance, given to you" (Sylvester, 1993, pp. 160–161).

I shall, therefore, focus on the fabrication of an image, on the way in which the material is worked on and constructed, on the conditions that make its accomplishment possible, and on the way in which those particular conditions play a decisive role in the impact of the work of art. As I do so, I would like to allow any possible harmonics to be heard between pictorial creation and analytical listening, and to show how the analyst may enhance his/her capacity for listening by becoming more sensitive towards the work of mental processing that initially is not done via words, yet never collapses into a reductive homology. In this approach, the idea is not to throw some psychological light on the aetiology of any given creation or on the psychopathological processes active within the work of art; I want to follow as closely as possible what is usually referred to as the painter's technique, confronted with the task of "making reality real", to use Bacon's own words. That task—of "making reality real"—is, in a different way, also part of the theorisation of psychoanalysis as well as of its practice. Freud has often been—quite correctly—criticised for being more concerned with the analysis of the content of a work of art than with the way in which it comes into being. He himself said so, particularly at the beginning of *The Moses of Michelangelo*:

> I may say at once that I am no connoisseur in art, but simply a layman.
> I have often observed that the subject-matter of works of art has a

stronger attraction for me than their formal and technical qualities, though to the artist their value lies first and foremost in these latter. ... Nevertheless, works of art do exercise a powerful effect on me, especially those of literature and sculpture, less often of painting. (1914b, p. 211)

His great dislike of modern art, which was seeing the light of day in the same years as he was working on his own ideas, can be seen in some of his correspondence. In a letter to Oskar Pfister dated 21 June 1920, in which Freud wanted to thank him for sending him a small volume about expressionism, Freud wrote:

For I think you ought to know that in actual life I am terribly intolerant of cranks, that I see only the harmful side of them and that so far as these 'artists' are concerned I am almost one of those whom at the outset you castigate as philistines and lowbrows. (Freud, E. L., 1961, pp. 330–331)

This is what he wrote in 1922 to Karl Abraham, who had sent him a drawing made by an expressionist painter:

I have received the drawing that is supposed to show your head. It is hideous. I know what an excellent person you are. It shocks me all the more that such an insignificant shadow on your character as your tolerance or sympathy for modern 'art' should have to be punished so cruelly. (Falzeder, 2003, pp. 461–462)

It is really quite astonishing to see the very person who took great pride in having inflicted an important narcissistic wound on humanity, through his invention of psychoanalysis, react so virulently to a pictorial attack on his own aesthetic models, accused of being an intolerable narcissistic wound. As Gombrich (1987, p. 221) points out, "Indeed, to the end of his life Freud looked at art and literature through the eyes of Goethe and of Schopenhauer", his culture having its roots in the classical traditions of the German *Bildung*. We often get the impression that what he says about art and the interest he showed in art were, to some extent, still far behind his own ideas, as though in that particular domain he did not allow himself to be influenced by the retroactive impact of his own theory of the psychical apparatus. Freud's aesthetic ideas are perhaps not visible in what he said explicitly about art; we ought perhaps to look for them in the way that he conceived of the mind, in the way in which he "invented" it, in his thinking about dream-work and in the structuring of his case reports. When, recently, I re-read the Wolf Man case, I felt that the way in which Freud reports on the case in itself gives the reader a sensation of vertigo, related both to the wish to go deeper and deeper and to the repeated theme of the loss of limits.

The invention of the psychoanalytical setting and its application to the session, through the implementation of specific modalities of mental activity and intersubjectivity, mean that psychoanalysis is a mode of practice that gives access to an experience. It is in the domain of that experience that certain things take place in a way that might clarify some aspects of the aesthetic experience, and which themselves are part of that aesthetic experience. None the less, whatever the affinities between those two experiences, it is impossible to argue that, in itself, psychoanalysis is an aesthetic experience. As Winnicott quite rightly put it,

> The idea of psycho-analysis as an art must gradually give way to a study of environmental adaptation relative to patients' regressions. But while the scientific study of environmental adaptation is undeveloped, then I suppose analysts must continue to be artists in their work. An analyst may be a good artist, but (as I have frequently asked): *what patient wants to be someone else's poem or picture?* (1975, p. 291, my italics)

Freud suggested that hysteria should be looked upon as a caricature of art; it is not purely by chance that it was Sándor Ferenczi who took up that idea. That point of view, which lays emphasis on the conditions under which psychical reality is produced, is no doubt the most fruitful way of exploring works of art from a psychoanalytical perspective. According to Ferenczi:

> Another problem hitherto considered only from the psychological side, that of artistic endowment, is in hysteria illuminated to some extent from its organic side. Hysteria is, as Freud says, a caricature of art. Hysterical 'materializations', however, show us the organism in its entire plasticity, indeed, in its preparedness for art. It might prove that the purely 'autoplastic' tricks of the hysteric are prototypes, not only for the bodily performances of 'artists' and actors, but also for the work of those creative artists who no longer manipulate their own bodies, but material from the external world. (Ferenczi, 1927, p. 104)

Because of the creative impulse itself, that material from the external world does not remain a pure exteriority. The very act of painting obliges us to take another look at the categories "interior" and "exterior". This is what Leonardo da Vinci had to say about that: "Our life is made by the death of others. In dead matter insensible life remains, which, reunited to the stomachs of living beings, resumes life, both sensual and intellectual" (Richter, 1970).

Material and matter

Here is a very basic description of the various components required to produce a painting. First of all, there has to be a surface on which to paint. This will be more or less flat, more or less rough, more or less porous. It will be fixed or mobile, perhaps the wall of a cave, the coated ceiling of a chapel, a panel of wood, or a cloth spread out. Next, the matter: dry matter—the pigments, mainly of mineral origin, that have to be dampened. This produces a moist matter that is more or less a kind of paste. To ensure that the dry matter and the liquid do not separate out while drying—and, therefore, to ensure that they do not come off the surface on which they have been laid, some kind of binding element is required, something to fix them together. This will usually be of animal origin, either from the skin of a dead animal, glue from the skin or from a fish, or from an egg. From that dead animal, hairs will be taken—these will form the sensitive part of the instrument with which the bound material will be applied to the surface so that it stays there.

It is obvious that such a description, no matter how minimal, is not neutral. It might even stir up in the analyst's ear a fondness and an appetite for projective theoretical speculation about which one has to be careful. But it has to be said that all those ingredients—or almost all of them—could be used to fabricate the psychical apparatus: a surface for projection, bodily matter, binding and unbinding, inscription and erasing, life and death, murder, immobility, and movement, egg. His/her appetite whetted, the psychoanalyst can see immediately in that pictorial matter something that has to do with the flesh, throbbing, lively, mentalized, animated, and, perhaps, even inflated by the painter's gesture. Raw material, not yet processed or representative, but which already contains in its very thickness some inscriptions that have to do with its origins; we are at the limits of the organic, corporeal, and psychical dimensions where, in a form of which we know nothing, a drive will emerge as a psychical representative, not yet as an ideational representative, in which the affect, discriminating pleasure from unpleasure, already offers an initial matrix for the creation of symbols.

Freud spoke of that kind of flesh in his description of the mechanisms that come into play in dream-work: "We call it 'regression' when in a dream an idea is turned back into the sensory image from which it was originally derived" (1900a, p. 543). A little further on, he adds, "Dreams, which fulfil their wishes along the short path of regression, have merely preserved for us in that respect a sample of the psychical apparatus's primary method of working" (p. 567).

The surface, the element on which the pictorial matter is placed, may, in a similar way, bring to mind the dream screen described by Bertram Lewin: "The dream screen, as I define it, is the surface on to which a dream appears to be projected. It is the blank background, present in the dream though not necessarily seen" (Lewin, 1934, p. 420). Lewin associates that screen to the phenomenon of falling asleep described by Isakower: just as we are about to fall asleep, we have the impression of an enormous mass that is coming so close that it might crush us, and our mouth feels full of something that does not come from outside.

> The state in question . . . is one in which sensations very different from those of waking life are experienced in certain regions of the body and conveyed to the subject by more than one of his senses. The principal bodily regions concerned are the mouth, the skin and the hand. (Isakower, 1938, p. 332)

This would appear to be a revival of the primary sensations of contact with the breast. According to Lewin, the screen, that blank background, is the surface of the breast; during sleep, it represents the breast but it is also sleep itself, representing the wish to fall asleep, the reproduction of sleep in early childhood.

From that dream screen, we could move towards other representations which constitute anchorage points in Freud's metapsychology: the protective shield against stimuli, the Pcs system, an intermediate zone of exchange between the Ucs and the Pcp–Cs systems. All of this has to do with skin, epidermis, endodermis, or endothelium.

Very early in his artistic career, towards the end of the 1940s, Francis Bacon decided to use the side of the canvas that had not been coated with a primer—and he went on to paint like that for the rest of his life. The other side of the canvas, however, always had to be coated. If we stay with the skin metaphor, we could say that he did not paint on the epidermis, but on the inner face of the skin turned towards the inside of the body. He liked to paint, as he put it, on "raw canvas" because the nature of its absorption had an impact on the image, which penetrated into the very substance of the raw canvas, becoming impregnated with it rather than being simply tacked on to its surface. He always emphasised the importance of the texture of painting, directly related to his aim of capturing reality as a hunter lays a trap to capture an animal—but with the idea of capturing it alive. "As an artist you have to, in a sense, set a trap by which you hope to trap this living fact alive" (Sylvester, 1993, p. 57) In that process of entrapping, the texture of painting plays a vital part, compared to the texture of a photo for example; "paint comes across directly onto the nervous system" (1993, p. 18) in a way that has nothing to do with a process of illustration. A living painting should be as far removed as possible from illustration. "An illustrational form tells you through the intelligence immediately what the form is about, whereas a non-illustrational form works first upon sensation and then slowly leaks back into the fact" (Sylvester, 1993, p. 146).

The picture that in the end emerges—the painter works away without any conscious intention of illustrating anything—

> has a life completely of its own. It lives on its own, like the image one's trying to trap; it lives on its own, and therefore transfers the essence of the image more poignantly. So that the artist may be able to open up or rather, should I say, unlock the valves of feeling and therefore return the onlooker to life more violently. (Sylvester, 1993, p. 66)

In order to reach that point, the painter has to enter into a very specific state of mind before beginning to paint. The "kind of haze" that he describes has an uncannily close relationship to the analyst's free-flowing state of body-mind:

> I used to have music on sometimes, but I'm not musical. Really I prefer just being alone here. . . . I work in a kind of haze. I don't want the work to be hazy, but I work in a kind of haze of sensations and

feelings and ideas that come to me and that I try to crystallize. (Sylvester, 1993, p. 194)

Bacon always maintained that conscious activity and intentional-ity had to be put on hold when doing a painting that would be other than a mere reproduction of something. When Sylvester asked him if this was a kind of trance, Bacon dismissed the idea because, in his view, it was too much like mysticism, which he hated. Sylvester then spoke of instinct, to which Bacon replied, "All art surely is instinct, and then you can't talk about instinct, because you don't know what it is" (Sylvester, 1993, p. 97).

The state that he described—and that he tried unsuccessfully to define—implies that any purposive idea be put on hold. To that extent, it is similar to free-floating attention, to a kind of self-hypnosis that would enable us to dream without falling asleep and, at the same time, on the edge of the field of consciousness, to have some critical faculty on the alert. The process of thinking is transferred to the hand that moves, to the movements of the brush, to the changes brought about in the pictorial matter.

> With oil painting being so fluid, the image is changing all the time while you're working. One thing either builds on another or destroys the other. Because moving – even unconsciously moving – the brush one way rather than the other will completely alter the implications of the image. . . . It's really a continuous question of the fight between accident and criticism. (Sylvester, 1993, p. 121)

The painter's task, then, is that of making reality emerge in all of its native force. According to Bacon, it is in the actual process of fabricating the painted image that lies the capacity for producing something real.

> To me, the mystery of painting today is how can appearance be made. I know it can be illustrated, I know it can be photographed. But how can this thing be made so that you catch the mystery of appearance within the mystery of the making. (Sylvester, 1993, p.105)

Whatever the intention at the outset, it is the unexpected which emerges in the course of the work that plays a decisive role in the appearance of the image; the very conditions of its emerging bestow on it a greater or lesser intensity of reality.

> It actually does come about in the working. And the way it works is really by the things that happen. In working you are really following this kind of cloud of sensation in yourself, but you don't know what it really is. (Sylvester, 1993, p. 149)

But, as soon as the image begins to take shape, disruptive techniques have to be invented in order to break up the emerging that becomes too easy. "Half my painting activity is disrupting what I can do with ease" (Sylvester, 1993, p. 91)

Putting brushes to one side, Bacon then began to use various other techniques: projecting handfuls of paint on to the canvas, wiping it with rags, a scrubbing brush, a hand broom. "I can only hope that the throwing of paint onto the already-made or half-made image will either re-form the image or that I will be able to manipulate this further into, anyway, for me, a greater intensity." (Sylvester, 1993, p. 90).

The aim of assaulting the canvas like that, of tormenting images that have just begun to take shape, is to produce greater intensity and, through that, more reality:

> The violence of painting . . . is an attempt to remake the violence of reality itself. And the violence of reality is not only the simple violence meant when you say that a rose or something is violent, but it's the violence also of the suggestions within the image itself which can only be conveyed through paint. (Sylvester, 1993, p. 81)

The principle and the aim of that pictorial violence are "unlocking the valves of feeling", "unlocking of areas of sensation", or even "[unlocking] the areas of feeling which lead to a deeper sense of the reality of the image", "[returning] the onlooker to life more violently" (p. 66).

These might remind us of the techniques used by those artists working on action-painting, or abstract expressionism, who were contemporaries of Bacon—particularly, perhaps, Jackson Pollock, who devised the techniques of dripping and of throwing. But Bacon dismisses in no uncertain terms that kind of abstract painting. The random inscription of gestures, movements, and rhythm on the canvas is only part of pictorial work. If we stop there—which is the case of abstract painting—we miss out on the fundamental duality of painting. According to Bacon, the inevitable destiny of abstract painting is aestheticism.

Abstract painting is an entirely aesthetic thing. It always remains on one level. It is only really interested in the beauty of its patterns or its shapes. . . . I think that abstract artists believe that in these marks that they're making they are catching all these sorts of emotions. But I think that, caught in that way, they are too weak to convey anything. I think that great art is deeply ordered. (Sylvester, 1993, p. 58)

Painting is a duality; the painter is faced with the task of representing something—using elements that are not representative, figurative, or rational—in order to record a fact. Analysing a portrait by Rembrandt, Bacon shows that it is wholly made up of "a coagulation of non-representational marks which have led up to making this a very great image" (p. 58). "I think that the mystery of fact is conveyed by an image being made out of non-rational marks. . . . And abstract expressionism has all been done in Rembrandt's marks" (p. 58).

The image that emerges from the raw material, from its primary substance, maintains an organic link to that umbilicus of dreams and sensations that tie it indefinitely to the unknown and prevent it from being a mere reproduction of an internal or external image, the clear-cut divide between inside and outside having lost all relevance. The painter then has the same kind of approach as the tightrope walker.

[This] image is a kind of tightrope walk between what is called figurative painting and abstraction. It will go right out from abstraction, but will really have nothing to do with it. It's an attempt to bring the figurative thing up on to the nervous system more violently and more poignantly. (Sylvester, 1993, p.12)

The flesh, the cry, the mouth

I would like to show how Bacon's technique, aimed at making figures climb out of their own flesh, gave rise to forms that reflect a mythical representation of the questions that preoccupy contemporary Western culture.

In 1944, Bacon produced a triptych that appears to have occupied a fundamental place in his work. Some forty-four years later, not long before he died, he produced another version of it. Between those two dates, he accomplished the whole of his artistic work. At first sight, nothing has changed—but something has indeed been modified. As at the end of an analysis? "We are always hounding ourselves," said Bacon in 1983 in a conversation with Hugh Davies. "We have been made aware of this side of ourselves by Freud . . . whether his ideas led to therapeutic results or not."

We are always hounding ourselves. The 1944 triptych has three animal figures, which also represent the male sexual organs. The extremity of the organ that is also the animal's neck displays an open mouth with teeth, frightening, crying out. A screaming penis, a devouring vagina. One wears a headband that blinds it, the other has an ear at the corner of the mouth. The triptych is called *Three Studies for Figures at the Base of a Crucifixion*. For Bacon, they are the Eumenides, but in Aeschylus's tragedy, they are more evocative of the Erinyes, the sight of which made the Pythia of Delphi step back when, as she entered the sanctuary, she caught sight of them beside Orestes, who killed his mother, crouching down by the Omphalos, the navel-stone of the Earth, blood dripping from their hands; they are women, she thinks, no, they are the Gorgons, but . . .

> But these are wingless, black, and all their shape
> The eye's abomination to behold.
> Fell is the breath—let none draw nigh to it-
> Exude the damned drops of poisonous ire.
>
> (Aeschylus, *Eumenides*)

By placing these monsters of maternal hate at the foot of the cross, Bacon was not producing a work of narrative painting, the story-telling painting that he disliked so much. He was producing an explosive condensation of two myths of origin of our societies, Greek and Christian. Their roots go deeply into his flesh, and he restores them to us with violence, forcing us to think of them together; he puts us within the power of the generation of the myth and, at the same time, in the genesis of its pictorial creation.

This is what Apollo has to say:

> Not the true parent is the woman's womb
> That bears the child; she doth but nurse the seed
> New-sown . . .
> Birth may from fathers, without mothers, be:
> See at your side a witness of the same,
> Athena, daughter of Olympian Zeus,

Never within the darkness of the womb
Fostered nor fashioned, but a bud more bright
Than any goddess in her breast might bear.
(Aeschylus, Eumenides)

It is that woman, born out of her father's head, who succeeds in calming the Erinyes and in entering into an alliance with them once they become the Eumenides.

Mine is the right to add the final vote,
And I award it to Orestes' cause.
For me no mother bore within her womb,
And, save for wedlock evermore eschewed,
I vouch myself the champion of the man,
Not of the woman, yea, with all my soul,
In heart, as birth, a father's child alone.
Thus will I not too heinously regard
A woman's death who did her husband slay,
The guardian of her home.
(Aeschylus, Eumenides)

Tradition was something that obsessed Bacon, but not in any purely academic way.

Of course, I think that, if one could find a valid myth today . . . it would be tremendously helpful. But when you're outside a tradition, as every artist is today, one can only want to record one's own feelings about certain situations as closely to one's own nervous system as one possibly can. (Sylvester, 1993, p. 43)

By following as closely as possible the meanderings of his own nervous system, Bacon, the painter of raw meat lying on the butcher's stall, knew also how to bring out from the flesh of his representations that highest symbolic level of the emblematic figures of a theatre of cruelty that belongs to our own civilisation. He who never ceased to bear witness to the hard grind of his everyday work as a painter, he who, to put it another way, emphasised the importance of processing what is involved in producing a painting, remained nostalgic for immediacy. His ideal of pictorial creation was also the instantaneity of a birth-vomiting-ejaculation-projection, which, in some ways, reminds us of Athena's birth. "My ideal would be just to pick up a handful of paint and throw it at the canvas and hope that the portrait was there" (Sylvester, 1993, p. 107).

The image of raw meat emerged "by accident" in 1946, while he was painting a bird of prey landing in a field.

> Suddenly the lines that I'd drawn suggested something totally differ-ent, and out of this suggestion arose this picture. . . . It suddenly suggested an opening-up into another area of feeling altogether. And then I made these things; I gradually made them. (Sylvester, 1993, p.11)

The bird of prey had just captured one of the essential images of Bacon's oeuvre; from then on, he would never stop elaborating on it. Raw meat made an immediate appearance in the form of a crucifixion, in the presence of a brute of a man, all we see of whom is his mouth, open and grunting. Slaughter-house, murder, devouring, sacrifice.

In Bacon's oeuvre, there is a movement from meat to flesh, from flesh to spirit—and perhaps even to the Holy Spirit. The vector of that movement is a breath, a breath that carries a cry: a cry of distress, of suffering, of pain, of despair, of delight. From the growl of a hideous beast, the snoring of the Erinyes, the supplication of Christ on the cross: "Why hast thou abandoned me?" The cry addressed to the father, to filiation, to transmission is what tautens and underpins the movement of that exclamation. From Abraham to Christ, from Orestes to Freud's myth of the primal horde, it is the oscillation between sacrifice and murder that is at stake here. The reversal of the one into the other. From the totemic meal to the Eucharist.

Artaud described Van Gogh's eyes as being those of a butcher: "In the depths of his plucked-looking butcher's eyes Van Gogh devoted himself uninterruptedly to one of those dark alchemistic operations which took nature for object and the human body for kettle or crucible" (Artaud, 1964, p. 10)

We have seen how Bacon not only projected but also reconstructed his very flesh in the texture of his pictorial material. What would emerge from that flesh involves images of the flesh, representations of the body, of the flesh and of the spirit, the relationships between them, and the generating not only of bodies, but also of the spirit. He shows how the spirit can come from itself, how a body can come from another body without being simply a kind of excrement, a piece of raw meat. Self-procreation, parthenogenesis, sexual begetting.

Bacon, like a child without a father, set out to conquer his filiations. A ground-breaking encounter with a painting, *The Portrait of Pope Innocent X*, placed Velasquez at the eminent yet perilous place of the paternal figure, of a chosen master.

> One wants to do this thing of just walking along the edge of the precipice, and in Velasquez it's a very, very extraordinary thing that he has been able to keep it so near to what we call illustration and at the same time so deeply unlock the greatest and deepest things that man can feel. (Sylvester, 1993, p. 28)

That encounter would enable him to become part of a tradition, not an inherited one, but one that he acquired, conquered, climbed on to. Bacon seized hold of that image, "the most beautiful painting in the world", and subjected it to every kind of treatment that eyes looking at an image can inflict upon it. He did not copy or reproduce it—he absorbed it, became imbued with it, ill-treated it, and made it scream: "But tell me, who today has been able to record anything that comes across to us as a fact without causing deep injury to the image?" (Sylvester, 1993, p. 28)

The ferociousness of the look in the eyes became a ferociousness of the mouth. What became condensed in the representation of the cry that shot through Innocent was the memory of an old book of medical plates illustrating diseases of the mouth, the detail of a screaming character in Poussin's *Massacre of the Innocents*, and the sequence of the Odessa stairway in *The Battleship Potemkin* in which a static shot shows a governess silently screaming. There is, of course, the image of the baby carriage hurtling down the stairs, but Bacon does not mention that because anything that tells a story simply bored him. When Sylvester asked him if his interest in the figure of the Pope had anything to do with his feelings for his father, Bacon did not understand the question. He had never thought of the Pope as being "il papa". But Sylvester's question did encourage him to give some autobiographical details. Bacon, who was never particularly interested in "psychology" or in biography in general, did, all the same, in just a few sentences, go directly to the heart of the matter:

> The thing is, I never got on with neither my mother or my father. They didn't want me to be a painter, they thought I was just a drifter, especially my mother. . . . My father was very narrow-minded . . . I disliked

him, but I was sexually attracted to him when I was young. . . . It was
a sexual thing towards my father. (Sylvester, 1993, p. 71)

The face, distortion, and destruction

"I disliked him, but I was sexually attracted to him." The calm lucid-
ity of that statement, which expresses a fundamental distortion of the
libido (which we could translate into psychoanalytical language as the
masochistic component of a negative Oedipus complex—but that is
not nearly as good as "I disliked him, but I was sexually attracted to
him"), evokes in us, of course, the torsions and distortions inflicted on
bodies and faces in Bacon's paintings. That libidinal cathexis, maintained in spite of the displeasure attached to it (in all logic we could
transform that statement into: maintained against the displeasure and
also maintained because of the displeasure) which here is to be seen
as belonging to the feminine masochistic dimension, evokes also that
of primary masochism; Rosenberg has shown that this lies at the very
heart of any possibility of mental processing:

> The aspect that seems to me to be essential is that the binding of the
> drives is dependent on the object (its representation). The object is
> therefore doubly cathected by the drives: on the one hand, by the
> death drive, which tends to dismantle it, smash it to pieces and
> dissolve it, and, on the other, by the libido, which strives, in parallel
> with sexual aims, to preserve the object of cathexis and maintain it.
> The libido tries to bind together, while the death drive tries to unbind.
> The object thus becomes the condition, the cement of the binding of
> the drives, its mediator. . . . Through the equivalence between the
> primary binding of the drives and primary erotogenic masochism, the
> primary ego is masochistic—if it were not, it could neither exist nor
> last. . . . Masochism lies at the frontier where binding can take place; it
> is through binding the life drive to the death drive that the first endur-
> ing psychical knot can be set up. (Rosenberg, 1990, p. 78, translated for
> this edition)

There is, in that point of view, a fundamental link between
masochism and artistic creation. With regard to the impact of a work
of art on the viewer and what it can communicate, evoke, and awaken,
I shall simply mention an anecdote reported by Yukio Mishima in his

autobiography *Confessions of a Mask* (1958). One day when he was all alone and at a bit of a loose end—he was twelve years old at the time—he picked up a book on art that his father had brought back from a foreign trip.

> I began turning a page towards the end of a volume. Suddenly there came into view from one corner of the next page a picture that I had to believe had been lying in wait there for me, for my sake.
>
> It was a reproduction of Guido Reni's "St. Sebastian", which hangs in the collection of the Palazzo Rosso at Genoa.
>
> . . .
>
> That day, the instant I looked upon the picture, my entire being trembled with some pagan joy. My blood soared up; my loins swelled as though in wrath. . . . I felt a secret, radiant something rise swift-footed to the attack from inside me. Suddenly it burst forth, bringing with it a blinding intoxication. . . . Fortunately, a reflex motion of my hand to protect the picture had saved the book from being soiled. This was my first ejaculation. (1958, p. 38)

From that day on, Mishima devoted himself frantically to masturbation, filling his play with sadomasochistic daydreams in which the deliciously prolonged tortures were followed by sacrificial ceremonies and cannibalistic meals:

> There in my murder theatre . . . the sacrificial victim must send up long-drawn-out, mournful, pathetic cries, making the hearer feel the terrible loneliness of existence. Thereupon my joy of life, blazing up from some secret place deep within me, would finally give its own shout of exultation, answering the victim cry for cry. Was this not exactly similar to the joy ancient man found in the hunt? (p. 93)

The image of the bird of prey reappears here in this theatre of murder in which sexuality seizes hold of the devices of destruction in order to save the person from falling into the melancholic abyss that is waiting for him. We can see also two other representations, which we sometimes find in Bacon's paintings: the arrow and the stain left by spunk. Mishima projects the image from a projectile activity in which the eyes follow the path of the arrow in order to "eat into the tense, youthful flesh" (1958, p. 39), make a hole in the canvas, then come back, completing the movement of the drive, on to the person him-self—here, into the hole of the pupil of the eye, all the way to the blankness of the retina, thus creating a "blinding exhilaration". Are the very graphic arrows that can be found in some of Bacon's paintings perhaps reminiscent of a pictorial tradition that is associated with the representation of St Sebastian transfixed by penetrating gazes? Who is Sebastian supposed to be protecting with the thickness of his body, transpierced as it is? That question obviously brings us back to the crucifixion, via a painting that Bacon did in 1963 and which carries the title *Lying Figure with a Hypodermic Syringe*. Bacon was in complete dis-agreement with the projective/anecdotal explanations that saw in that painting a denunciation of drug addiction: "I put the syringe because I want a nailing of the flesh onto the bed" (Sylvester, 1993, p. 78).

He wanted the flesh to be nailed to the bed, to be riveted to the cloth. That echoes what Artaud (1964) said about Van Gogh:

Carded by Van Gogh's nail,
the landscapes show their hostile flesh,
the growl of their disembowelled windings which some
   strange unknown force is elsewhere in the act of metamorphosing.

Among the drawings of the crucifixion that Picasso did, Bacon preferred the one dated 7 October 1932, as he said to Jean Clair: "I particularly like the one in which you see a piece of cloth with simply a safety pin" (Clair, 1992, translated for this edition).

In the drawing, there is almost nothing left. A scrap of cloth on the branch of a tree, fastened to it by a safety pin. Above it, a detail of a crucifixion in which all we see is a bone, with a bolt that holds together two pieces of bone. Over and beyond the fantasy represen-tations of sexual intercourse—a sadomasochistic primal scene—given the state of utter destitution that we have reached, all that remains is the need to connect two elements together. Fastening, pinning flesh to the canvas becomes the image of a desperate attempt to preserve some kind of cohesion, of connection, before sinking not into chaos, but into psychical death. With her concept of the pictogram, Piera Aulagnier said some very powerful things on that subject. In her analytical sessions with psychotic patients, she was particularly attentive towards certain alarm signals, which she called "blank signals" (Aulagnier, 1986): "'Signals' that manifest the impact of terror experienced by the I confronted with the appearance at its frontiers of the representation of something that cannot be put into words" (p. 343, translated for this edition).

In situations like that, she found it necessary to suggest, as quickly as possible, a representation in words, a "speech act" that would come "as near as possible to the pictographic representation, to the representation of corporeal things".

> An image will convey what I am trying to say: that of a man who suddenly discovers that his feet have taken him to the edge of a precipice, while behind him an explosion has cut off any possibility of turning back. Before vertigo takes over and thrusts him headlong into the abyss, he can only remain petrified, empty of all thought, all action suspended, with the hope of stopping once and for all any movement forwards or backwards. It is at times like those that the input that I have described as necessary becomes imperative: suggest to that person an image that again turns his eyes towards the outside, enabling him to recover his 'sight' in a way that brings towards him a part of the affect that accompanied the representation 'in itself'" (the part impossible to put into words). (Aulagnier, 1986, p. 348, translated for this edition)

That is what Piera Aulagnier called "painting with words". That spoken representation makes for the reconstruction of an exterior that can be thought about and cathected and where once again an object can exist. I shall later show how Winnicott saw that exteriority with respect to internal destructiveness and the constitution of the object.

And the stain left by spunk? It is spread all over Bacon's paintings, ostentatious, thrown at the last moment, a triumph and a blot. But let us be careful: following the model of "this is not a pipe", we should immediately say "this is not a stain left by spunk". It is a streak of white paint thrown on to the canvas. But, again, we could say "this is not a streak of white paint" . . .

For Clair, the safety pin is a safety pin, unlike Bacon's syringe:

> Everybody talks about religious art. Art is religious, as that other mystical atheist, Jean Cocteau, said. A real crucifixion is the result of Picasso's anger with painting. A work of art made up of nails, bits of cloth, things torn, wood, blood, rancour. (Clair, 1992, translated for this edition).

He could have added to his list the safety pin, so mundane and unexpected, that attaches Christ's perizonium, the emblem of that religion, of that link, of that fastener that brings together the destiny of *el nino*, the Child, and the image of the Celestial Father, hiding the specific features of his masculinity. This is another way of putting what Bacon said of his father: "I disliked him but I was sexually attracted to him".

That brings us back to distortions; it is time to turn to Winnicott—and this, for at least three reasons. In the first place, he was interested in Bacon's artistic work; second, because, by saying that the mother's face is a mirror for her child, he made psychoanalytical theory take a qualitative leap forward by freeing it from the mirror and its specular symmetry—whether Freud's conception of the analyst-as-mirror reflecting to the patient the latter's unconscious, or Lacan's "mirror stage"—by arguing that identity and identification have, from the outset, to do with the relationship with another living and talking human being; third, because he made the somewhat enigmatic and bold statement: "I personally do my work very much from the body-ego" (Winnicott, 1965, p. 161).

Bacon painted many portraits—it is, perhaps, that part of his work that is best known. Portraits of people close to him and with whom he was in an intense relationship, as a friend or as a lover. Isabel Rawsthorne, Lucian Freud (Sigmund's grandson), Franck Auerbach, George Dyer, John Edwards, Henrietta Moraes, Muriel Belcher, and Michel Leiris. He painted two portraits of Michel Leiris: "I'm always hoping to deform people into appearance; I can't paint them literally. For instance, of those two paintings of Michel Leiris, the one which is less literally like him is in fact more poignantly like him" (Sylvester, 1993, p. 76).

In his discussion of those portraits with David Sylvester, Bacon said, "One of the terrible things about so-called love, certainly for an artist, I think, is the destruction" (1993, p. 76). In that same interview, Bacon said that all of the people whom he portrayed, and whom he loved, were dead. The pictorial work required in order to make the reality of the object emerge has to destroy the object. Bacon was so intensely conscious of that requirement that he preferred to paint portraits of the people he liked using photographs of them, without the person actually being present, so afraid was he that he might hurt them or even kill them:

> I very much prefer working from the photographs than from them. . . . I find it easier to work than actually having their presence in the room. I think that, if I have the presence of the image there, I am able to drift as freely as I am able to through the photographic image. (Sylvester, 1993, p. 38)

The presence of the model inhibited him for the following reason: "If I like them, I don't want to practise the injury that I do to them in my work before them. I would rather practise the injury in private by which I think I can record the facts of them more clearly" (Sylvester, 1993, p. 38).

At that point in the interview, Sylvester tried to drive Bacon into a corner and force him to acknowledge his ambivalence. In so doing, Sylvester made use of ideas that, implicitly and in all probability without his realising it, echo the Kleinian concepts of attack and reparation. In his reply, Bacon brushed aside the theory that Sylvester was suggesting—and, in so doing, revealed himself to be much more of a follower of Winnicott than he could have imagined: "That is too logical. I don't think that's the way things work. I think it goes to a deeper thing: how do I feel I can make this image more immediately real to myself?" (p. 43)

Why Winnicott? In the first place, because in what Bacon has just said there is the idea of the possibility of using the object; that utilisation of the object is related not only to a feeling of reality, but also to a feeling of being oneself real. All of this has to do with destruction. Freud was the first to point out that "the external world . . . and what is hated are identical" (Freud, 1915c, p. 136), to which Winnicott added that the object must survive destruction in order for any experience of reality to occur and, above all, to continue existing independently of the destiny of the object:

> It is generally understood that the reality principle involves the individual in anger and reactive destruction, but my thesis is that the destruction plays its part in making the reality, placing the object outside the self. . . . It is the destructive drive that creates the quality of externality. . . . From this moment, or arising out of this phase, the object is *in fantasy* always being destroyed. This quality of 'always being destroyed' makes the reality of the surviving object felt as such, strengthens the feeling tone, and contributes to object-constancy. The object can now be used. (Winnicott, 1999, pp. 91, 93)

Bacon's portraits and self-portraits are representations of those corporeal things that cannot be put into words, of those obscure self-perceptions of the id (and of the self), of those wastelands of the soul, the frontier zones between the various psychical agencies; they are ways of being-to-oneself that lie below words, not organic life but mental life in a form unknown to us which, all the same, succeeds in expressing itself as a form, perhaps because it is, in fact, made up of forms. What makes it possible for the artist to produce the shape that confers a perceptible reality on them—it is not represented, but is certainly present in what we call technique—is that destructiveness which never stops destroying in fantasy so as to bring the inside outside. The feeling of gratitude that the viewer looking at a painting may experience towards the artist—a feeling of gratitude mingled with elation—is due to the fact that someone has succeeded in showing that. It can, therefore, be represented.

We have to be able to tolerate remaining in a certain state of mind in order to allow representations to emerge from their own flesh and make their appearance. To be more precise, we have to be able to accept formlessness, touch its outline, elusive and ill-defined, the vagueness of its frontiers, and let ourselves make contact with regions of our mind that are usually kept far away by our internal geography. We have to be able to tolerate the chaos that reigns therein and the extraordinary displacements of energy to which it gives rise, and to move around in what Winnicott called "the area of formlessness" (1999, p. 33). Bacon said, "I feel at home in this chaos because chaos suggests images to me. And in any case I just love living in chaos."

With respect to the psychoanalytical experience as we encounter it in the context of an analytical session, Winnicott often argued that we must have the ability to accept chaos and formlessness in order to help the analysand wait for the right moment, the moment when he/she will discover something in a creative way. In addition, he emphasised the importance of non-communication, not only in the infant's early development but also in the psychoanalytical experience. That experience of active non-communication exists in every human being, from the most to the least pathological; it protects the possibility for secretly and silently communicating with objects and with subjective phenomena: "Although healthy persons communicate and enjoy communicating, the other fact is equally true, that *each individual is an isolate, permanently non-communicating, permanently unknown, in fact unfound"* (Winnicott, 1965, p. 187).

In painters—and in every artist, in fact—the initial impetus that sets them to work and establishes the conditions under which they will best be able to finish their work has more to do with non-communication, as so defined, than with the need to communicate. It was perhaps with that in mind that Bacon was able to say "I am profoundly optimistic, but about nothing".

Violence of reality, violence of painting; the painter tears out, slashes and rips apart the veil, the screens that sift existence and filter reality: "I sometimes think, when people say my work looks violent, that I have from time to time been able to clear away one or two of the veils or screens" (Sylvester, 1993, p. 82).

Yet, Bacon wanted those paintings to be looked at from behind a glass screen. Was that intended to be a protective screen? If so, perhaps a protection that functions in both directions; protecting the viewer from the excesses of the painting, and protecting the painting from the destructive look in the viewer's eyes . . . That is possible, but, more fundamentally, perhaps, the glass screen places in front of the canvas a surface on which the viewer's face will be reflected, as in a mirror, while at the same time allowing the viewer to see, showing through, the reflection of his/her internal world in the face of the mother, the canvas.

"Francis Bacon . . . is seeing himself in his mother's face, but with some twist in him or her that maddens both him and us" (Winnicott, 1999, p. 114).

Let us once again turn to Antonin Artaud (1964):

Van Gogh, a madman?

Let him who once knew how to look at a human face take a look at the self-portrait of Van Gogh. I am thinking of the one with the soft hat.

I do not know of a single psychiatrist who would know how to scrutinize a man's face with such overpowering strength, dissecting its irrefutable psychology as if with a knife.

Van Gogh's eye belongs to a great genius, but from the way I see him dissecting me, surging forth from the depths of the canvas, it is no longer the genius of a painter that I feel living within him at this moment, but the genius of a certain philosopher never encountered by me in this life. (p. 59)

In concluding this chapter, I would like to say something of the setting, of the framework, and of what Bacon referred to as the artificial. A word or two first, perhaps, about vocabulary. What surrounds a painting is the *frame*; when we refer to the analytical *setting*, the use of the progressive tense of the verb indicates both movement and duration, an action which is being carried out and which in fact never stops being carried out. In this case, the action is that of setting up something. The word *setting* can also evoke the environment—a nice setting, for example. In what I am now about to explore, I shall show how Bacon constructed a setting that was conducive to the emergence of reality. Any exploration of how to establish the optimal conditions under which a given experience can occur is relevant also, *mutatis mutandis*, to the questions that arise in psychoanalytical practice when we are establishing the analytical setting, even though this, as such, has nothing very much to do with the frame of a painting.

What appears within a painting that has nothing to do with the frame but which depends fundamentally on the way in which the painter made it appear? For Bacon, what always underlies the question of figuration—and of the emergence of that figuration—has to do with a mass, a quantity of energy, envisaged in terms of force and intensity. For example, when Bacon thinks about the function of painting in a world in which the mechanical means of reproducing reality are more and more sophisticated, the idea that first comes into his head has to do with intensity.

> [A] painter, if he is going to attempt to record life, has to do it in a much more intense and curtailed way. It has to have the intensity of ... you can call it sophisticated simplicity.... You have to abbreviate into intensity. [The painter] has to re-invent realism. He has to wash the realism back onto the nervous system by his invention, because there isn't such a thing in painting any longer as natural realism. (Sylvester, 1993, p. 176)

In order to reach that level of intensity something has to be switched on, and this is possible only via the setting up of a wholly artificial structure that will close up on the subject of the painting as though it were a bait; then, the subject having disappeared, all that remains is reality. There is, however, no immediate reference to reality. There is a kind of tension between different dimensions of different realities that coexist:

> Well it's in the artificial structure that the reality of the subject will be caught, and the trap will close over the subject-matter and leave only the reality. . . . You have to start from somewhere, and you start from the subject which gradually, if the thing works at all, withers away and leaves this residue which we call reality and which perhaps has something tenuously to do with what one started with but very often had very little to do with it. (Sylvester, 1993, p. 180)

The analytical setting is also an artificial arrangement: artificial, but not arbitrary. The concept of *Durcharbeiten*, working through, is the touchstone that connects temporality (that of the deployment of what is possible) with the move that takes quantity (mass of energy) towards psychical quality. That processing lies at the very heart of Freud's description of the drives.

Durcharbeit in association with the analyst's professional attitude will enable what Freud called "the other scene" to come into the space and time of the session, defined as the setting, and unfold there.

It is through a similar kind of combinatory structuring of forces and framing that Bacon was able to put on canvas some representations of the other scene. That is perhaps the fundamental difference— but not the only one—between the 1944 triptych and the 1988 version of it. In the first version, the expressiveness of the figures and the stridency of the colours burst through the canvas. They throw themselves at the viewer's face (as they were thrown onto the canvas) with a tremendous sense of immediacy and a feeling of proximity. In the later version, there is a whole construction of the space and a framing, which create a sense of remoteness, of distance. The colours are darker, there is no stridency any more—just a quality of silence that makes us feel uneasy. Is this the approach of death? For Bacon, who thought that "great art is profoundly ordered", is it a victory for classicism? These figures are less like the Erinyes—but have they, for all that, turned into the Eumenides? In the central figure we see a new element: where the neck joins the body, there is a metal plate with two bolts, and another at the top of the tripod. Is this an echo of Picasso's *Crucifixion* that Bacon liked so much?

Distortions are part of what Bacon called artificial. The more he progressed in his work, the more the paradoxical tension between the artificiality of the means and the realistic intensity of the effect is strongly asserted.

> For instance, in a painting I'm trying to do of a beach and a wave breaking on it, I feel that the only possibility of doing it will be to put the beach and the wave on a kind of structure which will show them so that you take them out of their position, as it were, and re-make the wave and a piece of the beach in a very artificial structure. In this painting, I have been trying to make the structure and then hope chance will throw down the beach and the wave for me. But I just hope that this painting, no matter how artificial it is, will be like a wave breaking on a seashore. (Sylvester, 1993, p.148)

Sometimes elements of raw reality get inside the frame, but as soon as they are brought inside it, what remains of their rawness? What is marvellous about the chaos in his studio is the dust that gathers. It can be gathered up, mixed with some paint, and, once it dries out, used like pastel. Pure dust is the perfect colour for a grey suit of clothes. It is a kind of pastel, in fact, but it probably lasts longer than pastel. Perhaps not. It is difficult to estimate how long things will last. How could we convey something of the slightly furry quality of a flannel suit? "And then I suddenly thought: well, I'll get some dust. And you can see how near it is to a decent grey flannel suit" (Sylvester, 1993, p. 192).

In T. S. Eliot's *Four Quartets*, a work that Bacon really appreciated, we read the following lines:

> Dust in the air suspended
> marks the place where a story ended

It is tempting to end this chapter with the suspending in the air of that poetic talisman, but, for Bacon, what would be missing is the disruptive touch, the necessary splashing when the painting is too perfect. Towards the end of their final interview, Bacon reminded David Sylvester that art is cruel because reality is cruel; it is, perhaps, for that reason that people like abstract art so much, because it is impossible to be cruel in the abstract. Psychoanalysis cannot evade that fact. Bringing into play, in a psychoanalytical process, the theatre of cruelty as it takes place on the other scene has to do with affective athleticism and cannot be reduced to the abstraction of a matheme, whatever the resources of intelligence that we take from the *Geistigkeit*, the life of the spirit, in order to throw light on the scene.

1. The word used by Freud in German is *Trieb*, which is distinct from another German word: *Instinkt*. The decision to translate *Trieb* to instinct is, like any translation, questionable. My preference is for *drive*, which is closer to the French translation of *Trieb* to *pulsion*.
2. For further considerations on Lacan's approach see Chapters One, Five, and Six.
3. We find some aphorisms pointing in the same direction in Ferenczi's paper "Mathematics", in *Final Contributions to the Problems and Methods of Psycho-Analysis*, 1955.
4. There is a homophony in French between *panser* (to bandage) and *penser* (to think). Keeping this homophony in mind, the translation runs thus: "I bandaged him (i.e., I held him in my mind), God healed him".
5. "Neither of these"—that is, neither gratifying nor suppressing the need for love (Freud, 1915a, p. 166).
6. Freud's word in German is *Indifferenz*, which Strachey translated into English as *neutrality*.
7. Daniel Zaoui: "Le pur et l'impur, quelques correspondances bibliques et freudiennes" ["Pure and impure, a few biblical and Freudian correspondances"]. Unpublished paper, 1991.
8. As described by de M'Uzan in his chapter "The slaves of quantity" (de M'Uzan, 1994).

9. "It is perhaps the transformation into libido, or into a form of energy the aim of which is pleasure, a part of the energy necessary for the structuring of a living species which gave birth to that particular animal we call man" (Aulagnier, "The two principles of identificatory functioning: permanence and change", in Aulagnier, 1986).

10. The question may well arise as to whether this tendency to stand back from oneself is aseptically confined to the actual session, with no impact on the analyst's love life and social relationships in his/her personal life.

11. It is important to note that Winnicott approached that issue in a manner similar to that of creativity, that is, starting with the question of life itself.

> What I say does affect our view of the question: what is life about? . . . I am claiming that these same phenomena that are life and death to our schizoid or borderline patients appear in our cultural experiences. It is these cultural experiences that provide the continuity in the human race that transcends personal existence. (1999, pp. 99–100)

12. We owe that description to Serge Leclaire. It matches my own experience of watching Lacan "on stage" clumsily manipulating the bowels of the Borromean knots.

13. Lacan wrote his doctoral thesis on the case of a paranoiac, a woman who had attempted to murder a famous actress. He called her Aimée, literally "Loved".

14. Georges Bataille had been actress Sylvia Bataille's husband before she married Jacques Lacan.

15. [The psychoanalyst] takes the description of an everyday event as a fable addressed as a word to the wise, a long prosopopeia as a direct interjection, and, contrariwise, a simple slip of the tongue as a highly complex statement, and even the rest of a silence as the whole lyrical development it stands in for. It is, therefore, a propitious punctuation that gives meaning to the subject's discourse. This is why the ending of the session—which current technique makes into an interruption that is determined purely by the clock and, as such, takes no account of the thread of the subject's discourse—plays the part of a scansion which has the full value of an intervention by the analyst that is designed to precipitate concluding moments" (Lacan, 2006, p. 209).

16. The word "*mort*" in French can refer either to death—"the image of death"—or to the "dummy" in a card game (translator's note).

17. My aim here is to indicate Lacan's way of expressing the complex set of problems brought about by the requirement that the analyst be neutral; this finds many echoes in Freud's pessimistic thoughts expressed in *Civilization and its Discontents* (Freud, 1930a). For further discussion on this point, see Chapter Three, "The psychoanalyst and his/her discontents".

18. According to Elisabeth Roudinesco (1990), Lacan sent his doctoral thesis to Freud who simply let him know, in a very formal manner, that he had received it. The same happened to André Breton, but that did not prevent him from going to Vienna to meet Freud.

19. These circumstances are briefly summarised in the book that Gilbert Diatkine wrote about Lacan (Diatkine 1999).

20. Elizabeth Roudinesco gives a more complex and even more tragic account of the end of that analysis, completely distorted as it was by the political issues that were very much part of the Paris Society at that time.

> We know today, thanks to a letter from Loewenstein to Marie Bonaparte, dated February 22, 1953, and quoted by Célia Bertin, that Lacan's election to the ranks of the titular members had been the subject of violent conflict within the SPP. Against the advice of his analyst and thanks to pressure from Pichon, Lacan received his nomination to compensate for that of Heinz Hartmann, who had taken refuge in Paris. The latter, fleeing the Nazis once again, would emigrate, like Loewenstein, to the United States to become a founder of "ego psychology". In exchange for his full affiliation, Lacan promised his analyst to continue his interminable analysis, which was becoming increasingly difficult. Naturally, as soon as he secured his appointment, he abandoned Loewenstein's couch. Furious at being betrayed, Loewenstein regarded Lacan as a cheat and was to comment on the event in 1953 in his letter to the Princess: "What you tell me of Lacan is depressing. He always constituted for me a source of conflict: on the one hand, his lack of character, on the other, his intellectual value, which I prize highly though not without violent disagreement. But the problem is that even though we had agreed that he would continue his analysis after his election, he did not come back. One does not cheat on so important a point without dire consequences (let this remain between us). I hope that his trainees who have been analysed in a rush, that is, not analysed at all, will not be accepted." (Roudinesco, 1990, p. 122)

21. This follows on from Winnicott's concept of transitionality. It is also what Michel de M'Uzan develops in terms of the mutative effects of interpretation, in particular via his concept of the chimaera.

22. That word comes into my mind as I write these lines, a memory from Lacan's seminars. He himself used the term in order to protest against the fact that people were trying—wrongly, in his view—to "trash" him through references to structuralism. (Roudinesco, in *Lacan envers et contre tout* (2011) uses the (invented) words *poubellicant, poubelliquer, p'oublier* (≈ publier/to publish), with the idea of *poubelle*—rubbish bin—present in their sonorities. There is also in one of Lacan's seminars in St Anne the word *poubellication* (≈ publication) (Translator's note).)

23. That is the major criticism that Lacan makes of this mode of perception of the reality of the Other.

24. It is interesting to remark on the fact that that trend claims to be in the forefront of the protest movement against the American psychoanalytical establishment, represented by the inheritors of Hartmann, Kris, and Loewenstein's ego psychology.

25. So real that I would argue that they play a very important role in the development of the brain and the quality of neuronal circuitry, and, indeed, in the entire development of the biological body via the neuro-immunological and neuro-endocrinal systems.

26. All the more so if we consider that "primal repression" is only the psychical aspect (and metapsychological wording) of a complex set of biological phenomena that are in the process of self-organisation in the early stages of body–mind development.

27. This theoretical point of view does not preclude other aspects, in particular the role of intrapsychic unconscious conflict in sexual dysfunctions. It only highlights how the later oedipal conflictuality is deeply permeated in its construction, and determined in its form, by the early shapings of communication in the initial developments of the bodily ego. The parents' unconscious oedipal conflicts are active right from the very beginning and *they determine the mother's capacity for penetrability, permeability, and receptivity. In that respect, the process of shaping is not dual but always triangular.* This is also true of the pre-forms of the primal scene as described later in this chapter.

28. By using the word "significance" instead of "meaning", I am trying to convey the difference in French between *signification* and *sens*.

29. Mentioned by Judith Dupont in her introduction to volume 3 of the Freud–Ferenczi correspondence (Falzeder & Brabant, 2000).

30. In French, *"le dicible"*, that is, that which can be uttered in words.

31. In a footnote to her 1985 paper, Aulagnier writes,

    This "anticipated mother" is comparable to what Bion defined as a pre-concept: in both cases, a relation-based matrix awaits and precedes what will be one of its supports. But the similarity goes no further than that. Bion's hypothesis involves a vision that to some extent reminds us of Kant's conception of intuition. My idea is more "materialistic" and implies the presence of the "element of reality" that is provided by a somatic experience. (1985, p. 119, translated for this edition)

32. The zone of cortical representation of the face is adjacent to that of the hand and arm. The neurobiologist Vilayanur Ramachandran, who has studied the remarkable plasticity of the somaesthetic (or somatosensory) system, showed that a young man whose arm had been amputated above the elbow still felt sensations, four weeks after the amputation, in the amputated limb when he stroked his cheek with a cotton-bud.

33. Compare what Freud described as the patient's "faith" in his paper on "Psychical (or mental) treatment: "If this gives us grounds for blaming the patients' faith, we must yet not be so ungrateful as to forget that the same force is constantly at work in support of our own medical efforts" (1890a, p. 291).

34. Re-entry is the third tenet of Edelman's Theory of Neuronal Group Selection (the other two are: the formation during the development of the brain of a primary repertoire of extremely variable neuronal groups that contribute to neuro-anatomy—developmental selection, and the forma-tion under the influence of experience of a secondary repertoire of neuronal circuits resulting from the strength of connexions or synapses—experiential selection). Edelman defines re-entry as

the ongoing recursive dynamic interchange of signals that occurs in parallel between brain maps. Reentry depends for its operations on the intricate networks of massively parallel reciprocal connec-tions within and between neuronal groups. . . . It alters and is altered by the activity of the target areas it interconnects. . . . This interchange synchronizes and coordinates the functions of the various maps. Reentry plays the central role in our consciousness model, for it is reentry that assures the integration that is essential to the creation of a scene in primary consciousness. (Edelman & Tononi, 2000, p. 106)

35. The word "demand" comes up once again in the definition of drives that I shall study later on. It is correlative with the idea of work, but I would argue that it includes the notion of a demand internal to the organism that, as regards the physiological dimension, is equivalent to the ideal in

the psychical dimension. Having to find some way of satisfying a drive-related need compels the neural matter to develop further.

36. Recent developments in immunology may perhaps lend some scientific credibility to Freud's "stubbornness":

> The idiotype is the internal image of an aggression experienced by earlier generations, which no doubt will never occur again but which remains attached to zones that we refer to as idiotypic. This enables us to explain the presence of the 'natural antibodies' found in the newborn, which represent the aptitudes for a capacity for responding to aggression; these do not come from the newborn's genetic inheritance—they are passed on at birth by the child's mother. (Claquin, 1989, translated for this edition)

37. The immune system has many properties typical of sense organs or of a mobile brain, referred to the perception of the internal space of the body! . . . There are some remarkable phenotypic analogies between the nervous system and the immune system in so far as both of them take in and process a practically unlimited quantity of data, receive and emit signals, and set up their normal mode of functioning in *a historical dimension that takes into account the onto-genesis and the events arising in the history of the individual* because both, *in fine*, have *memory* available to them. (Gachelin, 1985, p. 58, translated for this edition, my italics)

38. In French: *un garde-manger*, literally "a keep-food".

39. Piera Aulagnier's metapsychology is an ensemble of concepts tightly articulated together. It is, therefore, very difficult to isolate one concept in order to define it. For the reader who is not familiar with her theory, I think it useful to give three excerpts from *The Violence of Interpretation* (2001) in order to convey the meaning of auto-engendering. I do not agree with Alan Sheridan's translation of "auto-engendrement" to "self-procreation". I have replaced it with "auto-engendering" and "auto-engendered":

> Although I see the activity of representation as the task common to the psychical processes, it may be said that its aim is to metabolise into an element homogeneous with the structure of each system an element of a heterogeneous nature. . . . My model defends the hypothesis according to which psychical activity is constituted by three modes of functioning, taken together, or by three processes of metabolisation: the primal process, the primary

process and the secondary process. The representations resulting from their activity will be respectively the pictographic representation or pictogram, the fantasy representation or fantasy, the ideational representation or statement. . . . The three processes that I postulate are not present in psychical activity from the outset; they follow one another in succession and their activation is provoked by the need felt by the psyche to become aware of a property of the object outside it, a property that the previous process had to ignore. (p. 4)

Every existent is auto-engendered by the activity of the system that represents it; this is the postulate of auto-engendering according to which the primal process functions. (p. 6)

Whether we are dealing with the primal, the primary or the secondary, one may therefore give the same definition of the aim proper to the activity of representation: to metabolise heterogeneous raw material in such a way that it may become part of a representation that, in the final analysis, is only the representation of the postulate itself. (p. 6)

40. I would see this in terms of what Michel Fain called a "self-soothing procedure", a concept further developed and explained by Gérard Szwec and Claude Smadja.

41. Is it really merely by chance that the concept of mucus immunity is becoming more and more important in immunology? "The study of mucus immunity, that of bronchial epithelium, of the digestive tube, of the skin and its invaginations, is in fact becoming an absolute priority in immunopathology" (Gachelin, 1985, translated for this edition).

42. Damien had conveyed to me a bodily image of his perfectly controlled mother as hard and cold, an exciting negative traumatic "presence".

43. From a cellular perspective, one of the major anomalies has to do with disorders in membrane permeability to chlorine. The sweat test consists in measuring the concentration of chlorine in a sample of at least 100 mg of sweat. In order to do this, the patient is enclosed in a plastic bag so that sweating may occur.

44. On condition that the spectator has a "capacity for reverie" as solid as a rock!

45. In a video entitled *Autopsy* (1994), Sheree looks at Bob lying naked on a table and says, "He looks like he's dead, that's why he is so appealing."

46. A word employed mainly in American English as spoken in New York. It comes from Yiddish and means shameless audacity, cheek.

47. I agree with what Michel de M'Uzan writes in "A case of masochistic perversion":

> Erotogenic masochism can be considered to be an ultra-precocious mechanism linked originally to a positive function. With regard to masochistic perversion of the type represented by M [a patient] I would see in this the resumption of the archaic mechanism at the time of an attack on the integrity of the psychosomatic being . . . (de M'Uzan, 1973, p. 466)

REFERENCES

Aeschylus *Eumenides*. Internet Classics Archive, http://classics.mit.edu/
  Aeschylus/eumendides.html

Artaud, A. (1958). *The Theatre and Its Double*, M. C. Richards (Trans.). New
  York: Grove Press, 1964.

Artaud, A. (1964)[1947]. Van Gogh: the man suicided by society. In: *Artaud
  Anthology* (pp. 47–54), J. Hirschman (Ed.), M. Beach & L. Ferlinghetti
  (Trans.). San Francisco, CA: City Light Books.

Aulagnier, P. (1962). Angoisse et identification. Paper presented in Lacan's
  seminar "L'identification", 1961–1962, pp. 138–145.

Aulagnier, P. (1968). Remarques sur le masochisme primaire. *L'Or, 38*:
  47–54.

Aulagnier, P. (1985). Naissance d'un corps, origine d'une histoire. In:
  Corps et Histoire. Paris: Les Belles Lettres.

Aulagnier, P. (1986). *Un interprète en quête du sens* [An Interpreter in Search
  of Meaning]. Paris: Ramsay.

Aulagnier, P. (2001)[1975]. *The Violence of Interpretation. From Pictogram to
  Statement*, A. Sheridan (Trans.). London: Routledge.

Bataille, G. (1988). *Inner Experience*. Albany, NY: State University of New
  York Press.

Bernard, C. (1927). *An Introduction to the Study of Experimental Medicine*. London: Macmillan.

Bion, W. R. (1962). *Learning from Experience*. London: William Heinemann [reprinted London: Karnac].

Bion, W. R. (1963). *Elements of Psycho-Analysis*. London: William Heinemann [reprinted London: Karnac, 1984].

Bion, W. R. (2005). *The Tavistock Seminars 1976–1979*. London: Karnac.

Botella, C., & Botella, S. (2007). *La Figurabilité Psychique*. Paris: In Press.

Brabant, E., Falzeder, E., & Giampieri-Deutsch, P. (Eds.) (1993). *The Correspondence of Sigmund Freud and Sándor Ferenczi, Volume 1: 1908–1914*, P. Hoffer (Trans.). Cambridge, MA: Belknap Press of Harvard University Press.

Cannon, W. B. (1932). *Wisdom of the Body*. New York: Norton, 1963.

Changeux, J.-P. (2009). *The Physiology of Truth: Neuroscience and Human Knowledge*. Cambridge, MA: Harvard University Press.

Clair, J. (1992). Le pathos et la mort. Entretien de Francis Bacon avec Jean Clair [Pathos and death. Jean Clair interviews Francis Bacon]. In: *Corps crucifiés* [Crucified Bodies]. Paris: Réunion des Musées Nationaux.

Claquin, M. (1989). Processus biologique et processus psychique: quelques incidences d'un modèle immunologique [Biological process and mental process: some repercussions of an immunological model]. *Psychanalyse à l'université*, 14(54): 91–99.

Damasio, A. (1994). *Descartes' Error: Emotion, Reason, and the Human Brain*. New York: HarperCollins, 2005.

David, C. (1985). La sublimation: concept ou valeur? [Sublimation: a concept or a value?] *Topique*, 34: 61–74.

David, C., Fain, M., Marty, P., & de M'Uzan, M. (1968). Le cas Dora et le point de vue psychosomatique [Dora's case and the psychosomatic point of view]. *Revue française de psychanalyse*, XXXII(4): 679–714.

De M'Uzan, M. (1973). A case of masochistic perversion and an outline of a theory. *International Journal of Psychoanalysis*, 54: 455–467.

De M'Uzan, M. (1977). Contre-transfert et système paradoxal [The counter-transference and the paradoxical system]. In: *De l'art à la mort* [From Art to Death]. Paris: Gallimard.

De M'Uzan, M. (1994). *La Bouche de l'Inconscient* [The Mouth of the Unconscious]. Paris: Gallimard.

Diatkine, G. (1999). *Jacques Lacan*. Paris: PUF.

Edelman, G. M. (2004). *Wider Than the Sky: The Phenomenal Gift of Consciousness*. New Haven, CT: Yale University Press.

Edelman, G. M., & Tononi, G. (2000). *A Universe of Consciousness. How Matter Becomes Imagination*. New York: Basic Books.

Eliot, T. S. (1963). *Collected Poems*. London: Faber & Faber.

Falzeder, E. (Ed.) (2003). *The Complete Correspondence of Sigmund Freud and Karl Abraham 1907–1925*, C. Schwarzacher, C. Trollope, & K. Majthényi King (Trans.). London: Karnac.

Falzeder, E., & Brabant, E. (2000). *The Correspondence of Sigmund Freud and Sándor Ferenczi, Volume 3, 1920–1933*. Cambridge, MA: Belknap Press of Harvard University Press.

Ferenczi, S. (1909). *First Contributions to Psycho-Analysis*. London: Hogarth Press, 1952 [reprinted London: Karnac, 1994].

Ferenczi, S. (1927). *Further Contributions to the Theory and Technique of Psycho-Analysis*. New York: Boni & Liveright.

Ferenczi, S. (1955). *Final Contributions to the Problems and Methods of Psycho-Analysis*, M. Balint (Ed.). London: Karnac, 2002.

Freud, E. L. (1961). *Letters of Sigmund Freud 1873–1939*, T. Stern & J. Stern (Trans.). London: Hogarth Press.

Freud, S. (1890a). Psychical (or mental) treatment. *S.E., 7*: 283–304. London: Hogarth.

Freud, S. (1895d). *Studies on Hysteria. S.E., 2*. London: Hogarth.

Freud, S. (1900a). *The Interpretation of Dreams. S.E., 4–5*. London: Hogarth.

Freud, S. (1901b). *The Psychopathology of Everyday Life. S.E., 6*. London: Hogarth.

Freud, S. (1905a). On psychotherapy. *S.E., 7*: 257–270. London: Hogarth.

Freud, S. (1908d). 'Civilized' sexual morality and modern nervous illness. *S.E., 9*: 179–204. London: Hogarth.

Freud, S. (1909d). *Notes upon a Case of Obsessional Neurosis. S.E., 10*: 153–318. London: Hogarth.

Freud, S. (1912b). The dynamics of transference. *S.E., 12*: 99–108. London: Hogarth.

Freud, S. (1912d). On the universal tendency to debasement in the sphere of love. *S.E., 11*: 177–190. London: Hogarth.

Freud, S. (1912e). Recommendations to physicians practising psycho-analysis. *S.E., 12*: 111–120. London: Hogarth.

Freud, S. (1912–1913). *Totem and Taboo*. *S.E.*, *13*: 1–161. London: Hogarth.

Freud, S. (1913c). On beginning the treatment. *S.E.*, *12*: 123–144. London: Hogarth.

Freud, S. (1913f). The theme of the three caskets. *S.E.*, *12*: 291–302. London: Hogarth.

Freud, S. (1914b). *The Moses of Michelangelo*. *S.E.*, *13*: 211–238. London: Hogarth.

Freud, S. (1914c). On narcissism: an introduction. *S.E.*, *14*: 69–102. London: Hogarth.

Freud, S. (1915a). Observations on transference-love. *S.E.*, *12*: 157–171. London: Hogarth.

Freud, S. (1915c). Instincts and their vicissitudes. *S.E.*, *14*: 111–140. London: Hogarth.

Freud, S. (1918b). *From the History of an Infantile Neurosis*. *S.E.*, *17*: 3–122. London: Hogarth.

Freud, S. (1919a). Lines of advance in psycho-analytic therapy. *S.E.*, *17*: 157–168. London: Hogarth.

Freud, S. (1920g). *Beyond the Pleasure Principle*. *S.E.*, *18*: 7–64. London: Hogarth.

Freud, S. (1923b). *The Ego and the Id*. *S.E.*, *19*: 3–66. London: Hogarth.

Freud, S. (1924c). The economic problem of masochism. *S.E.*, *19*: 157–170. London: Hogarth.

Freud, S. (1927c). *The Future of an Illusion*. *S.E.*, *21*: 3–56. London: Hogarth.

Freud, S. (1930a). *Civilization and its Discontents*. *S.E.*, *21*: 59–145. London: Hogarth.

Freud, S. (1933a). *New Introductory Lectures on Psycho-Analysis*. *S.E.*, *22*. London: Hogarth.

Freud, S. (1937c). Analysis terminable and interminable. *S.E.*, *23*: 211–253. London: Hogarth.

Freud, S. (1939a). *Moses and Monotheism*. *S.E.*, *23*: 3–137. London: Hogarth.

Freud, S. (1940a). *An Outline of Psycho-Analysis*. *S.E.*, *23*: 141–207. London: Hogarth.

Freud, S. (1940b). Some elementary lessons in psycho-analysis. *S.E.*, *23*: 279–286. London: Hogarth.

Freud, S. (1940e). Splitting of the ego in the process of defence. *S.E.*, *23*: 273–. London: Hogarth.

Freud, S. (1941f). Findings, ideas, problems. *S.E., 23*: 299–300. London: Hogarth.

Freud, S. (1950). Draft M, Notes II. Extracts from the Fliess Papers. *S.E., 1*: 175–280. London: Hogarth.

Freud, S. (1950a). *Project for a Scientific Psychology. S.E., 1*: 283–397. London: Hogarth.

Fridman, W.-H. (1991). *Le cerveau mobile. De l'immunité au système immunitaire* [The Mobile Brain: from Immunity to the Immune System]. Paris: Hermann.

Gachelin, G. (1985). *Corps et Histoire* [The Body and History]. Paris: Les Belles Lettres.

Gachelin, G. (1995). Psychosomatique et modèles en immunologie [Psychosomatics and models in immunology]. *Revue Française de Psychanalyse, 8*: 7–23.

Gombrich, E. H. (1987). *Reflections on the History of Art*. Berkeley, CA: University of California Press.

Green, A. (1973). *Le discours vivant* [Living Discourse]. Paris: PUF.

Green, A. (1999). *The Work of the Negative*, A. Weller (Trans.). London: Free Association Books.

Isakower, O. (1938). A contribution to the patho-psychology of phenomena associated with falling asleep. *International Journal of Psychoanalysis, 19*: 331–345.

Lacan, J. (1991). *The Seminar of Jacques Lacan: Freud's Papers on Technique*, J. Forrester (Trans.). London: Norton.

Lacan, J. (2006). *Ecrits*, B. Fink (Trans.). London: Norton.

Laplanche, J., & Pontalis, J.-B. (1973). *The Language of Psycho-Analysis*, D. Nicholson-Smith (Trans.). London: Hogarth Press.

Ledoux, J. (1998). *The Emotional Brain: The Mysterious Underpinnings of Emotional Life*. London: Weidenfeld & Nicolson.

Lewin, B. (1934). Sleep, mouth, and the dream screen. *Psychoanalytic Quarterly, 15*: 419–434.

Little, M. (1990). *Psychotic Anxieties and Containment: A Personal Record of My Analysis with Winnicott*. Northvale, NJ: Jason Aronson.

Miller, P. (1999). La douleur: une thérapeutique de survie? *Revue française de psychosomatique, 15*: 39–49.

Miller, P. (2012). How Emmy silenced Freud into analytic listening. In: C. Seulin & G. Saragnano (Eds.). *On Freud's "On Beginning the Treatment"* (pp. 103–119). London: Karnac.

Mishima, Y. (1958). *Confessions of a Mask*. London: Penguin.

Nacht, S. (Ed.) (1959). *Psychoanalysis of Today*. New York: Grune & Stratton.

Pessoa, F. (1960). *Obra Poetica*. Rio de Janiero: José Aguilar.

Poincaré, H. (1907). Intuition and logic in mathematics. In: *The Value of Science* (pp. 15–25). New York: Science Press.

Prochiantz, A. (1995). *La biologie dans le boudoir* [Biology in the Boudoir]. Paris: Odile Jacob.

Richter, J. P. (1970). *The Notebooks of Leonardo Da Vinci, Volume II*. London: Dover.

Rosenberg, B. (1990). *Masochisme mortifère et masochisme gardien de la vie* [Deadly masochism and life-preserving masochism]. *Monographies de la Revue Française de Psychanalyse*. Paris: PUF.

Roudinesco, E. (1990). *Jacques Lacan and Co.: A History of Psychoanalysis in France, 1925–85*, J. Mehlman (Trans.). London: Free Association Books, 1990.

Roudinesco, E. (2011). *Lacan envers et contre tout* [Lacan, despite all opposition]. Paris: Le Seuil.

Segalen, V. (1915). *Equipée, Voyage au Pays du Réel* [Adventure. Journey to the Land of the Real]. Paris: Gallimard, 1983.

Sylvester, D. (1993). *The Brutality of Fact. Interviews with Francis Bacon*. London: Thames and Hudson.

Vygotsky, L. (1962). *Thought and Language*. MIT Press.

Winnicott, D. W. (1954). Metapsychological and clinical aspects of regression within the psycho-analytical set-up. *International Journal of Psychoanalysis*, 36:16–26. Reprinted in: *Through Paediatrics to Psycho-Analysis*. International Psychoanalytical Library, 1975.

Winnicott, D. W. (1956). Primary maternal preoccupation. In: *Through Paediatrics to Psycho-Analysis*. International Psychoanalytical Library, 1975.

Winnicott, D. W. (1965). *The Maturational Processes and the Facilitating Environment*. New York: International Universities Press.

Winnicott, D. W. (1967). The location of cultural experience. *International Journal of Psychoanalysis*, 48: 368–372.

Winnicott, D. W. (1975). *Through Paediatrics to Psycho-Analysis*. International Psychoanalytical Library.

Winnicott, D. W. (1988). *Human Nature*. London: Free Association Books; New York: Schocken Books.

Winnicott, D. W. (1998). *The Spontaneous Gesture: Selected Letters of D. W. Winnicott*, F. R. Rodman (Ed.). London: Karnac.
Winnicott, D. W. (1999). *Playing and Reality*. London: Routledge.

INDEX